CURRICULUM PLANNING FOR ELEMENTARY EDUCATION

ENCYCLOPAEDIA OF ELEMENTARY EDUCATION SERIES

CURRICULUM PLANNING FOR ELEMENTARY EDUCATION

Edited by
M. Husain

ANMOL PUBLICATIONS PVT. LTD.
NEW DELHI - 110 002 (INDIA)

ANMOL PUBLICATIONS PVT. LTD.
4374/4B, Ansari Road, Daryaganj
New Delhi - 110 002
Ph.: 23261597, 23278000
Visit us at: www.anmolpublications.com

Curriculum Planning for Elementary Education

First Edition, 2004

ISBN 81-261-1530-0

[Responsibility for the facts stated, opinions expressed, conclusions reached and plagiarism, if any, in these volumes is entirely that of the Editor. The Publishers bear no responsibility for them, whatsoever.]

PRINTED IN INDIA

Published by J.L. Kumar for Anmol Publications Pvt. Ltd., New Delhi - 110 002 and Printed at Mehra Offset Press, Delhi.

Contents

Preface

'Elementary education' is much debated universal issue, which is given emphasis as a fundamental right of each and every human being. All the nation-states the world over have made statutory provisions to ensure that none could be deprived of elementary education. Many world organisations are playing vital role in advancing the status of elementary education. Despite all these measures a large number of children in different parts of the world are still deprived of basic education.

This work in three volumes intends to focus on some vital issues pertaining to the theme. Attempts are made to gather the well researched material, based on the empirical findings of different scholars of repute from various settings.

As the information is drawn from various authoritative sources, no claim is of originality. We are deeply beholden to all those whose works and views are cited or substantially borrowed herein for making the work comprehensive and more useful. Besides these, we are grateful to one and all who have rendered the assistance while executing the plan of the work. Finally Mr. J.L. Kumar, Managing Director, Anmol Publications Pvt. Ltd. deserve all appreciation for undertaking the publication of this venture.

—Editor

1
Elementary Curriculum Planning: Theoretical Bases

To the school or individual teacher embarking on planning a curriculum a challenging, if not overwhelming, task lies ahead. Teachers have to plan for a diversity of children, organizations and pedagogical principles and practices. How can teachers understand and plan for the world of the primary school, to operate successfully within it? Given that constituents of a 'good' teacher or a 'good' school are dependent on the values of the evaluator, how will success be judged? Notions of 'quality' in teaching and schools are varied, and must be interrogated to expose the value systems which support them. This involves a reflective and critical stance towards teaching; success begins with an understanding of the rationales which comprise primary teaching and then using these to inform planning. Planning thus takes place in accordance with the outcomes of reflection and the development of a questioning attitude to, and critical awareness of, teaching at the stages of planning, implementation and evaluation.

The existence of potential variety in primary teaching should promote a positive attitude and generate an open mind rather than the uniformity of practice which characterizes many primary classrooms (Galton, Simon and Croll, 1980). In this, no one method has universal acceptance or applicability; no simple formula can be provided for successful teaching. Teaching and planning must develop out of a consideration of appropriacy to teachers' personalities, the children in their care, and the types of classroom environments and climates which teachers wish to develop. Enjoyment of teaching and learning rests on the intelligent decisions which teachers are continually having to make. This chapter introduces some conceptual tools for understanding the primary curriculum and the several principles and constraints which have brought it to its present position and which govern its planning.

Primary education and its planning is the product of many trends and influences (Blyth, 1965), some mutually supporting and others conflicting; they are the contexts in which discussion of the primary curriculum are set. An analysis of these contests—ideological, epistemological, psychological, sociological, managerial and evaluative—paints a composite picture of the primary curriculum as fluid, negotiable, complex and, significantly, changeable; there are very few constants apart from the child and the teacher. Such fluidity and negotiability must be reflected in curriculum planning. A plan becomes a proposal rather than a blueprint or tidy package.

IDEOLOGICAL CONTEXTS

The curriculum is value based. It is founded on the principle of protection and neglect of selected values. Curriculum planners need to expose such values before evaluating how they are brought into the planning debate. A value or ideology can be defined as 'that system of beliefs which gives general direction to the educational policies of those who hold those beliefs' (Scrimshaw, 1983; p. 4). Different ideologies can coexist with a degree of harmony; different elements of the curriculum being built on different ideological foundations. Alternatively, one can adopt a less consensual line, seeing ideologies not as sets of beliefs of various social groups but—from a Marxian perspective—as that set of values issuing from the dominant powers in society which has imperceptibly permeated the whole class structure; this has the effect of sustaining the dominant class in power (Centre for Contemporary cultural Studies, 1981).

The significance of this interpretation for curriculum planners is to direct attention to the power of certain groups to make major curriculum decisions, to ask 'whose values are protected in the curriculum?' Educational ideologies will contain values, beliefs and assumptions about children, learning, teaching, knowledge and the curriculum. A curriculum is taken to be all those activities designed or encouraged within the school's organizational framework to promote the intellectual, personal social and physical development of its pupils. It includes not only the formal programme of lessons, but also the 'informal' programme of so-called extra-curricular activities as well as those features which produce the school's 'ethos'.

More specifically, Meighan (1981) contends than an ideology addresses seven components which concern curriculum planners:

1. A theory of knowledge: its content and structure—what is considered worthwhile or important knowledge, how it is organized (e.g. by subjects or integrated areas) and who shall have access to it.

2. A theory of learning and the learner's role—an active or a passive style, doing or listening, co-operative or competitive learning, producing or reproducing knowledge, problem-solving or receiving facts.

3. A theory of teaching and the teacher's role—formal to informal, authoritarian or democratic, interest in outcomes or processes, narrow or wide.

4. A theory of resources appropriate for learning—first hand or second hand.

5. A theory of organization of learning situations—criteria for grouping pupils.

6. A theory of assessment that learning has taken place—diagnostic or attainment testing, written or observational assessment, defining what is to be assessed.
7. A theory of aims, objectives and outcomes—a view of what is desirable for society, the child, and knowledge.

One can determine how characteristics of different educational ideologies will address these seven main components. Scrimshaw (1983), for example, suggests that ideologies differ in their emphasis on the individual learner, knowledge and society. While these are clearly not discrete, nevertheless the emphasis is useful, and is one way of organizing the potentially disparate number of ideologies which appear in educational literature. Many of these are substantially the same ideology under a different name and are presented in summary form in Table 1.1. The difference between knowledge (a) and knowledge (b) in Table 1.1 lies in the access to high status knowledge. Advocates of knowledge (a) would restrict high status knowledge to an elite minority, whereas advocates of knowledge (b) would make it accessible to all pupils. The difference between society (a) and society (b) lies in the perspectives on society. Society (a) tends to regard the existing societal *status quo* as desirable and worth perpetuating and improving while society (b) will look to its alteration, its future evolution.

Ideologies Emphasizing the Individual Learner

Ideologies in this sphere represent the 'developmental tradition' in primary education (Blyth, 1965). In them the transmission of knowledge is secondary to discovery and to following the child's impulses, needs and interests. Stress is laid on learning by doing, spontaneity, free expression and developing the child's own nature spontaneously: 'give your scholar no verbal lessons; he should be taught by experience alone' (Worthington, 1884; p. 56). Knowledge is not imposed from without, but is uncertain, pragmatic, tentative and provisional; it is that which the child discovers rather than reproduces.

Table 1.1
Clusters of Educational Ideologies

Ideology	Emphasis
Progressivism Child-centredness Romanticism	Individual child
Classical humanism Conservatism Traditionalism Academicism	Knowledge (a)
Liberal humanism	Knowledge (b)
Instrumentalism Revisionism Economic renewal	Society (a)
Democratic socialism Reconstructionism	Society (b)

Emphasis is placed, then on originality and authenticity of the child's experience and awareness, on diversity of response and provision, on creativity, enjoyment and the development of the emotional side of the child's personality. The process of learning is as important as the outcomes of learning—the knowledge products. Hence education is seen as intrinsically worthwhile; valuable in itself rather than for what it leads to in later life.

In their challenge to rationalism, objectivity, abstract analysis and universalism, these ideologies celebrate empiricism, subjectivity, personal meanings and particularism. Childhood becomes a state in itself rather than a preparation for adulthood: 'the child is the father of the man' (Wordsworth, 1807). Adults can learn from children and their childhood innocence (Aries, 1973). For curriculum planners such views refute the value of an imposed curriculum: 'put the problems before him and let him solve them himself...let him not be taught science, let him discover it' (Rousseau, in Blenkin and Kelly, 1981; p. 19).

Schools have to protect children from the harmful and unpleasant aspects of the outside world (King, 1978) which might corrupt them. Hence they cocoon the child in a comfortable and secure environment separate from the vagaries of the world outside the classroom. If children fail at school then the school rather than the child is to be censured. One can detect the inspirational and optimistic rather than the analytic tenor of child-centred ideologies; indeed analysis reveals how dangerously loose these ideologies can be. For example, how can one derive and plan a curriculum from needs and interests which may be trivial, ephemeral, irrelevant or morally unacceptable? How will children judge what their needs are until they have a measure of knowledge? How can a curriculum be constructed from aims such as 'development', 'growth', or 'discovery' (Hirst and Peters, 1970)? Will it not lead to Bantock's (1980; p. 44) fears that 'temporary interest and immediate need are the guiding principle implict in the attempt to "psychologize" learning; hence the emphasis on motivation and endogenous development too easily fosters a magpie curriculum of bits and pieces'?

Further, in sheltering children from the corruption of the outer world, how adequate an education is being provided for future citizens? How justified is the exclusion or neglect, however partial, of the world beyond the classroom or immediate environment, regardless of the desirability or undesirability of that world? Similarly, in concentrating on the 'here and now' of the child's existence, how fair or responsible are teachers being to the received wisdoms of prior generations? Children may want, and need, to know about conflict and change as well as consensus and stability.

In approaching child-centred ideologies, then, one has to pare away the romanticism and exhortation, address the criticisms, and then see how they can be usefully employed in curriculum planning, avoiding the curriculum myopia to which such ideologies are prone. The thrust of many of these ideologies towards practical discovery and experimental learning, problem-solving, a process approach to the curriculum, identifying, meeting and developing children's needs, abilities and individual personalities, flexibility rather than uniformity of teaching, and the provision of a stimulating environment, become the elements which curriculum planners can use.

Ideologies Emphasizing Knowledge

In these ideologies one can detect a strong sympathy with conservative notions of protecting and perpetuating the best of the past as experienced in the present. Their antecedents lie in the 'preparatory' tradition (Blyth, 1965) of primary education and derive too from Plato's 'Republic' through Jesuit education, the mandarins of classical Chinese history (Weber, 1972), Matthew Arnold, T. S. Eliot and Bantock. They are unequivocally divisive and elitist, arguing for a separate and elite education into 'high culture' and a high cultural heritage for a chosen minority, giving them access to power and privilege:

> education should help to preserve the class and to select the elite. It is right that the exceptional individual should have the opportunity to elevate himself in the social scale and attain a position in which he can exercise his talents to the greatest benefit of himself and society. But the ideal of an educational system which would automatically sort out everyone according to his native capacities is unattainable in practice.... It would disorganize society, by substituting for classes, elites of brains, or perhaps only of sharp wits.
>
> (Eliot, 1948, pp. 100-1)

Its curriculum is academic and intellectual, non-vocational even though its clients may go on to prestigious positions in employment; it recognizes the permanence of knowledge and of high status knowledge in particular. Children have to be initiated into the received wisdoms of their forbears, the initiation rites of passage often being formal examinations. Subject loyalty is strong, discipline oriented and reliant on instruction rather than experiential learning (Lawton, 1973). Standards are clear, excellence of academic achievement is emphasized, and stress is laid on the development of rationality through a curriculum marked by uniformity rather than diversity (Jenkins, 1975). This curriculum runs counter to social justice and equality of opportunity (Lawton, 1983). For the masses who cannot aspire to this, a 'folk' curriculum (Bantock, 1975; 1976) is offered whose result is effectively to debar them from entering the corridors of privilege, providing what is often regarded as low status, practical, vocational and everyday knowledge. Ideologies in this area, then, emphasize a 'dual' curriculum (Scrimshaw, 1976).

Against this perhaps bleak picture an alternative ideology in this area advances a knowledge-based curriculum whose emphasis is less on a stratified than on a unified society, with egalitarian principles at its core. In liberal humanism high culture is to be accessible to all through a common curriculum: 'If, as Tawney said, we think the higher culture fit for solicitors, why should we not think it fit for coalminers?... Every child should be initiated into those forms of experience which together constitute this higher culture—the arts, mathematics, the human and physical sciences, philosophy' (White, 1982b; p. 26). For curriculum planners the significance of debates about knowledge is to clarify which knowledge should be in the curriculum, how it should be organized and who should have access to it.

Ideologies Emphasizing Society

The ideologies in this group share a common belief that education is valued for what it leads to rather than solely being an end in itself. One can discern two clear directions which society-oriented ideologies take. Instrumental ideologies—instrumentalism, revisionism, and those stressing economic renewal—emphasize the need for education to fit learners to society, particularly in economic terms. Education thus exists to provide a skilled workforce to expand the nation's economic strength; hence resources are developed for vocational [Department of Education and Science (DES) 1985c], scientific and technical education. Weight is laid on the relevance and utility aspects of education (Scrimshaw, 1983). The intentions of education are not to alter radically existing society, rather to improve the efficiency of existing organizations, institutions and economic structures (Oliver, 1982).

Contrasted to this are more radical society-oriented educational ideologies. Figuring high at times of social rebuilding or social upheaval, e.g. post-war renewal of society, reconstructionism posits a view of education as a major force for planned change rather than stability in society; what society ought to be rather than what it is (Scrimshaw, 1983). Society in need of reconstruction requires an educated populace whose curriculum has a strong social core with a stress on citizenship, egalitarianism, democracy and participation in decision-making. In this world teachers are catalysts and guardians of social change; creators rather than transmitters of knowledge. There are dangers in this approach. Such a vision is potentially unstable as it is always looking to the future; it is predicated for its success on an educated citizenry—which is perhaps both its greatest strength and its greatest weakness; it relies on a high level of control—running the risk perhaps of centralization or even indoctrination. Finally, one has to question the extent to which education can shoulder the burden of chaining society. Do not macro changes require macro and manifold organizations and institutions to change? Reconstructionist ideology, with its positive, perhaps idealistic, tone and central role for education, requires curriculum planners to think from afresh the content, aims and pedagogy of curricula from the perspective of their benefit to society (Hewlett, 1986). From an analysis of key characteristics of different ideologies one can map their expression onto Meighan's (1981) components of ideologies outlined earlier, and they are presented thus in Table 1.2.

Table 1.2
Ideologies interpreted by their component issues

Ideology	Progressivism, child-centredness, romanticism	Classical humanism, traditionalism, academicism, conservatism	Liberal humanism	Instrumentalism, revisionism, economic renewal	Reconstructionism, democratic socialism
Emphasis	Individual child	Knowledge—unequal access	Knowledge—equal access	Society—*status quo*	Society—changed.
Theory of knowledge	Empiricist, active, evolutionary, subjective, emphasis on processes integrated curricula	Disciplines, non-vocational, academic, high culture, emphasis on products, rationalistic	Common culture curriculum	Utilitarian, economically relevant, vocational, scientific, technological	Revolutionary, problem-solving, active, socially relevant, vocational
Theory of learning and of the learner's role	Experiential, spontaneity, emphasis on skills and processes, co-operative, intrinsic motivation	Obedience, passivity, conformity, uniformity	Induction into key areas of experience, active and co-operative learning	Induction into vocationally relevant areas	Apprenticeship, practical, co-operative, problem-solving
Theory of teaching and of the teacher's role	Guide, provider of multiple resources, facilitator, catalyst of child's self-chosen curriculum	Instructor, information, transmitter, authoritative, formal tutor	Guide, provider of resources, facilitator	Instructor, trainer, transmitter of vocationally relevant experiences	Guide, catalyst of social changes, disseminator of centralist philosophy, instructor, trainer

Table 1.2 (Contd.)

Theory of resources	First-hand, diverse, extensive	Second-hand, restricted	First and second hand, multiple, extensive	Narrowly relevant to content, practical, vocational	Highly focused to task in hand, vocational
Theory of organisation of learning situations	Diverse, flexible, informal, co-operative, group work, discovery methods	Class teaching, formal, uniform, competitive	Open, flexible, diverse	Narrow, practical, relevant to task, class and individual teaching, uniformity	Individual and group work as relevant to task
Theory of assessment	Diagnostic, multiple criteria, informal, profiling	Written, formal, attaiment testing, examinations	Diagnostic, norm and written, formal or informal	Formal, written and oral, practical	Flexible, formal or written as appropriate, attainment testing
Theory of aims, objectives and outcomes	Self-expression, individuality, creativity, development of whole personality	Received curricula, elitist, non-vocational, high culture	Equal access to key areas of knowledge, egalitarian	Extrinsic worthwhileness, relevant to economic good, efficient worker	Extrinsic worthwhileness, relevant to social good, citizenship, common good

Ideological analysis affects primary curriculum planning extensively—at the levels of aims, content, pedagogy and evaluation. The analysis so far reveals the multiplicity of values which underpin the curriculum. There is no exclusive relationship between the ideologies and the everyday activities of primary schools; the same activity in school can support a variety of ideologies, just as one ideology can give rise to several activities. Further, different areas of the curriculum can, and will, serve different educational ideologies. The effect of this analysis is twofold: first, it reveals, importantly, that the curriculum is not a closed system, but that it is open, negotiable, problematic, and has to be constantly reviewed, questioned and discussed. Second, ideological analysis reveals potential conflicts in curriculum decision-making. If one queries why certain ideologies are over-represented or under-represented in the primary curriculum, one is thrust back on to an examination of the power structures operating in curriculum decision-making, to identify whose decisions are holding sway. As mentioned earlier, ideological investigation can reveal the nature of the power of dominant interest groups; ideological analysis is thus political analysis (Mannheim, 1936).

Schools and teachers are caught up in this, like it or not. The study of ideologies, while it separates artificially practices in the interests of conceptual clarity, assists teachers and planners to adopt the reflective and critical stance advocated at the outset of this chapter as a requisite of 'good' teaching. Curriculum planners will need to ascertain the power behind curriculum proposals emanating from diverse sources.

EPISTEMOLOGICAL CONTEXTS

While ideological contexts of the curriculum are fundamental to an understanding of primary practice, they are allied clearly to epistemological contexts—concerns with knowledge, its forms and structures. One can approach this area by posing the question 'what do we mean by knowing?'—a central question for curriculum planning. From Ryle (1949) can be taken two familiar terms to describe knowing: 'knowing that' and 'knowing how'. 'Knowing that' is concerned with what can be stated in propositions and facts, e.g. I know *that* the Prime Minister lives at 10, Downing Street; I know *that* this fridge is broken. Much educational knowledge is necessarily of this type. The weakness of 'knowing that' is its lack of utility: we may know the theory of something, e.g. driving, and yet be unable to drive in practice. Similarly, we may know the practice of something, e.g. that a fridge works, but not know why or how. What is required is Ryle's second type of knowledge, 'knowing how': understanding, possessing 'skills, techniques, trained capacities to perform in practical situations where pupils' expressive capacities are relevant and useful' (Skilbeck and Harris, 1976; p. 67). 'Knowing how' is the ability to do things well or correctly, e.g. to drive, to ride a bicycle. The implications of this for curriculum planners are twofold. First, we need to redress the balance in education, which presently over-represents 'knowing that'—inert ideas (Whitehead, 1932)—in favour of a greater emphasis on 'knowing how'—processes. Second, we can learn abut things—'knowing that'—by adopting appropriate processes—'knowing how'. For example, children can learn the value of co-operation by behaving co-operatively; perhaps through group work, they can learn about music by playing or writing it. In similar vein, Smith (1971) contends that the best way for children to learn about reading is by actually reading. Ideas and concepts are used actively rather than aggregated and stored.

A second key epistemological dichotomy in primary education contends that knowledge is reached through reason, thought and reflection, independent of the senses—which are notoriously fallible. A central area of rationalist enquiry is mathematics. For example, if we ask 'How do you know that 91 minus 36 equals 55?' it is inappropriate to reply 'I looked at it and saw it', but 'I figured it out'. One resorts to calculation, not seeing or hearing; one reasons it out. As Flew (1971) comments: 'propositions of this kind are discoverable by the mere operation of thought, without dependence on what is anywhere existent in the universe.

Though there never was a circle or triangle in nature, the truths demonstrated by Euclid would forever retain their certainty and evidence' (p. 384).

In rationalism knowledge is independent of the observer. It claims to provide universal truths; the development of rationality thus becomes a central educational aim. With its emphasis on logic and reason, rationalism appeals strongly to mathematics and to the spheres of values, aims and morals, where reasoning might be a better way of investigating the issues rather than relying on observed experience. However, the main thrust of rationalism for curriculum planners is to argue for the unchallengeable right of some subjects to be included in the curriculum—either because they develop rationality or because they are intrinsically and objectively worthwhile.

Subjects are included in the curriculum because they have objective value regardless of human perception. The problem with this is that while it may suggest the inclusion of mathematics or morality in the curriculum or require curriculum planners to address the problem of how to develop rationality in children, it is difficult to see how using the rationalist argument can in practice offer guidelines or guidance on what to select for the curriculum. At a philosophical level, objective intrinsic worthwhileness is impossible to demonstrate; conceptions of rationality, rational thought and behaviour differ; they are context-dependent. It is difficult therefore to argue the rights of any subject to be included in the curriculum by appealing to universal truths (Blenkin and Kelly, 1981).

While rationality might be one way of achieving knowledge, there are some types of knowledge which are not available through rationality alone—sensory knowledge. Empiricism is premissed on the notion that knowledge is only acquired through sensory experience and reflection on perceptions. For the empiricist, knowledge must correspond to the observed facts of the case. If one accepts the empiricist view then there are five main implications for primary curriculum planners. Initially the objectivity or universal validity of knowledge is replaced by a version of knowledge which sees it as unique, tide to specific contexts; a far more tentative, hypothetical and evolutionary version. Knowledge is subject to constant modification and obsolescence. This is perhaps a more accurate picture of the contemporary knowledge and information explosion than rationalism would offer. Second, knowledge becomes equated with experiences; the direct and first-hand experiences of the child are central to any educational endeavour. Third, teaching styles will have to be revised to reflect the tentative view of knowledge, to resist the imposition of knowledge in favour of the creation and discovery of knowledge—a more problem-solving, discovery approach.

If truth or knowledge are uncertain, temporary and provisional, any attempt by teachers to impose such knowledge on children must be suspect and unsatisfactory, since it is likely to inhibit rather than to promote the continuing evolution of knowledge by offering it in a form that suggests it is fixed and static rather than revealing the fluid entity it really is (Blenkin and Kelly, 1981).

Fourth, teaching will have to move to a process rather than a product view of knowledge, concentrating on skills of knowledge-getting rather than outcomes, e.g. enquiry skills and evaluation skills. Knowledge is to be tested rather than passively accepted (Bruner, 1970). Hence children will be working, for example, as a historian works. Rather than simply learning facts and dates, they will be working in the scientific method of formulating and testing hypotheses, controlling variables and carefully observing results rather than solely reciting scientific facts and concepts. Fifth, empiricism renders selection and curriculum planning problematic as it runs the risk of an imposed curriculum which may not fairly reflect the tentative view of knowledge (Alexander, 1984). Therefore, curriculum planners may need to temper the excitement of empiricism with the demands of coping and survival strategies.

In planning for the primary curriculum, the further epistemological questions which are raised concern how knowledge is to be structured and organized and whether it is to be organized on subject or integrated lines. The arguments about the benefits of one or the other conceal the conceptual confusion surrounding both terms. Subjects can derive from the disciplines of knowledge, with their own central concepts, modes of enquiry, distinctive logical structures and truth tests. Such disciplines could be articulated thus (Hirst, 1965):

mathematical knowledge
physical sciences
human sciences
history
religion
literature and fine arts
philosophy

However, the number and constitution of the disciplines is a major problematic area in epistemology. For example, Peterson (1975) gives four—logical, empirical, moral, aesthetic—while Schwab (1975) gives three—investigative disciplines (mathematics and natural sciences), appreciative disciplines (arts) and decisive disciplines (social sciences). Phenix (1975) gives six:

symbolics (languages, mathematics, logic)
empirics (physical and social sciences)
esthetics (arts)
synnoetics (relational insight, interpersonal awareness)
ethics (morals)
synoptics (history, religion and philosophy)

To say, then, that subjects should represent the disciplines is therefore to invite potential confusion into planning. Alternatively, subjects can be interdisciplinary—e.g. geography, home economics, human and social studies (DES, 1985a, 1985b)—where they integrate knowledge from the disciplines into topics and themes (houses, farms, water)—the stuff of the primary curriculum. Thus there is a lack of clarity on the term 'subject' (Peters, 1969). If the notion of a 'subject' is ambiguous then it is equally so for the notion of 'integrated' knowledge. What is being integrated: is it the disciplines of knowledge or the children's experiences? If it is the former then the question must be raised of the extent to which teachers can successfully integrate knowledge which by its disciplinary pedigree cannot fairly be integrated; if it is the latter then one has to ask how teachers can ensure that children understand the integration and the integrating principle (Taba, 1962). For many children the integrated curriculum is incoherent, a random assortment of loosely connected or disconnected facts and activities.

Given this clouded starting point, primary teaching, devolved both on subject and on integrated lines, stems from different epistemological parentage. For subject teaching the arguments arrange themselves around the notions of quality, excellence, tradition, high standards, high culture, sensitivity to ways of meeting and developing curricula from an analysis of children's needs through informed knowledge. Against this it is argued that subjects preserve outworn traditional knowledge, that they fragment a child's experience, that they are representative of a concern more with knowledge than the learner; a measure of inflexibility in content and pedagogy. In short, they embody the conservative ideologies outlines earlier. On the other hand, integrated knowledge serves the child-centred ideologies which emphasize the whole child, unity of experience, and the need to develop both the cognitive and the affective sides of the child's personality. There is a direct line which can be drawn between 'preparatory' histories, conservative ideologies, rationalist epistemologies and subject teaching on one side, and 'developmental' histories, child-centred ideologies, empiricist epistemologies and integrated types of knowledge on the other (c.f. Alexander, 1984). Dependent on one's value position will be the emphasis given to either strand in the planning of curricula.

It is possible then to reaffirm the conclusion reached at the end of the ideological discussion, that the curriculum of the primary school is not predicated on a single set of values. It is epistemologically value saturated, and as such it is open, tentative and negotiable. Different areas of the curriculum are premissed on different epistemologies. Epistemological analysis clarifies the problematic nature of selecting content, although it does not, nor cannot, answer the questions which it raises. That is a matter for personal or collective debate, reflection and open-minded discussion—the hallmarks of high quality planning.

PSYCHOLOGICAL CONTEXTS

Curriculum planners need to have a clear understanding of how learning takes place and how it can best be promoted through teaching and learning styles. Such an understanding derives from psychological theory. The foci of such theory comprehend:

1. The nature of the learner
   - (a) cognitive and affective aspects
   - (b) individual differences
   - (c) individual needs
2. The nature of the learning process
   - (a) learning theories
   - (b) motivation—extrinsic and intrinsic
   - (c) active learning
   - (d) reinforcement and feedback
   - (e) readiness and matching
   - (f) measurement and diagnosis
   - (g) structuring and sequencing learning
   - (h) transfer of learning skills
   - (i) role of language
   - (j) nature of child development.

Behaviourist Theories

In these importance is attached to a very precise analysis and sequencing of what is to be learned, step-by-step learning, with each new learning being rewarded or reinforced. Learning is evidence by observable changes in behaviour; the desired learning objective is broken down into the steps or processes which lead to the achievement of that objective. The influence of this type of approach can be seen generally in the ways in which teachers sequence and reinforce the learning of desired objectives and skills, and in particular examples such as reading workshops, SRA laboratories, and reading and mathematics schemes which operate through a carefully controlled sequence of new material.

However, behaviourist theories have been castigated for several reasons. They cast the learner in a very passive role: children are receivers of programmes (Taylor, 1968) or predetermined sequences whereas 'the individual is best viewed neither as a passive recipient of information nor as a bundle of stimulus—response connections. Rather he should be regarded as an active participant in the knowledge-getting process' (Bruner, 1974; p. 397). It is difficult to see how programmed learning can develop critical awareness and independent thought in children—an increasingly significant feature in a plural society marked by controversy and conflict (Ing. 1981), and a central feature of the primary ethos. Moreover, it is hard to imagine just how workable the idea is that complex and abstract concepts can be broken down into sequential steps; either the number of steps is unmanageably long, or the steps are poorly sequenced, or, more damaging still, it risks having only trivial or low-level objectives addressed—the same argument that has been levelled at behavioural objectives (MacDonald-Ross, 1975). Like the problems of behavioural objectives, the behavioural theories of psychology confuse logical steps with psychological steps (Hirst, 1967). They imply only one pathway through knowledge and a didactic and prescriptive teaching style. They equate a classroom with a clinical laboratory, unsullied by the realities of primary schools (c.f. Pollard, 1985).

Cognitive Theories

There are two key figures in this discussion, Piaget and Bruner. From Piaget can be taken the notion that learning is an active process through manipulating actual experiences (Kamii, 1975). For Piaget, learning is achieved through a process of assimilation and accommodation of experiences. He lays stress on the importance of social relationships—peer-group teaching and group work—as one important way of breaking free from the egocentricity characteristic of young children. Piaget both contributes to epistemological theory and fuels child-centred ideologies, for in his theories of cognitive development, from sensori-motor to formal operations, children change their thinking qualitatively as they grow.

The ideological impact of this qualitative difference in thinking between children and adults is to argue that children have status as children rather than solely as miniature or future adults. Their needs as children must be met, differences must be respected. Piaget's 'stages' theory also lends itself to introducing the concept of matching (discussed later) and readiness; that one can match a child's work if one knows which stage of development she or he has reached or is ready to meet. The concept of matching has urgency if one considers the overwhelming evidence of poor matching found by Bennett, Desforges and Wilkinson (1984), where 54 per cent of number tasks and 55 per cent of language tasks were mismatched.

However, Piaget's work must be treated with caution (Donaldson, 1978). Nisbet (1983) regards the stage theory of development with suspicion, lest it become too narrowly prescriptive—'a disguised version of behaviouristic determination', (p. 83) trapping children's development by planning work for stages which they may have left in many conceptual areas (see also Alexander, 1984).

Like Piaget, Bruner argues for the centrality of the child constructing her or his own knowledge rather than receiving it from outside: learning is by active discovery. Epistemologically, this lays great store on process and empiricist views of knowledge, views embodied in his MACOS project (Jenkins, 1976), where emphasis is laid on enquiry, observation, judgement, evaluation and reflection. Knowledge is speculative, therefore what pupils derive from the material cannot be determined completely in advance (Kelly, 1980). Bruner develops a theory of instruction (1966; 1970) which, he claims, has four main features:

1. It should provide experiences which stimulate curiosity in children—a 'predisposition to learning'.
2. It should structure knowledge in a way which can be readily assimilated by children. Structures of knowledge may be learned, he suggests, in three main ways: the enactive mode (knowing something through doing it); the iconic mode (knowing something through seeing or constructing a picture or image of it); and the symbolic mode (knowing something through symbolic means, e.g. language).
3. It 'should specify the most effective sequences in which to present the materials to be learned' (Bruner, 1970; p. 113); this must have due regard to the need to match the logical aspects of subject to the learner's strategies of learning. Bruner, like Hirst (1967), insists that there is no single sequence of learning; learning depends for example on an individual's speed of learning, motivation, stage of development, previous knowledge and mode of learning.
4. It 'should specify the nature and pacing of rewards and punishments in the process of learning and teaching' (p. 114). Clearly, Bruner is alluding to the need for careful use of intrinsic and extrinsic motivation, a diagnostic approach to identifying

children's needs, and the need to provide positive feedback to children.

In regard to the contribution of these theories to curriculum planning, it can be seen that behaviourist theories lend themselves to training and instruction in a narrow sense of specific and measurable skills—a limited conception of education—whereas alternative theories seem more open-ended. Psychological theories underline the central need to diagnose, evaluate and meet children's needs and abilities; to utilize and generate motivation in children; to offer appropriate rewards and punishments; to cast learning in an active, experiential, discovery mode (DES 1985b); to make learning meaningful (c.f. Smith, 1978); to offer feedback to children; to develop and operate from a positive self-concept in children; to plan on the 'moderate novelty principle'—making tasks and reasons for them explicit and challenging and yet not too remote (Siann and Ugwuegbu, 1980); to accept that there is a place, albeit limited, for rote learning to make responses automatic.

There is an important connection between cognitive psychologies, child-centred and progressive ideologies and empiricist epistemologies. However, attention must be drawn to the very generalized nature of the psychological theories outlined, to question whether they offer teachers little more than platitudes. The theories appear so diffuse as to be able to underscore a variety of conflicting practices. They require reflection and application for their substance. They are not hard and fast truths; they are conflicting, provisional, incomplete and falsifiable. The ramifications of this are once again to suggest that the curriculum and its planning are open to debate, problematic and negotiable.

SOCIOLOGICAL CONTEXTS

The curriculum of a school fulfils social functions; it responds to social requirements and pressures for change. Thus curriculum planning must look to characteristics and constraints of society to find purpose and direction.

The advent of the micro-chip has accelerated the information revolution and the information-based society. Knowledge is expanding at an exponential rate, a move matched by its rate of obsolescence. Schools and society have to develop mechanisms to tolerate such movements. Further, much of this knowledge and its application points towards an increasingly technological mode of operation. The ramifications of this are huge. One major implication is that traditional skills, practices and values are rendered obsolete (Sivanadan, 1979; Stonier, 1982). Society is being compelled to revise its notions of leisure and employment; leisure appears to be a growth area while employment both fluctuates and changes its patterns. The moral problems are vast. Whether to move to full employment or unemployment where technology both deskills and has the potential to reduce the size of the workforce required, is as much a moral question as it is political, economic or technical (Entwistle, 1981).

Second, with knowledge expanding in all directions, increased specialization and fragmentation of interests is inevitable. The central unifying spine of society is ever more difficult to identify; plural values, plural cultures, lifestyles, economics, politics—all are hallmarks of a society marked by a slender reduction in inequality (Westergaard and Resler, 1976), an increased materialism (Apple, 1982) and a loss of social cohesion. Further, the signs of societal strain are clear—urban and industrial decline, rising crime, juvenile delinquency, riots on city streets, and a widening gap between rich and poor. Pluralism is spilling over into conflict. The implications of this again are to reassert the necessity for examining moral problems and values. Technology, with its capability and capacity to create and destroy life in ways scarcely envisaged a generation ago, throws into sharper relief pressing moral problems—abortion, war, health, pollution, poverty. Morality must not be the casualty of technological advance. Further, the extent to which fragmentation of interests can be tolerated needs to be examined.

The educational implications of this scenario are vast. Given that the curriculum at its best can only be a selection from the culture then the criteria for that selection are problematic. To what extent can diverse and conflicting values in society be represented in the curriculum? Whose values are protected in the curriculum, whose neglected? Is the move to a common national curriculum an attempt to retrieve social consensus and cohesion? What will be the nature of the schools' responses to a technologically advancing society? How far can schools act as agents of social change? How far can one look to schools to shoulder the burden of macro-sociological problems?

Curriculum planners can address these issues on many fronts. First, curricula need to represent diverse values and cultures in society—multi-ethnically and subculturally. This raised questions of the extent to which individual schools and communities can determine their own curricula, and the extent to which all schools should be developing in children an awareness of the multiplicity of cultures in society and the problems and possibilities that this offers. Second, at a major decision-making level, there is the need to address the notion of a common curriculum, its desirability, feasibility and practicability, composition and framing—be it through subjects, areas of experience, themes, learning experiences or learning environments [Curriculum Development Centre (CDC), 1980]. Third, there is a clear requirement for schools to enable moral debate to take place, to deal with moral issues explicitly as well as implicitly and opportunistically (Lawton, 1983). Fourth, schools must ensure that children have an understanding of political, social and economic systems and power structures in society (*ibid*; Harwood, 1985).

Fifth, the whole relationship of education and employment requires exploration and rationalization. Such a relationship is tension ridden, for while education celebrates developing individual potential and diversity, the exact opposite is true for vast areas of employment, where a narrow application of skills is practised and where individuality and personal development do not even enter the calculus. Schools make far greater demands on children, and have the potential for offering them richer personal rewards, than does working life. This is not to neglect the significant role that schools must pay in teaching numeracy and literacy, indeed, with the rise of the service sector this becomes more pressing. Sixth, just as there is the need to re-examine the relationship between school and work, so there is between education and leisure (Entwistle, 1981). Seventh, the whole nature of technological education needs to be examined to allow for developing in children both a general and specific understanding of technology and its social implications and applications (Lawton, 1983). Eighth, to be able to cope with the knowledge explosion and the rate of obsolescence of knowledge there is a need, recognized by Her Majesty's Inspectorate (HMI) (DES, 1985b) to teach children skills of information handling, studying, problem-solving and communication (Lawton, 1983). The move to skills-based teaching, though significant, cannot be done in a knowledge vacuum; rather the whole area of content selection becomes problematic. Finally, the effects of change in technology, employment patterns and prospects, information processing, social diversity and cultural pluralism are to put a premium on developing personal and social skills in children (DES. 1981)—adaptability, self-reliance, self-development, personal and environmental responsibility. Planning for the curriculum to promote personal development requires careful consideration of the positive value of child-centredness as an enabling curriculum for developing autonomy in children.

The implications of an analysis of broad societal trends reveal the problematic nature of the primary curriculum. If society is changing, fragmenting and unsure of its directions or its areas of commonality, then the same may be reflected in the primary curriculum. Aims, content, pedagogy, criteria for evaluation are uncertain. A curriculum rests on shifting grounds, yet it must set a firm foundation from reflective, articulate and insightful planners.

The analysis so far is presented in summary form in Table 1.3. The primary curriculum is, and should be, negotiable. Given the inability to offer a single and enduring conceptualization of the primary curriculum, any approaches to planning will inevitably be value saturated. However, they should fairly address the conceptual analysis presented earlier by:

1. Reflecting the negotiable character of the primary curriculum.
2. Addressing macro constraints on the primary curriculum and teachers.
3. Analysing ways in which the primary curriculum is developing.
4. Anticipating, preparing for and serving changes at a macro-societal level.
5. Being able to be translated into practice by curriculum planners.
6. Assisting teachers and planners to become critical and reflective in a desire to promote and perpetuate high-quality teaching.

Table 1.3
Ideologies and their background contexts

	Instrumentalism	*Conservation*	*Progressivism*
Focus of the ideology	Society	Knowledge	Child
Emphasis of the curriculum	Efficiency, usefulness, vocationalism, science and technology	Homogeneity, uniformity	Discovery, activity, diversity, needs and interests
	Common curricula	Dual curricula	Diverse curricula

Table 1.3 (Contd.)

	Instrumentalism	*Conservation*	*Progressivism*
View of the child	Child as embryonic adult	Child as deficient adult	Childhood as a state in itself
View of knowledge	Societally determined Socially relevant vocational, useful Empiricist Evolutionary Product and process Extrinsically worthwhile Trained Egalitarian Structured	Unchanging Received, vicarious Non-vocational Rationalist Closed Product Intrinsically worthwhile Initiated Elitist Subject-based	Evolutionary obsolescent Reflexive, first-hand Non-vocational Empiricist Open-ended, discovered Process Intrinsically worthwhile Discovered, experienced Individual Integrated
Psychological implications	Behaviourist Understanding Group and individual learning Extrinsic motivation Need for sequence Task-centred learning Programmed learning	Behaviourist and Brunerian Acceptance Class learning Extrinsic motivation Need for structure Competition Structured learning	Developmental and Piagetian Meaningfulness, discovered Flexible learning organizations Instrinsic motivation Need for diversity Co-operation Autonomous learning
Roles of teacher	Trainer, instructor, director	Expert, authority, director	Guide, facilitator catalyst
Roles of child	Apprentice	Neophyte	Agent of own learning
Sociological implications	Education for leisure, social sciences curriculum, multicultural and technological education	Curriculum change from within, seeking equilibrium	Development of creativity, autonomy, self-reliance, adaptability, skills-based teaching

In reviewing the discussions and issues presented so far a checklist of principles can be devised which, taken together, can be said to constitute the 'primary ethos' (Morrison, 1986b):

1. A view of childhood as a state in itself as well as a preparation for adulthood.
2. The use of discovery methods and practical activity.
3. Learning by doing—practical activity.
4. Problem-solving approaches to teaching and learning.
5. Learning in various modes; enactive, iconic, symbolic.
6. Integration and unity of experiences; the integrated curriculum.
7. The value of teaching processes and skills as well as products and bodies of knowledge.
8. A view of content and process as complementary facets of curricular knowledge.
9. A view of educational activities and processes as being intrinsically worthwhile as well as having instrumental and utility value.
10. The value of an enriching social, emotional and physical environment.
11. The need to develop autonomy in children.
12. The provision of a curriculum which demonstrates and allows for breadth, balance, relevance, continuity and progression, differentiation and consistency.
13. The emphasis given to individual needs, abilities, interests, learning styles and rates as well as a received curriculum.
14. The fostering and satisfaction of curiosity.
15. The value of peer group support.
16. The value of self-expression.

17. The need for intrinsic as well as extrinsic motivation.
18. The use of the environment to promote learning.
19. The importance of the quality and intensity of a child's experience.
20. The uniqueness of each child.
21. The view of the teacher as a catalyst for all forms of development.
22. An extended view of the 'basics' to comprehend all curriculum areas, not just the three Rs.
23. The need to develop literacy and numeracy through cross-curricular approaches.

Such a checklist endeavours to meet two demands outlines at the start of this book: the need to provide principles which underpin planning, and, in recognition of the desirability of open-ended, divergent perspectives on primary teaching, the need to offer substance for reflective thinking and debate by teachers.

MANAGEMENT CONTEXTS

Between the theoretical contexts outlined so far and the practical day-to-day planning and implementation of the curriculum is set the interface of the management of the curriculum. This can be defined as the most effective use and organization of a spectrum of resources to enable children's learning to be at its optimal level, from planning to implementation, outcomes, evaluation and curriculum change and development (c.f. Bush, 1986). The management of primary school curriculum planning will seek to find major ways of translating the theoretical constructs and constituents of the primary ethos outlined earlier into curricula which are worthwhile and effective. Hence the analysis presented so far has to be taken to substantive levels, to deal with the issues involved in managing the curriculum. This involves addressing three key questions:

1. What are the levels of curriculum management?
2. What are the tasks of curriculum management?
3. What are the styles of curriculum management?

The Tasks in Curriculum Management

The case has been put for regarding the primary curriculum as a negotiation, discussion or exploration of proposals for what teachers should teach and for what children should learn, based on participants' ideologies, epistemologies, views of learning and views of society. Hence the management of the curriculum will involve debate and decision-making on three factors (Day, Johnston and Whitaker, 1985):

1. The planning, philosophies and policies of the curriculum.
2. The operation of the curriculum.
3. The evaluation of the curriculum.

However, the debate does not rest there, for one can suggest that, because the curriculum is about people interacting in a given setting, and because the curriculum is open to debate, managing the curriculum should involve: managing people; managing organizations; and managing change (Everard and Morris, 1985).

Managing People

Managing people will involve utilizing and developing their interpersonal skills and sensitivities, leadership capabilities, expertise in curriculum areas, interests and aptitudes, enthusiasm and motivation, effort, decision-making capacities, and their abilities to identify and handle conflict (Morrison, 1986a). Managing organizations from a curriculum perspective rather than a routinely administrative perspective involves: the development, effective and appropriate use of team work (Bush, 1986); shared decision-making; open communication channels (vertical and lateral); dissemination channels for new ideas; clarity of aims, philosophies and powers; stable organizational structures in which people can operate; available resources of time, money, space and administration—the technology to support the meeting of the organization's goals (Elliott-Kemp and Williams, 1979); co-ordination of activities; and co-ordinated use of staff expertise.

Managing Organizations

Managing people, an idiographic, individualized concern, clearly relies on effectively managing organizations and vice versa. A path has to be set which reconciles and manages several key tensions (Dalin and Rust, 1983).

Consensus *versus* conflict;

Re-stabilization *versus* renewal of the curriculum;

The individual *versus* the organization;

Leadership *versus* the staff;

Process of planning and change *versus* the content of planning and change;

Shared ownership of the curriculum *versus* self-interest of individuals in the curriculum.

Managing Change

Both managing people and organizations are synthesized in the notion of managing curriculum change and development. Curriculum innovation, development and change can be articulated as a multifaceted phenomenon (Dalin, 1978), involving regarding it as:

1. An evolutionary process over time rather than as a single event—from invention through development, dissemination and diffusion, to adoption, implementation, institutionalization and recommendation (Hall, Loucks, Rutherford *et al.*, 1975).

2. System disturbing; changes in one are of a school's organization and curriculum setting off a chain reaction in other areas, i.e. that it affects a system rather than a single teacher or instance.
3. A multi-dimensional phenomenon; political, social, organizational, individual, technical.
4. A series of transformations of ideas into practices, institutions and materials.
5. Involving all members of an institution and the complex interplay between individuals and organizational structures.
6. Having to address the rate, staging, scale, degree and continuity of the process (Hoyle, 1976).

The complexity of change and innovation can be realized in answers to the questions:

- Innovations for whom? (Nor everyone might benefit from the change; one person's benefit is another's loss in curriculum management).
- Innovations by whom? (Who has the power legitimacy and credibility to initiate, implement and support change?)
- Who has to change? (Changes can upset power hierarchies).
- What has to change? (A school's aims and philosophies, organizations and administration, roles and role relationships, curriculum aims, content, pedagogy, resources, evaluation).

These many facets all point to the need for management of curriculum change to address the institution in which the change and development is taking place as well as the curriculum itself. This involves addressing the climate (Halpin, 1966) or 'organizational health' (Miles, 1965) of the institution; an institution which is unhealthy is unprepared for curriculum change and development. A school staff or any part of it wishing to innovate a piece of the curriculum may well have to set its institutional health in order before it can innovate in the curriculum; its health must be robust. Hoyle (1975a) reinforces this point where he comments that 'curriculum innovation requires change in the internal organization of the school. Change in the internal organization of the school is a major innovation' (p. 332).

An organizationally healthy school (Miles, 1965) will be clear on its goals, have adequate channels of communication, adequate resources of time, space, money, administrative services, staff (Fullan, 1982), comprise a cohesive staff, tolerate and resolve dissension, encourage teamwork, be able to identify problems, match leadership by the head with leadership by staff, involve staff in curriculum development and discussion, share affective and social relationships as well as institutional relationships, maintain high morale, respect teacher autonomy, foster creativity, be open to self-criticism, operate staff development and INSET plans, and be open to innovation—the list becomes endless!

Collegial Decision-making

The model, then, is of 'collegial' rather than 'hierarchical' decision-making (Campbell, 1985). To achieve this may mean overcoming differences of value of power, separately or in combination, tackling barriers to innovation: increased workloads, deskilling which innovation brings (MacDonald, 1975), inappropriate organizational arrangements, lack of resources, edging staff out of a natural reluctance to change, lack of capability to perform new roles (Gross, Giacquinta and Bernstein, 1971), to see change as a benefit, as unthreatening, as evolving from existing practice, as supported by many parties, as a means of increasing job satisfaction and professional development.

Thus a manager of change has to possess several qualities which can be said to lie in the fields of knowledge, skills and personality. This involves addressing the questions set out in Tables 1.4, 1.5, and 1.6. Stewart (1985) highlights characteristics of good managers in Table 1.7. A school which is seeking to improve its organizational development (Dalin and Rust, 1983) can utilize a variety of strategies:

1. Training or education, including lectures, exercises, simulations.
2. Process consultation, concentration on observing ongoing processes and providing feedback.
3. Confrontation, bringing together units or groups which have a history of poor communication.
4. Data feedback, involving systematic collection of information which is reported back to the organization.
5. Plan-making, dealing with planning and goal-setting.
6. Organizational development task force establishment, setting up *ad hoc* groups to provide structure for solving problems and carrying out plans.
7. Techno-structure activity, focusing on structural factors, work flow and means of accomplishing tasks (Schmuck and Miles, 1983).

Table 1.4
Knowledge required for managing change

Knowledge of:

1. People and their motivational systems—what makes them tick
2. Organizations as social systems—what makes them healthy and effective, able to achieve objectives
3. The environment surrounding the organization—the systems that impinge on and make demands of it
4. Managerial styles and their effects on work
5. One's own personal managerial style and proclivities
6. Organizational processes such as decision-making, planning, control, communication, conflict management and reward systems
7. The process of change
8. Educational and training methods and theory.

(*Source*: Everard and Morris (1985) *Effective School Management*, p. 180)

Table 1.5
Skills required for managing change

Skills in:

1. Analysing large complex systems
2. Collecting and processing large amounts of information and simplifying it for action
3. Goal-setting and planning
4. Getting consensus decisions
5. Conflict management
6. Empathy
7. Political behaviour
8. Public relations
9. Consulting and counselling.
10. Training and teaching.

(*Source*: Everard and Morris (1985) *Effective School Management*, p. 181)

Table 1.6
Personality characteristics required for managing change

1. A strong sense of personal ethics which helps to ensure consistent behaviour
2. Something of an intellectual by both training and temperament
3. A strong penchant towards optimism
4. Enjoyment of the intrinsic rewards of effectiveness, without the need for public approval
5. High willingness to take calculated risks and live with the consequences without experiencing undue stress
6. A capacity to accept conflict and enjoyment in managing it
7. A soft voice and low-key manner
8. A high degree of self-awareness—knowledge of self
9. A high tolerance of ambiguity and complexity
10. A tendency to avoid polarizing issues into black and white, right and wrong
11. High aLility to listen.

(*Source*: Everard and Morris (1985) *Effective School Management*, p. 181)

Table 1.7
Characteristics of good managers of change

1. They know clearly what they want to achieve
2. They can translate desires into practical action
3. They can see proposed changes not only from their own viewpoint but also from that of others
4. They do not mind being out on a limb
5. They show irreverance for tradition but respect for experience
6. They plan flexibly, matching constancy of ends against a repertoire of available means
7. They are not discouraged by setbacks
8. They harness circumstances to enable change to be implemented
9. They clearly explain change
10. They involve their staff in the management of change and protect their security
11. They don't pile one change on top of another, but await assimilation
12. They present change as a rational action
13. They make change personally rewarding for people, wherever possible
14. They share maximum information about possible outcomes
15. They show that change is 'related to the business'
16. They have a history of successful change behind them.

(*Source*: Stewart, in Everard and Morris (1985) *Effective School Management*, pp. 179-180)

Dalin and Rust (1983) stress the need for internal and external support for change to be provided to motivate, sustain and shape the direction of the change (c.f. Lavelle, 1984).

It is clear that such skills draw on an ability to state goals, to plan, organize, control, lead and direct people and projects (Everard and Morris, 1985). How this is done can be termed the 'style of curriculum management'.

Styles of Curriculum Management

These concern all parties in the planning process, and depend on the climate of the school and the nature of curriculum leadership in it. For instance, curriculum planners may adopt any of four styles (Loubser, Spiers and Moody, 1975; Tannenbaum and Schmidt, 1985):

1. Tell decisions—autocratic.
2. Sell decisions—paternalistic.
3. Consult decisions—consultative.
4. Share decisions—democratic.

The need to achieve both successful results and successful relationships will guide the selection of styles. There is a trade-off between the styles, whichever are chosen. For example a 'tell' decision can effect a bureaucratic, hierarchical model of planning which reinforces zones of power and influence. While this may be necessary, desirable or expedient, it risks alienating those who receive the decisions. 'Sell' decisions may suit a leader who wishes to foster friendly relations and yet maintain a firm rein on curricular practices; in fact, the opposite may result, the recipients seeing the style as non-genuine (Halpin, 1966), over-assertive, non-motivating and temporary. It is interesting perhaps that this is regarded as a very closed climate for planning and curriculum change (Halpin, 1966). A consultative model may reach many participants and hence foster involvement in planning the curriculum; alternatively, it could be perceived as 'the iron fist in the kid glove', as the locus of power is left undisturbed.

A 'share' decision will be democratic, with authority deriving from expertise [professional rather than positional authority (Bush, 1986)], but it may founder for want of time, or will to participate, or conflict of values. Planners will need to adopt styles which depend on the level of the curriculum debate—conceptual to practical, the type of organizational practices, and the stage of the planning and uptake—from first principles and opening debate to trialling, adoption, implementation and institutionalization.

Levels of Curriculum Management

While this is taken up more in Chapter 2 where levels of planning are established from the contextual to the practical, attention here is drawn to the notion of spheres of influence, levels of decision-making and use of staff expertise. The question requires curriculum planners to harness levels of the curriculum debate and decision-making to staff expertise and power. The task harks back to the styles of curriculum management—hierarchical to collegial.

If a hierarchical model is adopted then decision-making power is clear (see Figure 1.1). If a collegial style is present then equalization of power is its predicate (c.f. Bush, 1986), see Figure 1.2. This latter, or a variation of it which sets the head and deputy above the other scales which remain clustered together, may more fairly reflect the nature of primary schools where teachers regard each other as a community of equals (Lortie, 1975), regardless of the scale posts which may be awarded for curriculum or pastoral responsibilities. For the purposes here, curriculum planners will need to decide which levels and states of the planning debate are best dealt with by which people, external or internal to the school (Lavelle, 1984), and which people will take decisions about which aspects of the curriculum and its planning. For successful curriculum planning these levels need to mesh, to integrate, in the true spirit of primary education.

EVALUATIVE CONTEXTS

If curriculum planning is to be effective, and if the notion of effectiveness implies both matching, as discussed in later chapters, and curriculum development and renewal, then there is a built-in need to evaluate the curriculum—its planning, implementation and outcomes. Evaluation is the springboard to action, to planning. This need is being increasingly accorded recognition, priority and formalization,

Head teacher
↓
Deputy head teacher
↓
Scale three teacher
↓
Scale two teacher
↓
Scale one teacher
↓
Probationary teacher

Fig. 1.1: A hierarchical model of decision-making.

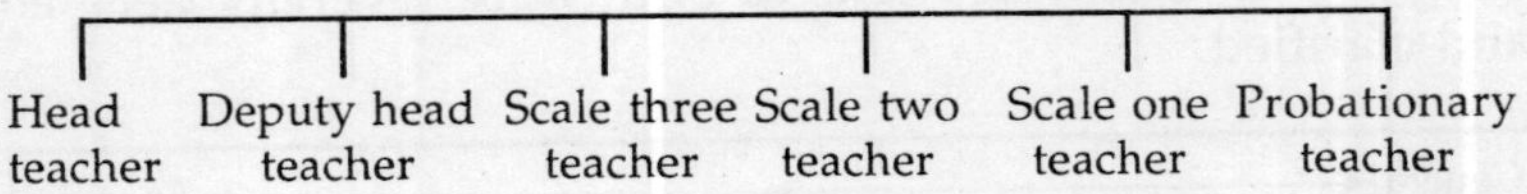

Fig. 1.2: A collegial model of decision-making.

both politically and educationally (DES, 1977; 1981; 1983). At a national level this is reflected in the establishment of the Assessment of Performance Unit (APU), the growth of central directives and reports (DES, 1985b; 1985c). At a local level Simons (1984) sees it reflected in increased testing of pupil performance, increasing public reporting by schools (by brochures, headteachers' reports, four-yearly reports), curriculum review and institutional evaluation. At an institutional level the emergence of school and teacher evaluation, appraisal and self-evaluation surfaced in the 1970s as a legitimate means of meeting the demand from, and response to, macro pressures for increased teacher accountability. Such pressures rode on the crests of several waves—political, economic and educational.

Initially the economic retrenchment of the 1970s required assurances from education of 'value for money' (Callaghan, 1976). In the optimism of post-war economic expansion and stability, education was the shining star in the human capital theorists' heaven—that investment in self-development yielded personal and economic satisfaction. At time of economic and fiscal difficulty, given impetus by the 1973 oil crisis, education became the scapegoat for an ailing society, criticized for its tenuous links with industry, its inability to prepare children for the world of work, and its alleged contribution to the relaxing moral fibre of the country's youth. Evaluation then became a form a reassurance (Holt, 1981).

Secondly, in education there was a burgeoning expansion of, and interest in. methods and methodologies of curriculum evaluation *per se*. Well-tried methods operated at the level of national large-scale projects (e.g. Schools Council); new methods emerged (e.g. Parlett and Hamilton, 1976), and the alleged merits and demerits of both were severally debated and clarified.

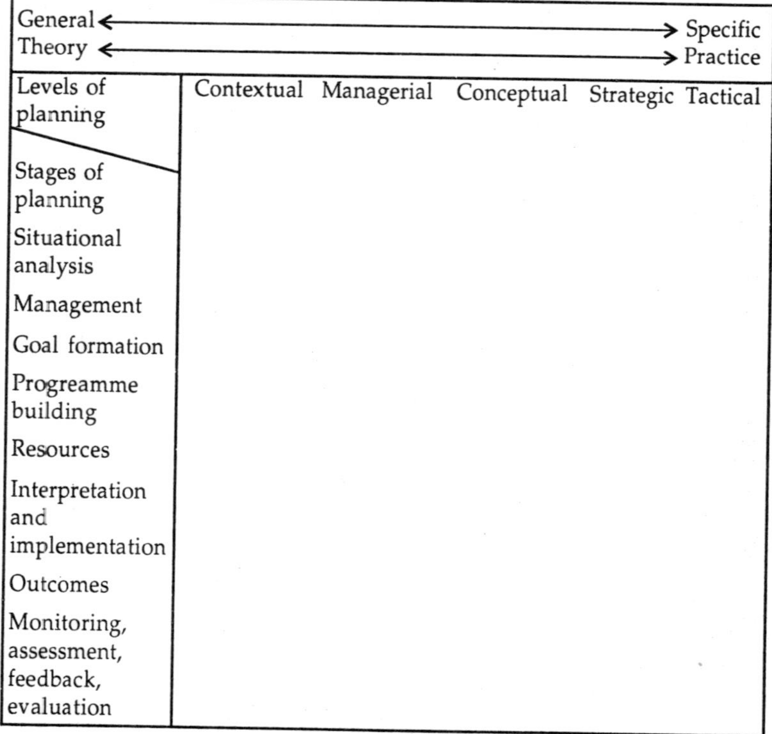

Fig. 1.3: Levels and stages of curriculum evaluation.

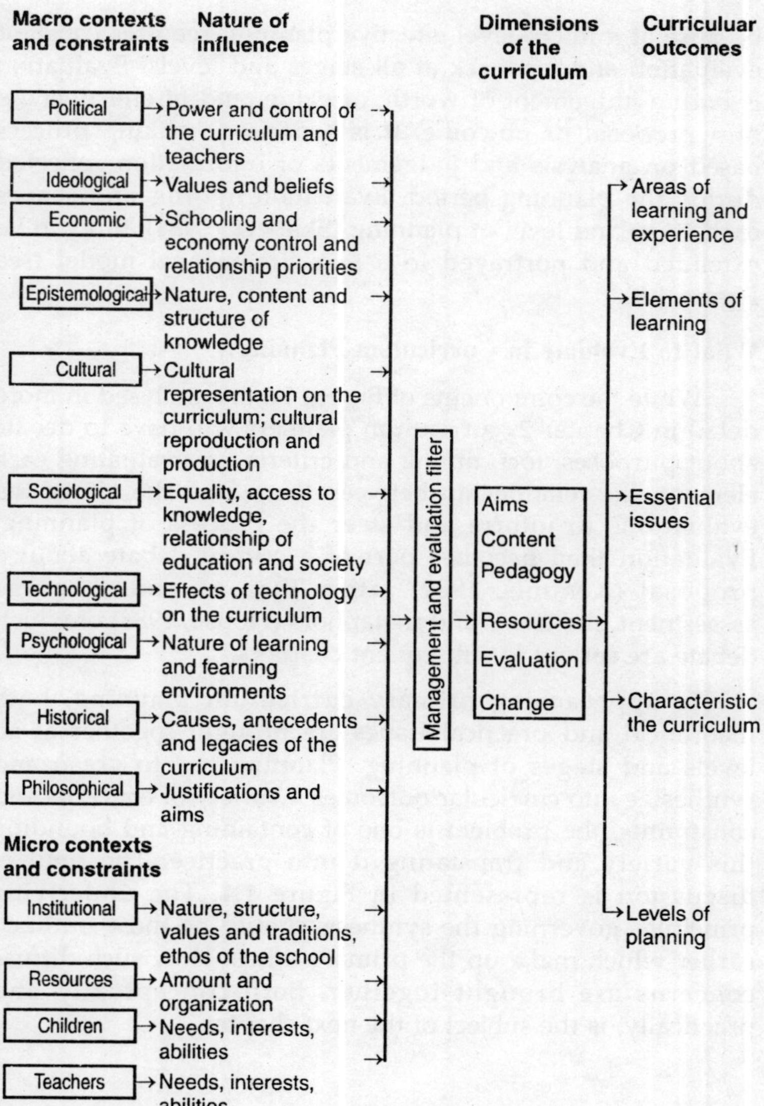

Fig. 1.4: Components of the curriculum debate.

For curriculum planners the urge to evaluate should be strong both because it meets macro-level demands and because at a micro-level effective planning requires constant evaluation and feedback at all stages and levels. Evaluation is both a judgement of worth, of value, and of effectiveness of a proposal or outcome. It is a decision-making process based on analysis and judgements of information collected during the planning period. Evaluation informs and shapes each stage and level of planning (Skilbeck, 1984); this can be extended and portrayed in a two-dimensional model (see Figure 1.3).

What to Evaluate in Curriculum Planning?

While the components of Figure 1.3 are analysed in more detail in Chapter 2, curriculum planners will have to debate about purposes, foci, timing and criteria for evaluating each element, the relationship between them, and the use of the evaluations to inform and steer the process of planning. Evaluation then becomes part of a critical debate about a proposal (Kemmis, 1982) rather than an end-of-course assessment, the terms and metaphors (House, 1985) of which debate are set out in subsequent chapters.

In approaching primary curriculum planning, both theoretical and practical issues are brought together at all levels and stages of planning. Planning has to grasp and synthesize into curricular outcomes a variety of concerns and constraints; the problem is one of containing and bounding this variety and translating it into practice. The field of discussion is represented in Figure 1.4. The underlying principles governing the synthesis should be those outlined earlier which make up the primary ethos. How such diffuse concerns are brought together, both conceptually and practically, is the subject of the next chapter.

2

Curricular Proposals

Today's educator must feel somewhat overwhelmed by the flood of curricular demands made on the schools. Philosophy cannot determine which of these may best deserve implementation, but it can help to clarify what they *mean*. Some of the concepts central to these proposals are part of the standard vocabulary of education while others, like *confluent education,* have revolutionary implications. It makes sense to invoke a mood of philosophical detachment long enough to get our bearings.

The Claim of "Generative" Subject-matter

The popular press often urges educators to get back to the three R's. In its simplistic form, such a demand need not be considered seriously. It may, however, serve to raise the question of whether there is such a thing as basic subject-matter. We have seen that teaching is a triadic affair which includes something taught, but this does not settle *what* should be taught.

One answer to the question of what should be taught is so-called generative subject-matter. Generative subjects are those that are so fundamental to education that they appear at every level and are a precondition of nearly everything else. Certainly, the three R's can claim something of that status, the development of some minimal competence in the symbols of thought and expression: speaking, reading, writing, and reasoning.

Concern for generative subject matter is part of a larger proposal made by Jerome Bruner in his *The Process of Education*. He makes two significant claims: (1) Learning at early stages, he says, "should not only take us somewhere; it should allow us later to go further more easily."[1] (2) Young students are fundamentally interested in and able to understand the logos of adult subject-matter. These are, of course, psychological not philosophical claims, but they fit with many of the things we have already noted about the meaning of "teaching" and "educating."

The fault of old-fashioned, adult-subject-oriented education Dewey and other progressive educators have criticized was that it allowed for Bruner's first proposition, but rejected or did not understand the second. Consequently, educators faced a dilemma: On the one hand, the student needed to learn certain things in order to become a knowledgeable adult, and, on the other, the student was not interested nor was he ready to grasp these subjects. The teacher was compelled to become an authoritarian indoctrinator. This posture made the educator vulnerable to the criticism of the progressives who seemed to bespeak the child's real nature. The trouble with many childish interests is that they are temporary, and they do not carry the educational process forward. Pandering to them often resulted in making education into a kind of entertainment.

If Bruner is correct, this dilemma can be overcome. Children, he says, *are* interested in understanding adult subjects, and, moreover, they can grasp them if the child's intuitive mode of thought is understood, and if instruction is oriented to that mode of understanding. This is how he puts it:

The early teaching of science, mathematics, social studies, and literature should be designed to teach these subjects with scrupulous intellectual honesty, but with an emphasis upon the intuitive grasp of ideas and upon the use of these basic ideas. A curriculum as it develops should revisit these basic ideas repeatedly, building upon them until the student has grasped the full formal apparatus that goes with them.[2]

This is what he calls the "spiral curriculum."

I have argued that the fundamental meaning of "educating" is the initiation of the student into the realm of human meanings. Bruner's research on the spiral curriculum makes this enterprise more practically plausible than most of the work done on the psychology of the curriculum prior to his time. If the child can indeed grasp in an intuitive way the logos of materials that he will need to know as an adult, and, if, further, he is interested in understanding these things, then, the whole business is put on a more substantial footing. The claims of generative subject matter can now be considered without falling back into an authoritarian approach that ignores the child's own way of learning. Instead of endless drill and rote learning, the young student can be really *taught* in the paradigmatic sense of the word. Hence, what he is taught will become more significant to him as he moves through the schools. The psychological point is that children are curious. They enjoy learning as such. The teacher need not stay with trifling interests because the pupil is young. Even at the tenderest age, his powers of understanding are unfolding, and he not only derives great satisfaction, but also sustains an enduring interest in exercising them.

It will still, no doubt, be true that the ratio of training to teaching will be higher in the early years than in the later ones, but appeals to understanding will never be absent. As the student matures, the teacher's role will gradually move from being a director of the learning process to that of a facilitator of learning. Ideally, at the end of the period of formal schooling, the student will be ready to learn on his own.

Bruner's work finds confirmation in the work of Benjamin Bloom and his associates in their two-volume work on the *Taxonomy of Educational Objectives*.[3] These volumes offer an analysis of the natural sequence of learning in both cognitive and affective areas. We shall consider later the question of affective education. Here we are concerned with the authors' conception of the sequence of learning from the simplest levels of understanding to the most comprehensive.

The *sequence* in congnitive learning, they claim, is as follows: (1) Knowledge of specifics: terminology and facts. (2) Knowledge of ways and means of dealing with specifics: organizing, studying, judging, and criticizing. These include (a) an early awareness of conventional terminology and methods for dealing with specifics, awareness of trends and sequences, such as the continuity and development of American culture; (b) knowledge of classifications and categories used in given subject fields; (c) knowledge of criteria by which facts, principles, opinions, and conduct are tested or judged; and (d) knowledge of methods of inquiry in such fields. (3) Knowledge of the universals and abstractions in a field: This involves knowledge of the major schemes and patterns by which phenomena and ideas are organized.

From another perspective, Bloom considers knowledge in terms of intellectual abilities and skills. The competences are traced *developmentally* as follows: (1) Comprehension as the lowest level of understanding. (2) Application: the use of abstractions in particular and concrete situations. (3) Analysis: the constituent elements or parts of any hierarchy of ideas are clarified. (4) Synthesis: the putting together of elements and parts so as to form a whole. (5) Evaluation: the development of standards of appraisal, both internal and external, appropriate to the scheme involved.

The significance of the *Taxonomy* is that it spells out both the inner structure of understanding and the outer structure of symbolic systems. This makes clearer the meaning of educating in our sense.

A final word on the subject-matter content of education. Present-day educators are under pressure to think of education in terms of personal development, social relationships, and so on. This claim is important and will be studied presently. However, the cognitive dimension is, as we shall see, a kind of special property of schools and universities. Without it, affective education would be a truncated affair.

Michael Oakeshott, in an essay on "Learning and Teaching," eloquently bespeaks this point:

> ...this inheritance is an historic achievement...it is what human beings have achieved...by exploiting the opportunities of fortune and by means of their own efforts. It comprises the standards of conduct to which from time to time they have given their preferences, the pro- and con-feelings to which they have given their approval and disapproval, the intellectual enterprises they have happened upon and pursued, the duties they have imposed upon themselves, the activities they have delighted in, the hopes they have entertained and the disappointments they have suffered....

A teacher, then, engaged in initiating his pupils into so contingent an inheritance, might be excused for thinking that he needs some assurance of its worth. For, like many of us, he may be expected to have a superstitious prejudice against the human race and to be satisfied only when he can feel himself anchored to something for which human beings are not responsible. But he must be urged to have the courage of his circumstances. This man-made inheritance contains everything to which value may be attributed; it is the ground and context of every judgment of better or worse.... He may be excused if he finds the present dominant image of civilized life too disagreeable to impart with any enthusiasm to his pupils. But if he has no confidence in any of the standards of worth written into this inheritance of human achievement, he had better not be a teacher; he would have nothing to teach.[4]

Oakeshott knows that the individual teacher cannot deal with this entire body of civilized meanings, but his rationale as a teacher lies within it. Learning is always related to, if not exclusively identified with, an historic inheritance, and "that what is to be handed on and learned, known and understood, are thoughts and various 'expressions' of thoughts."[5]

The above remarks about subject matter raise other questions. One of them is suggested by concept of *relevance.*

Relevance

There is a great cry today for *relevance* in the curriculum. What does this mean? Presumably, it means relevance to the student's needs, interests, and so on. We will look briefly at needs and interests, but, I think that the more basic meaning of *relevance* is that the student be able to see the value or significance of what he is studying. It is too easy a solution for the educator to arrange a curriculum around the subjects in which the student is immediately interested. Such a curriculum is in danger of being irrelevant in the larger sense; when the youthful interest has changed, all he has learned is outmoded. To short circuit the search for relevance by orienting everything to job finding or social success, and so on, is to eventually sell the student short.

Generative subject matter, leading to initiation into the realm of human meanings, has few rivals in its claim for relevance. Language, for instance, is relevant to almost every interest that will emerge throughout life. Failure to master the symbols of communication leads to permanent human impoverishment in almost every field. Or, consider the range of human experience that is deepened, enlarged, and made more joyous or more insightful by virtue of understanding the arts. As far as social studies—history, sociology, anthropology, and the like—are concerned, no one is going to ask an adult when Luther pinned his theses on the cathedral door, or when Galileo was forced to recant his discovery that the earth moved around the sun. But if a person does not know such things, he cannot understand what it means to be a modern man rather than a medieval man.

Compared with many so-called relevant topics introduced ad hoc into the school, these subjects are enormously significant. They are not immediately exciting to the untutored because their full relevance can only be grasped after long initiation. If education is what we have claimed it to be, the task of educators is to devise ways and means of initiating their pupils into these secrets as early as possible.

Interests

What of the child's interests? There are several problems connected with the notion of interests as a guide to curriculum. The psychological fact that the pupil must be interested is not the same thing as saying that the child's immediate interests are the proper focus of teaching. Human beings can be interested in almost anything, however mean or bizarre. One Nazi doctor was interested in how long children would live when deprived of fats in their diet. Human beings are often interested in things that are unworthy of their attention, and, conversely, they are uninterested in and perhaps unaware of many things from which they would benefit. Educating is interesting students in things that will be to their advantage as human beings.

We have seen that one of the things in which children are interested is understanding. To educate and to teach mean to build on this primary fact, otherwise, the educator becomes merely an entertainer.

Needs

How about a needs curriculum? This would seem to be more substantial a basis for education than mere interests. What are *human* needs? Students obviously have biological needs, but these are not of direct interest to the educator. The meeting of those needs is, primarily, the job of other social institutions. As soon as we talk about "social needs" or "growth," we enter a more debatable realm.

To speak of any specific human needs is to presuppose some view of human nature. The educator, who is a convinced social Darwinian, for instance, will have an entirely different view of what students need than, say, a Marxist or Christian. This will be true of every claim except, perhaps a few relating to biological necessities like food, air, and shelter. Even here, the claim that these necessities ought to be shared in some equitable way is not merely a fact of some science. It is a moral claim.

Today one might object that many social needs are obvious, such as the need for job training, for instance. But there are many needs in our society; some militant blacks, for instance, would say that there is a need for training in social militancy, not adaptation to a racist society.

The point is that the notion of *needs* is highly ambiguous. It does not, *by itself,* help the educator to organize his work. No doubt, in the broadest sense, any educational system that can justify itself before the bar of reason will have to serve something fundamental in human nature, and *needs* may stand for that something. I suggest that naming it in this way is not much help.

In conclusion, it must be pointed out that one typically human need is the *need to understand* or the *need to share meanings*. This would seem to be the need that *educating* in its essential meaning is directed toward. Moreover, meeting this need by cultivating the power to understand is a precondition for any large satisfaction of the wider range of human needs. Understanding is the *metier* of educating. If educators do not make this a prime objective, no other group in society is likely to do so.

Adjustment

Critics of modern education have focused frequently on the effects of making *adjustment* a curricular goal. The results, they claim, are mass conformity and mediocrity. This is not a philosophical issue, but it becomes philosophical if we ask what *adjustment* means. In an essay on "The Concept of Adjustment," C. J. B. Macmillan contends that there seems to be a "gross misunderstanding rooted in the concept of adjustment; educational theorists and their critics seem to talk past one another whenever the topic of personal or social adjustment enters the discussion."[6]

Adjustment in a psychological sense is any accommodation of the person to his environment. Even if the child becomes a truant, says Macmillan, he has in this sense *adjusted* to his environment by running away from it. For the purposes of education, it is necessary to add something to the purely descriptive meaning of the term. Whether consciously or not, the educator means by *adjustment* some *proper* relationship to other people and the environment. *Proper,* however, introduces a norm not immediately derivable from the psychological descriptions. To be sure of the meaning of *proper,* it is necessary to have some standards or criteria of that which is adequate or *good* human behaviour.

Running away is thought to be an improper response to the educational environment. The withdrawn student has also adapted, but in a way that the educator views as unsatisfactory. If we look at it from the teacher's point of view, we can ask whether, say, drugging the student should count as a *teaching* method. Many *overly active* students, we are told, are given drugs to quiet them so that they can conform to the classroom situation. Up to a point, this is innocent enough, but surely there comes a point where drugging a student so that he is passively submissive is contrary to the purpose of educating. Yet, from a purely descriptive point of view, this would count as *adjustment* of a sort.

Macmillan cites the discussion of adjustment in Laurence F. Shaffer and Edward J. Shoben's textbook, *The Psychology of Adjustment,* to show what psychologists mean by the concept. According to Shaffer and Shoben, life is a sequence of need arousal and need satisfaction. Behaviours are adjustive because "they reduce tensions."[7]

Macmillan argues that to substitute "reduce tensions" for "adjust" in the context of education is absurd. If you ask a teacher whether a given child is adjusting, the reply, "Yes, he is reducing his tensions," would be educationally unilluminating. Even to say that Johnny is adjusting in the sense of reducing the tensions aroused by the school routine would not help. As we have seen, running away would be one form of adjustment in this case. Thus, it would appear that the psychologist and the educationist mean different things by saying that "Johnny is adjusting to the school routine."[8]

The theory of tension reduction is too simplistic for educational purposes, failing to make distinctions that are educationally important, the distinctions, for instance, among the tensions of thwarting, of hunger, of intellectual attention, of anticipation, of joyful excitement, and so on. Distinctions like these, of great subtlety and variety, are common in ordinary language, as Austin and other analysts have pointed out. This is why it is possible to use the ordinary language analysis of analytic methods to criticize technical proposals when they are applied to a wider range of phenomena than is warranted.

Ambiguities of this kind in the concept of *adjustment* compelled Macmillan to conclude that psychological theory is "inadequate for use in theories designed to guide educational practice."[9]

Learning to Learn and Learning to Think

Criticisms of curricula based upon retention of information are congenial to the claims we have made for the meaning of both teaching and educating. These critics say that the schools should make a much larger place in the curriculum for what might be called cognitive competencies as distinguished from cognitive retention. What counts in education, they say, is not the information one can remember, but the skills one has attained in learning and thinking. There are other competencies that belong to the same family of related concepts: learning to solve problems, to inquire, to discover, to think critically, and to create. If we are to understand what is proposed when it is recommended that students' *learn to learn* or *learn to think,* and so on, there are some conceptual ambiguities to be clarified.

(1) Learning to learn is learning an activity not a sum of knowledge. It is learning *how* to do something. In this sense, we may think of it as a skill. It is a kind of competence in doing, like swimming or playing the piano.

(2) It is different from learning the skill involved in swimming. Learning to swim is to learn to do one thing, whereas learning to learn is becoming competent in a whole *class* of activities. Human beings can learn to perform an enormous range of activities from doing science or meditating, to horseback riding, or karate. What needs to be clarified is whether there is a single body of instruction that can make learning all these things easier.

When Dewey proposed his five steps of thought, he believed that he had exposed the natural structure of being intelligent in the world. When we say someone is "intelligent," we mean that he can learn something quickly. Dewey thought intelligence was a biological notion derived from the survival pattern of the race, and these five steps were a clarification of that basic pattern. He also thought science was the model of intelligent activity, and the five steps were a commonsense version of all scientific reflection. Dr. J. Richard Suchman and his group at the University of Illinois have followed Dewey in their studies of "inquiry training." They have elaborated these steps of thought into a teaching technique they claim can bring a student to a high level of competence in *problem solving* or *inquiry*. The technique consists in putting the student into a situation where a concrete problem serves as a focal point of his investigation. The adult environment must be responsive to the child's efforts without giving him ready-made answers. The teacher must make additional information available as the student requires and offer sequences of goals or plans of action, but he must not infringe upon the student's own territory by taking over the direction of his thought. Such man claims statistical proof that this method works well.

Perhaps it does, but this does not answer the question that we have raised: Is there a universal technique of intelligence? It is not sufficient to show that some techniques are capable of generality, or that the methods in some of the sciences are applicable to many commonsense situations. As valuable as this is, it does not establish that the person who masters such a technique has really *learned to learn*. He may have learned a technique that is more general than the activity of learning one type of material, but he would still fall short of having mastered the key to universal intelligence.

There are other dimensions of understanding that are not covered by such a pattern. The pattern of thought we are using in this book, conceptual analysis, for instance, does not follow these five steps, nor does it illuminate, without serious amendment, what it means to learn about values or to think in moral, aesthetic, or religious categories.

There are more serious objections to thinking of learning to learn or to think as a technique. We discussed these reasons when we searched for behavioral equivalents to thought. We learned in that discussion that there is simply no limit to the moves that intelligence makes in inventing and creating. This does not mean that there is no value in formulating strategies that have been widely useful in certain types of problems, but it is a chimera of the technician that all these moves can be spelled out. There is, furthermore, a contradiction in the desire to find a universal technique and the claim of the educational critics that contemporary education ignores the intelligence and autonomy of the student. In its final meaning, this proposal for teaching everyone a universal technique is like the very programming of the student that is so offensive to these educators.

Let us turn from this general question to a few specific ones. When it is proposed that students *learn to learn,* it is not clear just what is meant. Here are some possibilities: (1) It could mean this mastery of a universal technique; (2) it could mean simply that the student be disposed to keep on learning after he leaves school; or (3) it could mean a generalize capacity to understand.

There is a real difference between (1) learning to learn, and (2) learning to be a learner. Learning to be a learner, which is, I think, nearer to what educators who follow this line really seek, is significantly different from learning to learn. It would be perfectly sensible to say, "He 'learned to learn' in school, but he has done precious little learning since." Learning to *be* something is not the same thing as learning to *master* something. The latter includes, among other things, a discrimination among values and a decision with regard to them that leads to a disposition to be one kind of person rather than another. There is no reason to suppose that, say, *learning to swim* is the same as *deciding to be a swimmer*. Something like the later statement appears to be what is involved in the proposal *learning to learn*.

There is also a difference between the mastery of a general technique and a generalized capacity to understand. Consider the differences among the following:

1. Learning to "parrot" chemical formulae.[10]
2. Learning to do chemistry—the ability to perform chemical experiments, and so on.
3. Learning the logos of chemistry—learning not only to do chemistry, but to know what one is doing when he is experimenting, hypothecating, and so on.
4. Learning to perform in other fields of knowledge as well as chemistry.
5. Learning the logos of these other fields.

6. Learning the interrelationships of the logos of these fields to one another.

The last item would require a grasp of the wide variety of human modes of understanding. This would be what I have called the real meaning of *educating*, namely, to become initiated into the realms of human meaning.

One of the advantages of this last concept of *learning to learn* is that the sheer awareness of such a range of human meanings that comes about in a genuinely liberal education carries with it dispositional features. That is, there is a high likelihood, if not the certainty, that a person educated in this way will retain a taste for understanding after he has left formal schooling behind.

Creativity and Criticism

Before we leave this topic we should look at a couple of other items that illustrate conceptual analysis in education. The first is to ask what *creativity* means. Tests on *creativity*, for example, often include questions that explore the student's ability to think unconventionally about certain topics. One test asks the student to "Write down as many unusual uses as possible for a brick."[11] The criterion of creativity in this question is the largest number of such "unusual uses." Does this test creativity?

Creativity certainly involves breaking away from conventional patterns, but by itself it may mean madness as well as genius. In addition to *novelty*, creativity involves at least three other criteria. The unconventionally bizarre or crazy is not in itself a mark of creativity. Only if the new production has a more complex rationale and significance than what preceded it can it count as an instance of creativity. A new vase, a mechanical invention, or a new theory must not only be different, but it must possess a fresh beauty or usefulness. What is merely nonconformist in thought or action, the merely unusual, cannot count as creativity. What is also missing in the identification of creativity with mere unconventionality is the failure to recognize the high level of discipline manifested by inventors, poets, and painters. Their discipline includes not only the struggle for a personal technique suited to their talents, but also a rich background of knowledge in the art or science in which they are working.

There is, to be sure, a logos of creativity in the broad sense. Good descriptions of the "creative process" are available from such scholars as Brewster Ghiselin.[12] This logos, however, does not include precise techniques for guaranteeing creativity itself. What a person can learn from such descriptions are some general truths about people who have been creative in various fields, but there are no guarantees that one will become a poet, painter, or scientific discoverer.

Another concept that appears in many curriculum proposals is *learning to be critical*. If we think of this in terms of techniques, we might imagine that drilling students in stock critical moves would make them into good critics or develop their powers of critical thinking. John Passmore argues that this would be merely a form of indoctrination. Cleverness in analysis is not the same thing as being a good critic. "Being critical," Passmore writes, "is, indeed, more like the sort of thing we call a 'character trait' than it is like a skill. To call a person 'critical' is to characterize him, to describe his nature, in a sense in which to describe him, simply, as 'capable of analysing certain kinds of fallacy' is not to describe his nature."[13]

To learn to be critical is then dispositional as much as technical. To learn this depends much more on the attitude and example of the teacher and the atmosphere of the school than upon any concrete techniques. If the teacher thinks that *being critical* means merely finding fault with everything that confronts him, he will not set an example of the critical spirit. He may produce a crop of mere faultfinders. In order to develop criticism in the best sense, writes Passmore, "a teacher has to develop in his pupils an enthusiasm for the give-and-take of critical discussion."[14] The key element is the revelation to the student that the teacher himself can be wrong, that his authority is not infallible. Where this happens the teacher has an opportunity to demonstrate the critical spirit by revising what he has taught. He thus demonstrates in rational discussion that it is evidence and reason that count, not persons.

Confluent Education

The term "confluent education" is used by educators who propose that the curriculum should include affective as well as cognitive elements. They are more concerned with attitudes, values, personal awareness, and interpersonal relations than with knowledge. In life, they say, these things are separated, and if education is for living, then it would seem plausible that they should be joined there as well.

Here several analytical issues are raised. What, for instance, are the similarities and differences among (1) coming to know, (2) coming to value, and (3) coming to be. In an essay entitled "Coming to Value and Getting to Know," Alburey Castell contrasts these two activities.[15] To say, "I know *X*" is to say something quite different from "I value *X*." To be sure, he points out, if a person did not value some things like consistency, clarity, verifiability, and even knowing, he would not get to know anything. On the other hand, you cannot value something you do not know about. Thus, these two activities—knowing and valuing—are related, but different. In Castell's view, educators should realize that their real concern is with *coming to know,* that is, with what he calls "liquidating ignorance" rather than with valuing. He contends that trying to get someone to value something, except in the indirect sense mentioned above, cannot count as *teaching*. I think that this may be only partially correct.

The issue seems to me to lie in the question whether there is a logos of valuing as there is logos of knowing. I believe that there is. I will discuss this at some length in the next chapter, but here it will be enough to appeal to the

Taxonomy of Educational Objectives previously cited. Volume II of *Taxonomy* examines so-called "affective learning." The authors describes this process as follows: (1) There is first the receiving or attending to certain value experiences. (2) Then, some kind of response to the phenomenon in question and finding satisfaction in the response follows. (3) At the third stage, the items of evaluation begin to take on some consistency and stability. At this stage, the student notes his own preferences and makes tentative personal commitments. (4) Gradually, these evaluations evolve into a *system of values* through increased conceptualization, emerging in stage. (5) As a characterization of personality of the learner. The value complexes become more or less permanently a part of his unique value-attitude system. At this last stage, the individual has integrated these beliefs, ideas, and attitudes into a single philosophy or world view that is his own.

A glance at the taxonomy of cognitive learning reported earlier will show how many striking parallels there are between the two types of learning. This *Taxonomy* supports rather substantially the view that there is a rationale to learning values. Where there is a rationale there can be *teaching*.

To be sure, valuing is not something that can be grasped as a pure concept; it remains to the very last a type of data. This is also true in scientific knowing. In science, the data are not reduced to concepts, but their relationships are structured conceptually. When I know something scientifically, my knowing is never identical with the thing known, which remains a datum of my experience, but I am said to know it when the relationship of this sensory datum to other data is made clear through thought.

In this sense, teaching about valuing is not the same thing as inducing a specific kind of valuing in the student. However, it is so significantly close to the process by which valuing is changed and enriched that the closeness should be acknowledged.

Learning to Be

The same can be said of the concept *learning to be,* the search for character, personal identity, or self-knowledge. *Human becoming* has a rationale that has been recently elaborated in the work of psychologists, such as Erick Erickson, Carl Rogers, and the late Abraham Maslow, who have directed their research toward what they call "human potentialities." Like the cognitively oriented educators who decline to consider personal becoming as legitimate curriculum, these psychologists tend to despise cognitive learning. Rogers writes, "Anything that can be taught to another is relatively inconsequential, and has little or no significant influence on his behaviour."[16] He says that he has "lost interest in being a teacher," and that the outcomes of teaching "are either unimportant or hurtful." Insofar as he is underscoring the need for interest and participation in learning on the part of the learner, he is undoubtedly right. The tenor of his proposals is to limit education to the kind of thing he has found important in psychotherapy, namely, the process of *coming to be* rather than *coming to know*.

The proposal that these writers are offering to educators—to make education more affectively significant—is worth examining. The proposal as an educational matter hinges on the presence of a genuine rationale in the process of becoming, a rationale that can be taught. The schools are not the only institutions charged with helping human beings become more human by fulfilling their personal potentialities. This has been the traditional role of the family and the church. Lately, it has been taken over by the psychotherapeutic branches of medicine.

The question is this: What is the peculiar role of education in this matter? My reply is that the educator's primary role is with the *rationale* of personal growth, with the *understanding* of these personal processes that go on both in and out of institutions. Whatever has a rationale can be taught. Erickson, for instance, has elaborated the stages in human becoming from infancy to maturity. The rationale of that process is surely as important as the study of mathematics or history. Of course, the wise teacher knows that this rationale cannot be understood unless he refers to the present experience of the student as a kind of laboratory in which these concepts are tested and made comprehensible.

Habits

To close this discussion with a consideration of a term commonly used in connection with *character* education. We refer to the concept of *habit*. It is sometimes said that the teacher should inculcate good habits in his students. Some educators are of the opinion that an educated person is one who has learned a set of useful habits, especially, in Dewey's phrase, "the habit of intelligence."

In fact, the expression "habit of intelligence" seems to be a contradiction in terms. When we speak of a person having a habit of biting his nails or smoking cigarettes, we suggest not only something bad that he does, but also that the compulsion to do so is also bad. A habit is an activity that goes on without, or even in spite of, thought. Nor does it make much sense to cure bad habits by counter habits. A compulsion not to bite one's nails or a compulsion not to smoke would not necessarily be good. Nonsmoking is not the same as having a habit of not smoking.

A habit is a pattern of behaviour that is set off automatically by a set of stimuli. It, like the notion of conditioning, suggests automatically, and is chiefly appropriate to bodily processes or activities. No doubt, automatic reactions can be useful under certain conditions, such as battlefield behaviour or participation in a sport. The range of application of the notion of *habit* to education lies in this region of *training*. It does not make sense to speak of the "habit of honesty" or the "habit of thinking independently."

There are several reasons for this. The first is that being honest, for instance, is a norm controlled activity, in the sense that the actor behaves in certain ways *because* of certain norms. Honesty cannot be a simple reflex. To be honest means to know the meaning of such complex notions as *ownership, property, rights,* and so on, plus a set of principles that are applicable to a wide variety of situations. To be honest is not a reflex conditioned to fixed situations. It can be applied in new situations which one has never before encountered.

What has been said of honesty applies even more emphatically to the quality of being intelligent. Being thoughtful or honest are dispositions to behave in accordance with complex norms, not habits of reflexive behaviour in the presence of stimuli patterns. Given the stimuli, we can predict the behaviour in the case of a habit, but this is not true of the behaviour of an honest man. To be sure, there are things that can be predicted of an honest man; he will not steal in situations where theft is clearly defined. His positive acts are not predictable in this way. The honest thing to do in a complex situation cannot be predicted, it must be thought out in accordance with the notions of integrity of the actor himself. Of course, he may make a mistake that he will regret. Habitual behaviour cannot be mistaken. One may have a bad habit, but the habit cannot be mistaken. In the case of a disposition to behave in honest ways, a person may regret that he did not apply his norms accurately. What the educator is concerned with is not habits but dispositions, and dispositions include that ingredient of understanding that belongs to education.

What is a School?

This question is philosophically awkward because it is partly historical and partly analytical. What we are seeking is the distinctive role of the school in society. In primitive societies, we do not find that division into specialized institutions and agencies that characterize our own. Though, to some extent, there is much overlapping of function, each of the major institutions of society—the state, family business, church, and school—performs characteristic services unique to that institution. A modern society is impossible without schools for the simple reason that the degree of education required of its citizens is both too broad and too specialized to be left to other social institutions. This is its sociological rationale.

The school is the place of *teaching* and *educating, par excellence.* It is the place for systematically cultivating the human capacity to understand. Take this away and the schools' unique significance disappears. The school is a repository of past knowledge, the center for new inquiry, and the medium for initiating successive generations in the secrets of learning.

Society acts through the school to preserve and perpetuate itself. The school is one of the major links between generations, one of the agencies for initiation of the young into the ongoing society. If the society is dynamic like our own, rather than traditional, then this act of self-preservation cannot be one of merely coming to terms with things as they are. Society will inevitably have to prepare the individual to participate in the movement of society toward its own possible futures. This fact makes the debate over adjustment versus transformation somewhat *academic* in the bad sense. Whenever the student is adjusted to a moving stream, he is bound to need the skills and knowledge for moving wisely with society's preponderant currents of change.

The direction of these currents is not fixed or predetermined. A society has many potential futures at a given time. Educators cannot avoid making some decisions about which of those possibilities are to be actualized. For better or worse, educators have to direct their energies toward the things most worth knowing as a society's potentiality moves toward its actualization, that is, the information, skills, attitudes, and values that belong to the future desired by the members of that society.

When, for instance, we consider education in a democracy, we need at least some reasonably clarified notion of what defines a *democratic* state of affairs, and, to put it behaviorally, what concrete styles of life contribute to that social ideal. There is bound to be tension between the school and certain segments of the community. In racial matters, for instance, the schools of a democracy have no choice but to arrange some amicable, equal, and just relationship among the races, if they are to be faithful to the democratic proposition. Nor can they remain content with a nineteenth-century class notion of what constitutes American education.

Aside from the question of how to best prepare the young to contribute to the continuity of American society, there is another claim: the individual himself. It is not enough to look at him entirely from the social point of view. He has a right to expect that his schooling will endow him with some of the means for becoming a full human being. The happy coincidence of social needs and personal fulfilment is a consummation devoutly to be wished, but, as Freud observed, civilizations have a way of bequeathing a certain amount of discontent to its citizens. This tension between personal growth and social usefulness is bound to last as far as we can foresee, and it must be taken into account by the schools. Generations of human potential may not be sacrificed lightly to social expediency by any society that calls itself good, especially by a democracy that presumably exists for the welfare of its members. Thus, we have three themes that must be constantly woven into the composition of education: the present and the future needs of society and the potentialities of individuals.

Much of what we have said applies not only to schools, but to governments, churches, and indeed to all institutions. What may then be said of the school specifically? We can answer this by combining what has been said about the school's specialized function and meaning with the above observations about the needs of society and the individual. The school as society's institutionalization of understanding discharges its obligation to both the society and the individual by initiating its students into the rationale of the major realms of human meaning. In so far as such an understanding prepares the individual for his place in society, both present society and that of the future, and enables him to develop as an authentic person, the school has discharged its proper function.

All this does not mean that schools may not perform some non-educational tasks. It does mean that the central focus of its function and meaning should be perfectly clear. Otherwise, as we have seen in so many communities, the schools are burdened with all sorts of non-educational activities from baby-sitting to public entertainment. Communities are often tempted to burden the schools in this way because the schools have the children in custody for so many hours of the day. We have already seen that this captivity is one of the liabilities of compulsory education, and to use it to further dilute the process is educationally debilitating.

What is a University?

The meaning of education is more visible at the upper end of the process than at the beginning. This is not surprising. The seed is more manifest in the flower and fruit than in its early shoots. With the current ferment in higher education, it might be useful to see if there is some unique meaning to the notion of a university.

Suppose that colleges and universities were abolished and all their functions were parcelled out to other institutions. Would anything be lost? Let social clubs and marriage bureaus arrange the marriages that are now formed during college years. Let training for trades and professions be carried forward in institutes attached to the appropriate industries. Let the present tendency of the young to make a religion out of education be redirected to the churches. Citizenship training and related attitude formation could be parcelled out to informal community programs, television, and the press. Perhaps hardest of all, let athletic clubs take over the public entertainment aspect of intercollegiate athletics. What would be missing if the college and university were thus to disappear?

What would be missing would be any center where learning is enjoyed for its own distinctive worth, a setting in which the unfolding of the understanding is prized for itself. There would be no place that systematically cultivated the broad range of human meanings that have become the funded and growing treasure of civilized existence.

What are some of the presuppositions of such an educational center when it is functioning in accordance with its historic though unwritten charter? The first is freedom. Freedom is a *sine qua non* for genuine inquiry that pursues the meaning of any subject-matter without prejudice. Where the conclusion is foregone, the inquiry is precluded. It is also a necessary ingredient in the educational ideal of putting the student in complete possession of all his powers. He must be free to experiment with his own values and concepts, and to discover what the civilized tradition means to him. This is the basis rationale of the much debated tenure of professors and academic freedom. To the public tenure is often viewed as a guaranteed job or sinecure, but its real meaning lies in the effort to put the teacher beyond threats to his freedom to teach and to inquire, following, as Socrates said, the argument where it leads. It has no other justification.

A second, presupposition of higher education is respect for persons. Kant, in his second formulation of the famous categorical imperative, said that a rational man may never treat another person merely as a means, but always as an end in himself. He deduced this rule from his first formulation of the same imperative, namely, that a rational man will always universalize his actions, never making himself an exception. The logical connection here is simple: The man who appeals to reason appeals to it equally in every other man and must respect that other man as an agent of reason. No doubt, there are other grounds for respecting people, and one of them is connected intimately with the educational task: Without a high degree of mutual respect, genuine learning cannot go on.

A third presupposition of higher education is respect for truth itself as it unfolds to human inquiry. Truth, like justice, is no respecter of persons. In the presence of troth there is no appropriate response but acceptance, with only such reservations as are presupposed in the necessity for further inquiry. Moreover, truth has a universal element. It is no more a respecter of nations or cultures or races than it is of individuals. The university is thus a trans-national global institution. It stands for an ideal that judges the claims of all special groups and cultures.

A further presupposition of higher education is the unity of knowledge. This unity is not a present possession but an ideal. The quest of understanding presupposes the eventual ideal unity of the realms of meaning. The compartmentalization of knowledge into disciplines and sciences may be a convenience, but the university must protect itself against the fragmentation that such compartmentalization fosters. The learner is a single mind with the desire to see things in their togetherness, not mere *ad hoc* togetherness, but meaningful togetherness. This is hard to hold in focus in a world where knowledge explodes in so many directions. It was easier in the medieval university where this unity, according to John Henry Newman, "was realized and acted on...with a distinctness unknown before; all subjects of knowledge were viewed as parts of one vast systems, each with its own place in it, and from knowing one, another was inferred."[17] In the modern university there is no such single system, but there cannot be a university in the real sense that does not presuppose such a unity and that does not search diligently for it.

What of the current drive to turn the university into an active force for social change? Several factors have conspired to bring this about. One is the rising generation's tendency to make higher education into a kind of religious surrogate: a center of social ideals and repository of the means for achieving full personhood. This is not too surprising in the light of declining public enthusiasm for official religion coupled with the ideal notion of the university that I have just outlined. Another factor is the increasing criticism of modern society and the desire to see it changed without delay. When we consider that university is the first institution that young people encounter as they emerge into adulthood, it is natural that they should see it as the ready instrument for carrying out their hopes for the world and for themselves.

We have seen that education in a dynamic society is as inevitably committed to the future as to the past, and that social change is bound to be in part a by-product of the way educational decisions are made. However, it is another matter to turn the university into a political agency for direct social action. Even enlightened political action is inevitably partisan, and no matter how urgent it may be at the time, it is no substitute for the work of detached critical analysis that marks the unique task of a university. Moreover, the university's commitment to learning for its own sake can be perverted by making it a mere means to any end no matter how good the end may be.

Students are no doubt right in demanding a larger share in the decisions that must be made in university life, but there is a limit to what can be done within the confines of a university without perverting its essential charter. When students and faculty abandon their work as students of society and turn to political action, they leave the school behind and put their faith in a political institution rather than education. If the turn the university into a partisan enterprise, they will, to this extent, destroy it as a place of learning.

To be sure, involvement in affairs is one good way to motivate learning. If students and teacher remain in a neutral vacuum regarding the urgencies of society, learning will diminish accordingly. This is only to say that social involvement at the university serves fundamentally the purpose of stimulating learning. From the university's point of view, social change and even personal growth are happy by-products of growth in understanding. When the formula is turned around, the university as a unique institution disappears. To see this with great clarity, we have only to see the fate of the political universities of Germany and Russia under Hitler and Stalin.

As a recent Harvard report put it: "The university—any university—has a distinctive competence, a special nature. That competence is *not* to serve as a government, or a consulting firm, or a polity, or a pressure groups, or a family, or a kind of secularized church; it *is* to serve as a center of learning and free inquiry."[18]

We are presented with a paradox that must be accepted if university education is to survive. The paradox is this: Higher education can serve society best by being itself, that is, a place of learning and understanding. That its learning should be relevant to the urgencies of personal and social life goes without saying. If it turns into a practical program for self-growth or social change, it will lose its distinct reason for being. Unfettered learning is a great social solvent. No social program founded on untenable ideals or the distortion of facts can long endure the light of critical examination. For the same reason, a regimen of personal development that is unable to withstand the light of reason cannot survive.

The university is a unique institution with its own charter of existence. Humanity has a high stake in letting the university be the university.

All of this has a bearing on the lower schools as well. The ultimate significance of education at the lower levels is eventually to come to fruition in the kind of thing that a university represents. To be sure, many students will not extend their formal education beyond high school, but, insofar as possible, they should be initiated into the ideals of education for which the university stands.

REFERENCES

1. Jerome S. Bruner, *The Process of Education* (New York: Vintage Books, 1960), p. 17.
2. *Ibid.*
3. Benjamin S., Bloom *et al., Taxonomy of Educational Objectives,* Handbook I: *Cognitive Domain;* Handbook II: *Affective Domain* (New York: McKay, 1956, 1964).
4. Michael Oakeshott, "Learning and Teaching," in R. S. Peters (ed.), *The Concept of Education,* p. 162.
5. *Ibid.*
6. C. J. B. Macmillan, "The Concept of Adjustment," in Komisar and Macmillan (eds.), *Psychological Concepts in Education,* p. 60.
7. *Ibid.,* p. 65.
8. *Ibid.,* p. 68.
9. *Ibid.,* p. 61.
10. The phrase "learning to parrot" is used by Alburey Castell in "Pedagogy Follows Learning Theory," in Komisar and Macmillan (eds.), *Psychological Concepts in Education,* pp. 158-166.
11. Gribble, *Introduction to Philosophy of Education,* p. 97.
12. Brewster Ghiselin (ed.), *The Creative Process* (New York: New American Library, 1955).
13. John Passmore, "On Teaching To Be Critical," in R. S. Peters (ed.) *The Concept of Education,* p. 195
14. *Ibid.,* p. 198.
15. Remarks on a paper, "Value Conflict," by Harry S. Broudy, presented at a conference at the University of Oklahoma in November, 1963.
16. Carl Rogers, *On Becoming a Person* (Boston: Houghton Mifflin, 1961), p. 275.
17. Dwight A. Culler, *The Imperial Intellect* (New Haven: Yale University Press, 1955), p. 188.
18. *The University and the City* (Cambridge: The Office of the President, Harvard University, 1969), p. 6.

3

Models of Curriculum Planning

PROBLEMS OF CURRICULUM MODELS

Models must be useful, they must facilitate clear thinking and planning. Curriculum planning is an all-embracing term, for it comprehends many stages, many levels of abstraction, many levels of application, many foci of analysis; it originates from many different parties and loci of power, and has to meet demands from many sources. It would be invidious to suppose that a curriculum model could address realistically or honestly this range of problems and issues unitarily. Hence the notion of planning curricula with the assistance of models is pluralistic—many models to serve many concerns. The problems, raised, then, concern articulation of the dimensions of models and their clarity and appropriacy to the particular task in the curriculum planning process. The dimensions of curriculum planning models must link to the diverse nature of the term 'curriculum' and to the diverse nature of the planning process. What, then, are these dimensions?

A curriculum planning model must be certain of its range: is it referring to the whole curriculum or to a part of it? This begs the enormous question of defining the curriculum and its constituent parts. Definitions are both varied and broad. Some go for comprehensiveness, e.g. Kerr's suggestion of 'all the learning which is planned and guided by the school whether it is carried on in groups or individually, inside or outside the school' (Kerr, 1968; p. 16), and Orlosky's and Smith's (1978) view of it as the substance of a school's programme.

While such definitions have the attraction of allowing virtually anything into the curriculum, they offer only loose guidelines to thinking about the curriculum: that it must be planned, that it must include the hidden as well as the formal curriculum, and that it must involve a wide field of focus. Such definitions fail to address problems of selection and justification, participants and processes of curriculum planning and implementation. Other definitions err on the other side, being narrow and very tightly prescriptive: e.g. 'a programme of activities designed so that pupils will attain by learning certain specifiable ends or objectives' (Hirst, 1968; p. 40) or the *Oxford English Dictionary* definition as 'a course of study'.

Other definitions attempt to bridge the gap of the broad or the narrow. Skilbeck (1984) defines it as referring 'to the learning of students, in so far as they are expressed or anticipated in educational goals and objectives, plans and designs for learning and the implementation of these plans and designs in school environments' (p. 21).

Definitions of the curriculum thus cannot be relied upon to produce useful guidelines for modelling the curriculum. A curriculum planning model then must make explicit its range. It may contain reference to the whole school—a systemic and complex model (Dalin, 1978) which incorporates:

1. Participants and roles, school organizational, administrative and management structures and networks.
2. Contexts of the curriculum—historical, ideological, philosophical, sociological, cultural, political, psychological, and so on.
3. The relationships of the school and its curriculum to wider society.

4. Curriculum aims, content, pedagogies, resources, evaluation, development strategies and directions.
5. Styles and modes of curriculum planning and dissemination—problem solving, interactive and centre-periphery (Havelock, 1973).

Alternatively, it may refer to the whole school or to a particular part of the whole curriculum, either specifically, e.g. music or music in the infant years, or more generally, e.g. language across the curriculum. Further, it may refer to an individual teacher's curriculum in general or to an individual teacher's particular area of her or his total curriculum. The implications of being clear on the range of the curriculum being addressed are to point to the level of analysis of the curriculum statement, policy or plan. A whole school curriculum policy statement will almost necessarily be less specific than a curriculum area's or an individual teacher's statement and planning process. This refers back to the level or stage at which the curriculum model is pitched.

A curriculum planning model must be clear on its purpose, whether it is to be prescriptive or descriptive—a 'model for' planning (Figure 3.1) or a 'model of' planning (Figure 3.2). The former portrays, perhaps, an ideal view of curriculum planning—comprehensive and evolutionary—whereas the latter describes actual practice—which may be good or terribly poor. Significantly, the descriptive example overlooks the role of theory, evaluation and modification of theory and practice; it represents *ad hoc* and static curriculum planning. Further, such prescriptive and descriptive models must be clear on the level at which they are prescribing or describing, for planning models range from the contextual to the practical and specific.

It is possible to identify five levels of curriculum planning models which move from the general to the specific and from the abstract to the concrete classroom situation (Figure 3.3). It is a brave curriculum planner who attempts to incorporate all levels into a single model, for there are qualitative differences between each.

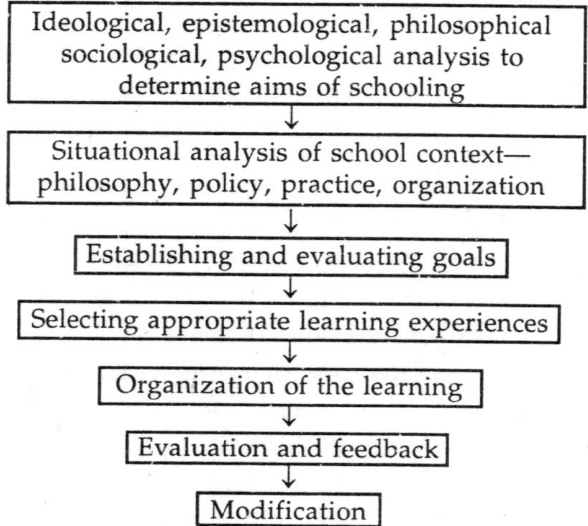

Fig. 3.1: A prescriptive model of curriculum planning.

LEVEL ONE: CONTEXTUAL LEVEL

These draw on the contexts set already and on the primary ethos which it described. They attempt a broad brush approach to factors in the planning process. Contextual models have a considerable pedigree in curriculum theory [despite Barrow's (1984) reservations about them)]; one can discern a clear line from Tyler (1949), through Taba (1962), Wheeler (1967) and Skilbeck (1976a). The essence of models cast in this mould is to establish clear foci and sequence of curriculum planning. For primary curriculum planners the models must be shot through at every stage with the principles of the primary ethos.

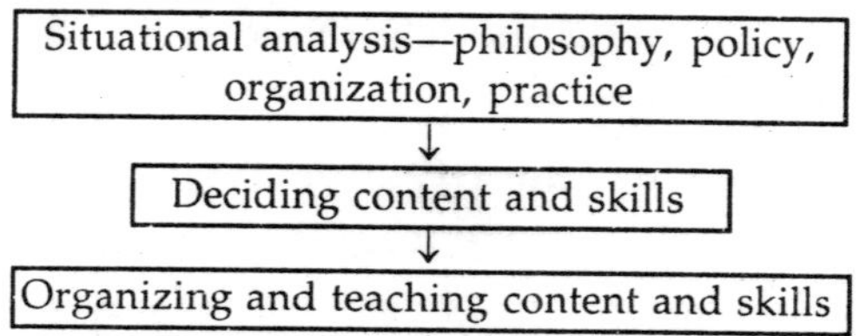

Fig. 3.2: A descriptive model of curriculum planning.

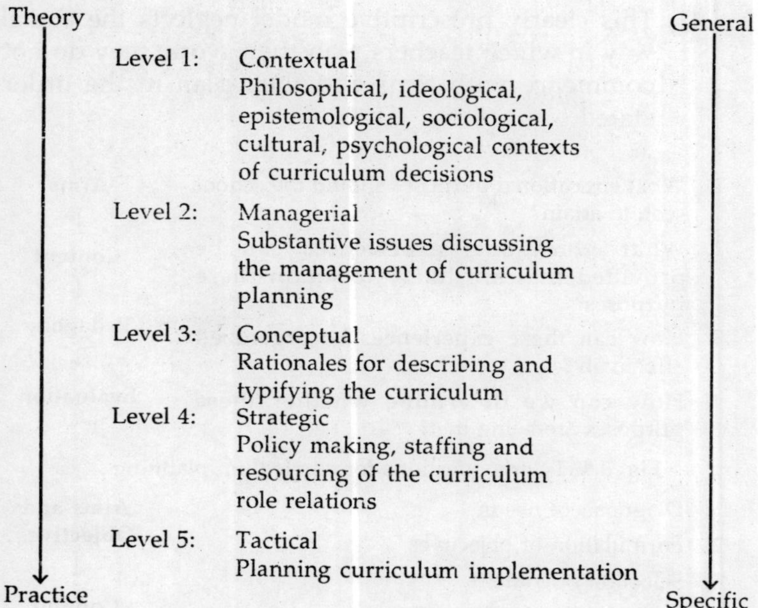

Fig. 3.3: Levels of curriculum planning models.

Tyler (1949) poses four famous questions as the basis for curriculum planning (Figure 3.4). Taba (1962) refined this into a seven-stage model (Figure 3.5). Both of these examples assume the reasonableness of starting with aims and finishing with evaluation—a means—end model—deciding on ends then designing means to achieve them. This has weaknesses, many of which are well aired (MacDonald-Ross, 1975; Sockett, 1976; Kelly, 1982; Lawton, 1983). For example:

1. Evaluation is seen as terminal (summative) rather than continuous (formative).
2. This model assumes that it is acceptable to determine children's end behaviours at the planning stage of the curriculum—which has the potential to deny their creativity, choice, needs and interests.
3. The educative process is seen as producing solely demonstrable, behavioural outcomes.

4. This clearly prescriptive model neglects the actual way in which teachers plan their work; they do not commence with aims and then plan in the order stated.

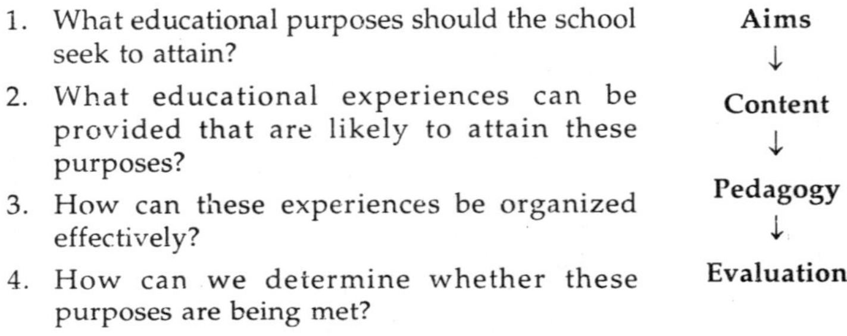

Fig. 3.4: Tyler's questions for curriculum planning.

1. Diagnosis of needs 2. Formulation of objectives	**Aims and Objectives**
	↓
3. Selection of content 4. Organization of content	**Content**
	↓
5. Selection of learning experiences 6. Organization of learning experiences	**Pedagogy**
	↓
7. Determination of what to evaluate and means of doing it.	**Evaluation**

Fig. 3.5: Taba's seven-stage model of curriculum planning.

Skilbeck (1982) attempts to reduce the excesses of this model by three means. His model is represented in Figure 3.6. The model includes two obvious improvements in Tyler and Taba; his inclusion of a fully fledged 'situational analysis' as an element of curriculum planning is an addition to the Tyler model; a situational analysis requiring an examination and incorporation of the contexts of curriculum planning and of internal pressures and constraints on curriculum planners. This ties curriculum planning firmly to the 'reconceptualist' notion (Pinar, 1975) that a curriculum is unique to a specific school and a group of teachers and pupils at a specific time and place.

Second, Skilbeck's feedback loop to reviewing the situation and situational analysis adds a dimensions absent in Tyler—the need to reconsider and reformulate aims and objectives. His third modification is not immediately apparent. Skilbeck encourages users to enter the model at the stage which is appropriate to their perceived needs; it is not necessary here to begin with aims and objectives. Similarly, he argues that users may go through the components in any order, even running some elements in tandem. The significance of this third point is striking; Skilbeck is breaking the mould of Tyler and replacing a prescriptive stage theory model with a more overtly interactive model. Interaction is assumed in the Tyler model, but it is in one direction only.

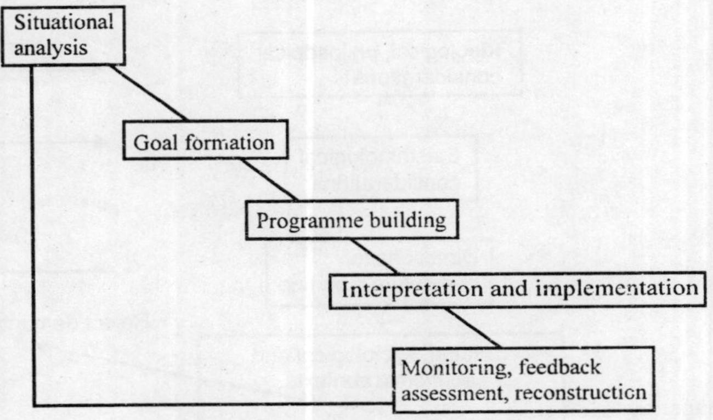

Fig. 3.6: Skilbeck's curriculum development model.

In Skilbeck's model participants are freer, more creative and responsive agents of planning; key elements of his model are mutually interacting. Skilbeck, though perhaps silent in his model on persons and their agency, sets the scene for explicit interactive models of curriculum planning; this can be taken forward into a proposal for an interactive model of curriculum planning at a high level of abstraction (Figure 3.7). This model sets interaction at the heart of the planning process. It embodies the heart of the curriculum reconceptualists' belief in the primacy of situated activity and the value of individuals' autobiographies entering the curriculum planning process. The teacher, embedded in cultures and social contexts, and through her or his perceptions of organizational constraints and own psychological make-up, addresses the pressures to follow directions in curriculum planning, accepting, modifying and resisting such demands. The teacher can offer feedback to review ideology, epistemology and philosophy. Such a model accords importance to a neglected area of curriculum planning—the personal and interpersonal dynamic and dialectic—long established in change and innovation theory (see Havelock, 1973; Hoyle, 1975a), but relatively poorly articulated in theories of planning (Pinar and Grumet, 1981).

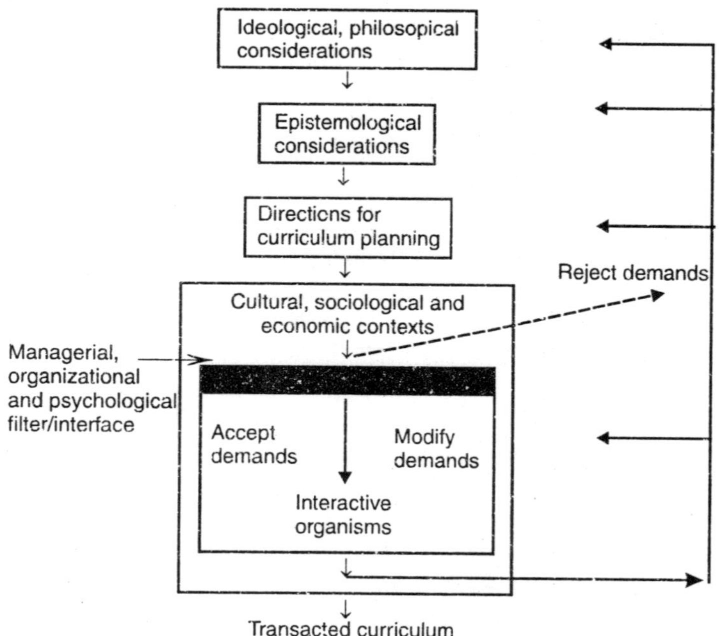

Fig. 3.7: An interactive model of curriculum planning.

Just as in change theory the interpersonal dimension has received growing attention, so in successful planning there must be a focus on the planners, participants and recipients. Thus the concept of the curriculum as being open, negotiable and problematic is kept wide, negotiation being (1) among the participants, (2) within each participant and planner, and (3) between planners, participants and recipients. The need for this negotiation is felt as sharply among teachers in internally generated curriculum planning as if it were to be externally generated.

LEVEL TWO: MANAGERIAL LEVEL

This has been discussed already, and the factors in the management of curriculum planning can be represented in Figures 3.8 and 3.9.

LEVEL THREE: CONCEPTUAL LEVEL

Curriculum planning needs to decide its definition of the curriculum. The Schools Council (1983) alludes to this when attempting to describe the curriculum in five ways:

1. The curriculum as subjects, e.g. English, mathematics, science, history. The strength of such a conception lies in its ability to enable teachers quickly to ascertain whether children are following a broad or a narrow curriculum. Similarly, children identify them easily. Whether describing the curriculum by subjects represents more a secondary than a primary style is open to debate.

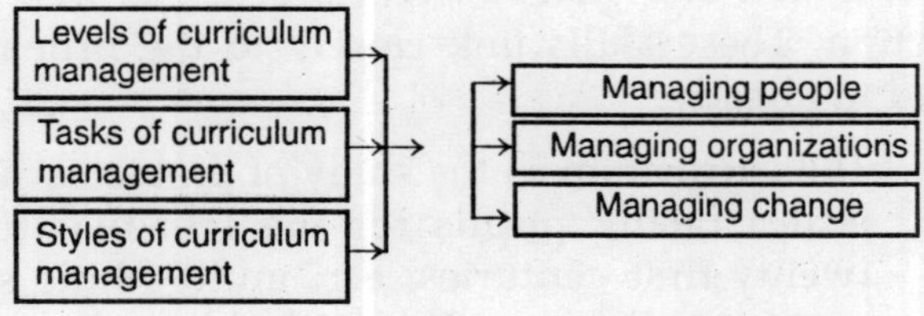

Fig. 3.8: Dimensions of management of curriculum planning.

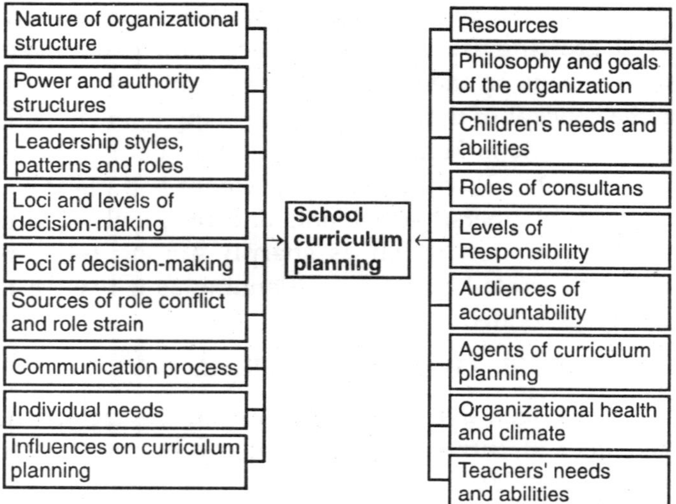

Fig. 3.9: Management factors in curriculum planning.

2. The curriculum as process, i.e. a focus on skills teaching. Such skills can be very specific, e.g. skimming and scanning in reading, or more general (DES, 1985b; para. 100):

    communication skills
    observation skills
    problem-solving skills
    physical and practical skills
    creative and imaginative skills
    numerical skills
    personal and social skills

The notion of a skill involves practice as well as direct instruction. These skills link closely to the primary ethos detailed in already.

3. The curriculum as the study of problems. These are issues facing pupils for the late twentieth and twenty-first centuries, e.g. multi-ethnic societies, computer literacy. Third World studies, ecology, conservation, pollution and energy utilization. The

proportion of the timetable which could, or should, be devoted to this is debatable as ideological pressures differ; conservative ideologies would underplay this area while reconstructionist—and society-focused ideologies would stress it.

4. The curriculum as areas of knowledge and experience. Whether their roots lie in epistemology, culture, tradition, or accepted practice. Given such discrepant sources it is scarcely surprising to find different classifications of what worthwhile knowledge should be taught. While there are clear discrepancies between the representations, it is striking how similar they all are. Indeed, they collectively and severally can be used as frameworks for common curricula (c.f. Proctor, 1984). The notion of areas of experience rather than bodies of knowledge accords perhaps more clearly that other conceptions with the value of experiences stressed in the primary ethos.
5. The curriculum through a child's eyes—a much neglected area, but one which emphasizes sensory experiences, friendships, locations, activities and enjoyments, i.e. the hidden curriculum. Such a perspective throws into sharp relief the problems of match—matching the teacher's intentions and curriculum planning with the perceptions and understandings which the child brings to, and takes from, the curriculum experience.

An alternative way of describing the curriculum has been suggested by Scrimshaw (1983), who offers five categories of the substance of children's learning:

1. Facts, beliefs, statements and theories, i.e. cognitive or academic learning.
2. Policies, principles and rules, i.e. learning social behaviour.

Table 3.1
A chronology of representations of the curriculum as areas of knowledge or experience

Peterson (1975)	*Phenix (1975)*	*Hirst (1965)*	*Lawton (1973)*
Logical Empirical Moral Aesthetic	Symbolics (languages maths, logic) Empirics (physical and social sciences) Aesthetics (arts) Synnoetics (relational insight) Ethics (morals) Synoptics (history, religion and philosophy)	Mathematics Physical sciences Human sciences History Religion Literature and fine arts Philosophy	Mathematics Sciences Aesthetics and creative Physical Social and political Ethical Linguistic Spiritual
DES (1977)	*DES (1978a)*	*CDC (1980)*	*Galton, Simon and Croll (1980)*
Mathematical Linguistic Scientific Social and political Physical Ethical Aesthetic and creative	Mathematics Language and literacy Science Aesthetic and physical Social studies	Arts and crafts Communication Health education Environmental studies Work, leisure and lifestyle Mathematical skills and reasoning and their applications Scientific and technological ways of knowing and their application Social, cultural and civic studies Moral reasoning and action, value and belief systems	Mathematics Language Arts and craft General studies (RE, history, geography, geography, social studies, science)

Table 3.1 (Contd.)

DES (1982b)	*Lawton (1983)*	*DES (1983)*	*DES (1985b)*
Mathematics	Social system	Mathematics	Aesthetic and creative
Language and literacy	Economic system	Language and literacy	Human and social
Religious and moral education	Communication system	Science	Linguistic and literary
Learning about people	Rationality system	Modern languages	Mathematical
Learning about the physical world	Technology system	Music	Moral
Learning about materials, plants and animals	Moral system	Arts and crafts	Physical
Art and craft	Belief system	Home studies	Scientific
Music	Aesthetic system	Physical health education	Spiritual
PE		History	Technological
		Geography and RE	

3. Ideas and concepts, i.e. an emphasis on understanding.
4. Skills, activities and actions, i.e. those areas which emphasize doing rather than reflecting.
5. Insights, feelings, emotions, attitudes and habits, i.e. development of the personality. This has resonances with the DES (1985b) which reinforce the need to consider 'elements of learning' in curriculum planning—knowledge, concepts, skills and attitudes.

An alternative to the previous conceptions can be found in a classroom-learning-based model (Ridley and Trembath, 1986). This draws on content, skills, concepts, problem-solving, interests and objects, pointing the way to level five models (tactical levels). It is rooted in practical applicability, thus providing a bridge from theoretical concerns and practical outcomes; the abstract to the concrete (Figure 3.10).

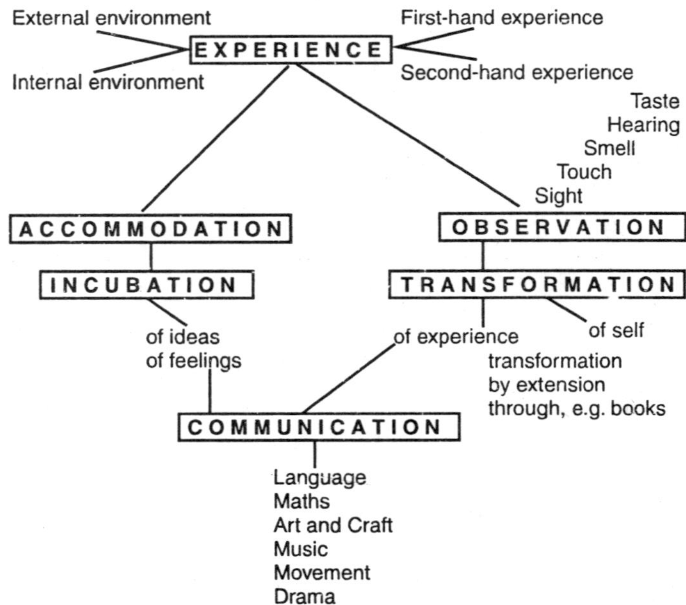

Fig. 3.10: A classroom-learning model of curriculum planning.

The model accommodates activity-centred approaches and at the same time recognizes the importance of knowledge within the process of learning. It points clearly to the importance of direct experiences coupled with the centrality of skills, the involvement and development of the child's personality and yet a concern for outcomes and products. It is a model which takes account of two significant polarities in describing the curriculum outlined earlier in the chapter—the curriculum as planned by the teacher and the curriculum through the child's eyes. It is thus a model which lies at the interface of theory and children's classroom experiences. It has a clear sympathy with the primary ethos outlined earlier, where conservative and instrumental ideologies are tempered with child-centredness and progressivism.

Conceptual levels of modelling the curriculum, then, are devolved upon decision-making about the structuring and classification of knowledge for children.

LEVEL FOUR: STRATEGIC LEVEL

This level synthesizes the previous three levels, analyzing personnel deployment, roles, resources and their optimal use, translating values and general organization of knowledge in the curriculum into specific policies at a whole staff level, i.e. tailored to a school's individual situation. It is represented in Figure 3.11 (c.f. Hicks, 1972). At this fourth level collective and individual responsibility for curriculum planning looks to all three previous levels for articulation of key rationales of, and problems and possibilities in, planning the curriculum, and to level five of individual teachers' curriculum planning and implementation. It must be responsive to constraints from all levels. Hence the model translates into school curriculum decision-making policy the interactive model outlined earlier at a contextual level.

LEVEL FIVE: TACTICAL LEVEL

The fifth level of the curriculum modelling process engages class teachers' planning in the long term, medium term, day-to-day and lesson-by-lesson stages. It is informed by all four previous levels, and reciprocally informs them. There are six typifications of curriculum planning at this level. They cover planning which is content-based, skills-based, problem-based, interest-based, objectives-based (c.f. Barnes 1982), activity-based, theme-based, informed by a 'classroom learning model'. A full curriculum plan will need to draw eclectically on all types.

Content-based Planning

Here the teacher approaches curriculum planning by examining the possibilities for learning in an identifiable corpus of content in terms of:

1. Activities.
2. Concepts.
3. Information to be emphasized.
4. Resources.

The origin of the content is problematic here. Does it derive from epistemology, a cultural analysis, or a child-centred ideology of what is engaging the child at a particular moment of time?

The question of who makes the selection is problematic; be it teachers, children, HMI, advisers, DES, governors or parents, there will be power and potential conflict brought into the curriculum arena.

Similarly, the form or expression of that content is problematic. Is it best expressed in areas of experience, subjects, schemas, concepts or processes? Taba (1962) offer some guidelines here, suggesting that at its lowest level content can be expressed in terms of specific facts and processes. At the next level it can be expressed in terms of basic principles—the structure of a subject; at its third level it comprises concepts—abstract ideas built up through a variety of experiences. At its highest level it constitutes thought systems and methods of enquiry; Taba here betrays

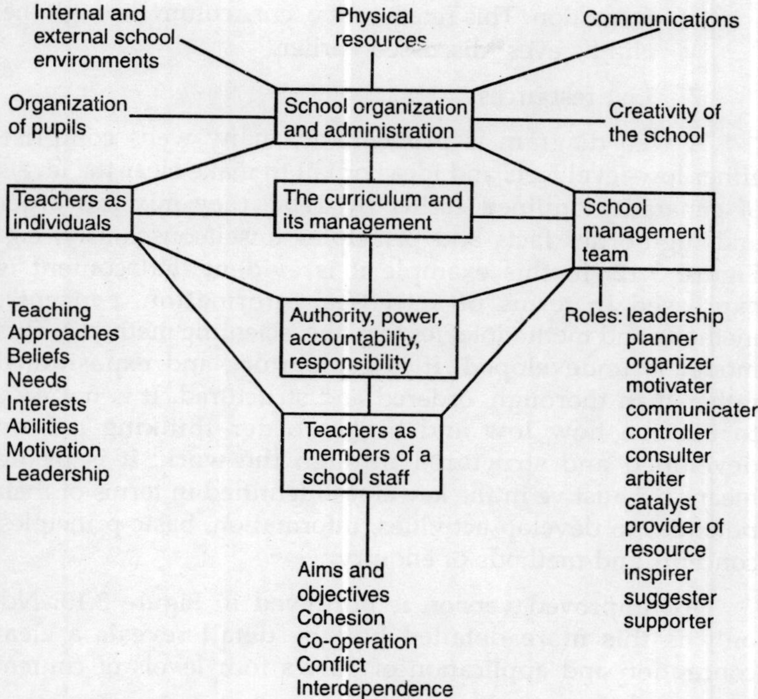

Fig. 3.11: Dimensions of curriculum policy-making at school level.

a sympathy to the discipline-centred approach to curriculum planning outlines by Hirst (1965). If one adopts a content based approach to curriculum planning, Barnes (1982) suggests that it can be staged thus:

1. Select the content.
2. Express the concepts and principles which arise out of the content.
3. Prioritize content and concepts.
4. Sequence the learning.
5. Contruct a web diagram of the content.
6. Scrutinize the content to see how far it allows children to perceive links between areas—concept

formation. This refers to the 'curriculum through the child's eyes' discussed earlier.

7. List resources.

A web diagram is problematic, many webs comprise either low-level facts and ideas or fail to make clear the levels of generality outlined earlier by Taba; they mix low-order and high-order facts and principles unselfconsciously; e.g. Figure 3.12. In this example it is evident that content is expressed in terms of activities, information, concepts, methods and methodologies (e.g. the 'scientific method'). This model is undeveloped; it is exploratory and expositional rather than thorough, ordered and structured. It is not easy to discern how low and higher order thinking can be developed and structured through the work; it is by no means exhaustive in the key areas identified in terms of their potential to develop activities, information, basic principles, concepts and methods of enquiry.

An improved version is portrayed in Figure 3.13. Not only is this more detailed but the detail reveals a clear conception and application of Taba's four levels of content

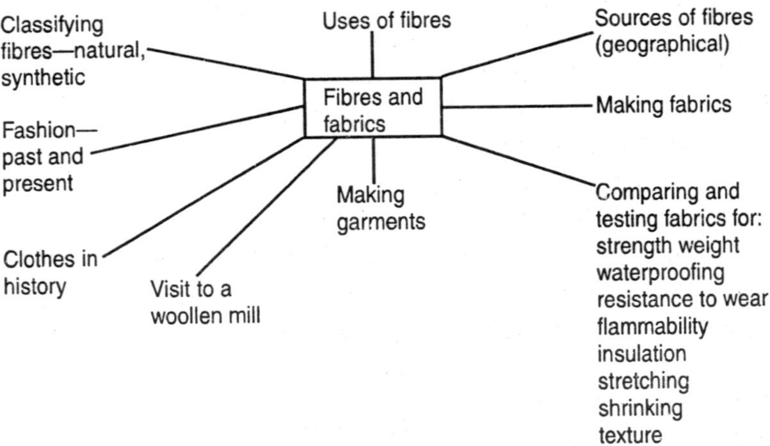

Fig. 3.12: A web diagram on 'fibres and fabrics'

expression. The application is comprehensive, i.e. it applies to all three areas described, the model is sequenced, and the cross-references give it coherence. A web diagram, then, will need to address areas of the curriculum, levels of thinking, activities, concepts, skills, knowledge, teaching and learning styles. Planning the curriculum by content makes for a potentially relevant curriculum; it compels teachers to analyse key concepts of curriculum programmes, can allow for progression and continuity, breadth and balance (DES, 1985b) and assists in the avoidance of repetition (Blyth *et al.*, 1976).

There are, however, difficulties with this model. Constructing a curriculum from a statement of content may be completely arbitrary, incoherent with the rest of the curriculum, biased, conservative, a received rather than a reflexive curriculum (Eggleston, 1977), neglectful of aims and objectives (purposeless), potentially neglectful of processes and skills, potentially closed to new knowledge, and certainly neglectful of the whole issue of matching.

Concept-based Planning

Here the starting point is a concept rather than a body of knowledge e.g. rhythm, power, change, balance. The concept can straddle few or many subject fields. The concept-based approach shares many of the advantages and disadvantages of the content-based approach. Additionally, the strength of this approach is its fittingness to the elements of the primary ethos which stress integration of knowledge and meeting the whole personality of the child. The major drawback of this approach concerns 'the curriculum through the child's eyes': to what extent will the integration be in the teacher's rather than the child's mind; to what extent is it acceptable or possible to attempt to integrate completely different, and often exclusive, disciplines in a way which is not contrived or artificial? For example, the concept of 'power' mentioned earlier will have completely different meanings for the social scientist, the historian, the musician, the religious educators, the scientist, the mathematician, the artist or the physical education teacher. How can these different perspectives realistically hope to be integrated or perceived in any unitary way by the child? The term 'power' is no more than a convenient label whose integrated meaning may be lost on the child (c.f. Schools Council, 1972). This points to the need:

1. To select concepts which are in themselves truly comprehensible to children and the exemplification of which are truly representative of the range of the parent concept.

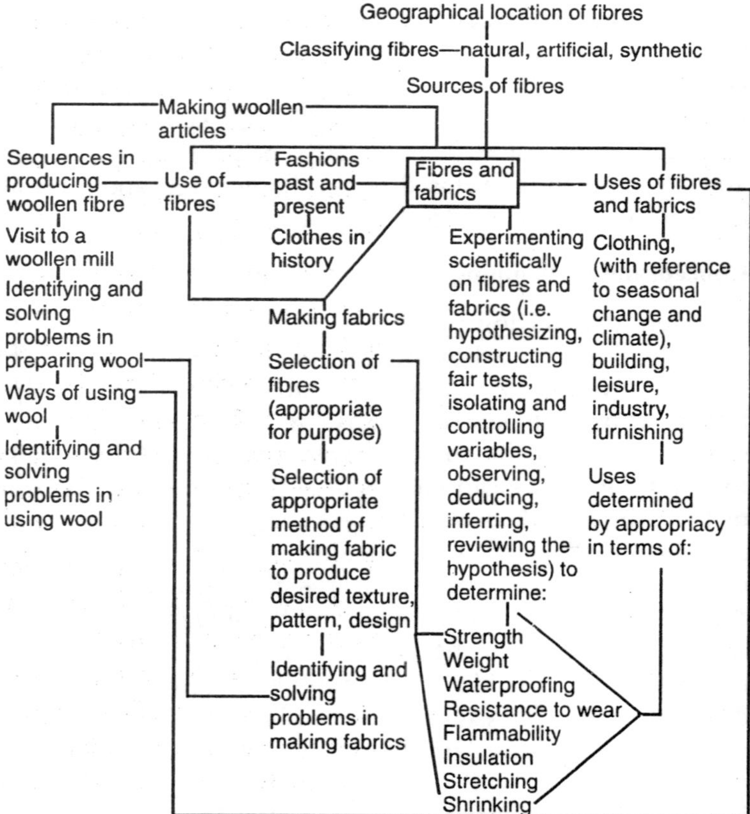

Fig. 3.13: A completed web diagram on 'fibres and fabrics'.

2. To ensure that the concept truly integrates knowledge in a way which is perceptible to children.
3. To select concepts which are not unrealistically abstract.

Skills-based Planning

Here planning begins from an analysis of skills to be learned or practised. This approach has considerable appeal to progressive ideology, for it dwells on activity, discovery learning, processes, and an emphasis on education as experience––the empiricist base or primary education rather than on outcomes (Blenkin and Kelly, 1981): 'Skill-focused teaching starts from data not conclusions, experience not books, and is open not closed' (Oliver, 1982; p. 131)

Clarification is needed at the planning stage of the level of the skills; from low to high order, and from highly specific (e.g. cutting and pasting) to highly general [e.g. 'to weigh and interpret evidence and to draw conclusions' (DES, 1985b; para. 100)]. This will then indicate some sequencing of the skills; that some skills will necessarily precede others. This begins to address the problem of progression, which, for skills-based teaching, is difficult. While skills-based teaching allows for flexibility, teacher and pupil autonomy, practical activity and potentially high relevance for children, there are a number of problems which must be faced in this approach. Initially the questions of the origins and directions of the skills must be addressed, for in skills-based teaching alone it is difficult to imagine how it would shape the curriculum; this is because it neglects to take account of the knowledge upon which skills can be worked. Skills-based teaching and learning cannot be practised in a knowledge vacuum; a pure skills-based approach simply does not address the questions of content, of deciding worthwhile knowledge, or of planning for the development and progression of knowledge. Its neglect of the knowledge dimension and its failure to address knowledge outcomes of skills could render the curriculum static and offer little guidance or basis for future curriculum development. The relationship between skills and knowledge must be drawn. Further, in considering the origins of the skills-based curriculum, there is the question of decision-making; who decides on the skills to be learned, taught or practised? If it is left to individuals alone then it runs the risk of being arbitrary—at the whim of decision-makers—which may fortuitously produce a broad and interesting curriculum, but which may also produce a curriculum which is narrow and lustreless.

There is a further problem in that evaluation of the skill development might either be trivial (focusing solely on the observable and the measurable) or over complex (focusing on the abstract, general and unobservable) which constitutes much of education. The direction in which skills-based planning points is to show initially its useful contribution to curriculum planning but its overall inadequacy as a total model for structuring and developing the curriculum.

There is perhaps a more acceptable alternative in the concept of a process approach to planning (Stenhouse, 1975). Planning the curriculum on a process model attempts to insert rigour into the pure skills-based model, to render less arbitrary the skills developed, and to move away from the simplistic view that skills alone can determine curriculum planning. It seeks to show that instead of skills being the starting point, curriculum planning can begin, so to speak, from the other end; that by studying the content and the structure of that content, certain skills will suggest themselves as being appropriate to the learning of that content, and consistent with the significant features of that content. This model addresses both the problem of knowledge and its selection, and principles of pedagogy. It marries progressive ideologies and those ideologies which emphasize a concern for knowledge.

For example, in music teaching the content of music concerns, among other factors, performances, appreciation and composition. It is suggested in the process approach that the skills required of children for a full understanding of these factors would be those of actual performance, appreciation and composition. The skills derive from an analysis of content and not vice versa. Similarly, in science teaching scientific methodology is premissed on the notion that scientific ideas and concepts are in principle falsifiable, that scientific knowledge is provisional; the scientist formulates a hypothesis, tests it and reviews the hypothesis, fitting it into a paradigmatic framework or reformulating the paradigm. Hence in science teaching, to be true to this methodology and rationale, children must be immersed in the scientific, critical method rather than simply accepting scientific 'facts' unquestioningly.

A further, much celebrated, example of the 'process' approach is the Humanities Curriculum Project (Stenhouse, 1968), which focused on controversial issues in society—war, poverty, race—open-ended matters for which there are no clear or finite answers. Given that the content is open-ended and in a sense indecisive or inconclusive, then the skills and pedagogy deriving from that content must be appropriate to dealing with that type of content. Hence the project decided that discussion was a principal teaching method, a principal skill to be learned and practised, and that, as neither teachers nor pupils could claim to possess the 'right' answers to controversial issues, the teacher should be a neutral chairperson, and that children should be learning skills of posing questions and prompting debate, articulating and reflecting rather than seeking fixed solutions to open problems. If the content were investigative and exploratory then the skills appropriate to that content should be investigative and exploratory.

One has to question here whether the process model suffers from the spectres of Tyler's and Taba's linear models of curriculum planning—with implicit objectives (Hirst, 1980; Skillbeck, 1984) and the selection of learning experiences appropriate to the content. Other problems ensue in the process model, notably that of assessment, for the teacher is cast into the role of diagnoser and critical friend rather than marker; a process rather than a product concern. Further, the question has to be raised of its suitability for all areas of the curriculum; is it perhaps only suited to the humanities and social science areas? Like the content-based model, it too does not question the origin of the content; it may be completely arbitrary. Thus, though there are considerable attractions to the process approach, as a model for curriculum planning it is incomplete.

Problem-based Planning

Here emphasis is placed on children-solving problems responsibly, e.g. a multiplicity of problems can be identified in mathematics, CDT, environmental studies or drama. In this approach teachers must be clear on seven points. Initially the educational aims of the problem-solving activity must be approached to clarify whether the emphasis is to be on the solution or on the process. This requires teachers to clarify whether they are in fact engaged in problem-solving or investigational work where a solution is not necessary. It also begs the question of whether in fact the problem is soluble; teachers in their planning must determine this as it will affect the aims of the activity, its criteria for success and resources to be used.

Second, teachers must be clear on the extent to which problem-solving approaches can become the basis for whole curriculum planning; are there some areas of the curriculum which do not readily lend themselves to problem-solving approaches? It is fundamental here to determine whether the problem-solving approach to planning concerns the aims of the curriculum or the pedagogical processes; whether the intention here is to develop in children the facility either to regard learning and behaviour from a solely problem-solving basis or to recognize that problem-solving is a useful method of tackling certan situations—a strategy rather than an aim. One has to question here whether, realistically, all learning could be problem-solving, as:

1. Children depend on past experience to recognize problems (Entwistle, 170).
2. Time pressures in school may prevent this ideal from becoming reality.

Third, the expression of the problem must be clarified. The problem must be clearly recognized, identified and operationalized, i.e. expressed in a way which suggests pathways to its solution. This will involve identifying key factors which cause the problem. For example, children might be investigating the problem of lack of leisure time amenities in their locality. It would be unacceptable to tackle this solely at the level of complaint ('there's not enough to do in the evenings'); it would need explication and exegesis, for example:

1. Is the problem lack of amenities or is it something else?
2. What are the alternatives to providing amenities?
3. Who is registering the complaints and why?
4. What are the aims of providing the amenities?
5. What are the present amenities?
6. How are they used?
7. Why are they not used or abused?
8. Who uses the present amenities?
9. What objections would there be to increasing amenities?
10. What additional amenities are required?
11. Whom would the additional amenities serve?
12. What are the advantages and disadvantages of proposed sitings?
13. How would they be financed?
14. On what criteria would provision be prioritized?

Fourth, the level of complexity of the problem must be anticipated, as it will affect the sequencing of the problem. For example, the problem of building a model house is far less complex than the planning, construction and arrangement of a model village. Fifth, related to the complexity of the problem is the range of the problem, for example, macro problems (perhaps those relating to Third World poverty, or housing and education in developing countries, or human rights) dwarf more localized problems. Attempts to address such problems might not be able to go beyond the superficial level in schools. This links to the sixth consideration, the extent to which the problem is realistically within the capabilities of children and teachers to comprehend and solve. Finally, there is the ideological question of who generates the problems. Are they teachers' or children's problems? If they are children's problems are they then perceived as such by the children? Thus the notion of problem-solving planning is itself problematic. While it may in fact describe more accurately than a didactic model the ways in which children learn, like other approaches, it does not straightforwardly provide a model which teachers and planners can accept at face value.

Interest-based Planning

Here work follows a particular interest or event, for example, the child's interests or a visit, a collection, a theatrical experience and so on. This form of planning is opportunistic, is overtly related to child-centredness, and provides for high pupil involvement and relevance. It respects pupil freedoms and choices; it is a model which is perhaps common practice in nursery and infant education, sadly reducing as children progress through the primary years. Its merits are clear. However, there are difficulties and problematic areas in this approach. Interests may be unsuitable or incomplete as basis for curriculum planning (Dearden, 1968; Hirst and Peters, 1970). The curriculum could become completely random, partial and fragmented.

The question is raised, then, of whether, like problem-based planning, the notion of interest-based planning is reflected more in the pedagogy than in the aims. Further, there is an ambivalence in the term 'interests' (Peters, 1966). It comprises both what interests the child and what is in the child's interests. The ambivalence is important for it reveals the decision-making process in the teacher—pupil relationship; a child's interests may be trivial, worthless, ephemeral, horrible, damaging or of limited educational value. It is part of the teacher's role to guide the child into developing what is in her or his interests and to see what is of value, be this unacceptable because of its instrumental ideological overtones or not.

For the curriculum planner who likes the security of predetermined outcomes, planning the curriculum by interests is not a suitable model, for the notion of novelty and uncertainty is inherent in it (c.f. Wilson, 1971). Its opportunistic appeal can be viewed as a strength or a drawback, dependent on one's ideological position. How one builds breadth, balance, coverage, consistency, structure, continuity and progression into interest-based planning is also difficult, as are timetabling and resource implications. The problem then—as with all the previous models is their exclusivity and partiality. The curriculum planner, stresing comprehensive guidance has thus to focus not only on what models address but what they neglect, and to realize that within each model no glib prescriptions or straightforward guidance can be found. This again reinforces the notion of the need for teachers to be eclectic, reflective and discerning.

Objective-based Planning

Here teachers begin from a clear specification of what they hope to achieve, or what the pupils will have learned or be able to do by the end of the lesson(s). Objectives describe the hoped for outcomes of education and curricula (Wiles and Bondi, 1984). The field of objectives-based planning and its relationship to aims, ideology and epistemology is vast. Planners need to consider the following:

1. The desirability and dangers of objectives-based planning.
2. The practicability of objectives-based planning.
3. The applicability of objectives-based planning to all areas of the curriculum.
4. The need to tailor objectives to the ages, abilities, needs and interests of children.
5. The scope of objectives—their range (high to low order, from specific to general, and from specifying products to specifying skills and processes (Figure 3.14).

While objectives make for clarity of thinking, there is a risk of confining education to that which can be stated specifically, of neglecting both the unobservable and the more spontaneous activities which make classrooms exciting, and of rendering the child a passive recipient of prepared experiences rather than an active creator of those experiences. There are powerful arguments both for and against objectives, and a clear need to clarify their nature, purpose, scope and potential.

This chapter has demonstrated that attempts to translate rationales of the curriculum into practice can be approached through the application of curriculum planning models. Modelling the curriculum is not straightforward. Models clarify and conceptualize but do not themselves provide simple solutions; each model is problematic. This is desirable, for it underlines one of the central themes of this book, that good teaching is not promised on the uncritical application of a series of practices, but that constantly it is a reflexive and enquiring activity. The problematic areas of teaching must be interrogated continually, School learning is about planned learning, planned learning that is at the same time organized and sequenced but also flexible and responsive to immediate and unpredictable situations. It is interactional, dependent on the inter-relationships between the teacher, the child, the context and the task. Hence no single blueprint for planning can be proposed, rather a series of issues can be outlined which planners need to address and use selectively in the way unique to their situation and purposes. Planners need to establish frameworks of concerns within which space is created for flexibility, teacher autonomy and development.

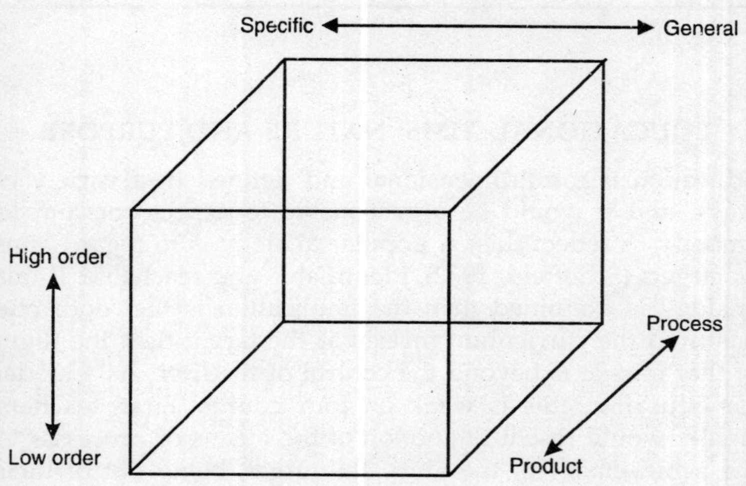

Fig. 3.14: The scope of objectives in curriculum planning.

4

Aims and Objectives of Curriculum

EDUCATIONAL AIMS: NATURE AND PURPOSE

Education is multidimensional and defined in a variety of ways, and it would be unreasonable to expect one aim to embody or reflect this. A popular analogy is to regard aims as targets (Schofield, 1972), identifiable and reachable. If this analogy is examined then the implication is that once one has fired the curriculum missile at the target then the flight of that missile is beyond the control of the firer. As a model for education this is weak on four counts. First, teachers rightly would resent the notion of the means or processes to the achievement of the aims, the target, being out of their control, the very nature of teaching implies the controlled transmission or discovery of knowledge.

Second, children and teachers interact with each other (Pollard, 1985), constantly shaping their own and each other's futures and situations. To suggest that teachers could plan a curriculum and not have to modify and refashion it in the light of changing situations and interactions is irresponsible and unrealistic, and neglects a key premiss that children develop in ways not always anticipated at the start of an educational programme. The primary ethos is against such behaviouristic prescriptivism.

Third, the notion of aims as targets is poor in that it suggests that aims are in fact reachable; in epistemological terms this means the learning of an identifiable and prespecified body of knowledge whose ideology would perhaps be conservative. The roots and bases for the primary curriculum are not as exclusive as this; they incorporate empiricism as well as rationalism progressivism as well as instrumentalism or conservatism, processes as well as products. The notion of finite aims lies ill at ease with progressive ideology or empiricist epistemology, for they are by definition open-ended and available for negotiation. In this sense aims are perhaps better regarded as signposts rather than targets; to be educated is not to have arrived, it is to travel with a different view (Peters, 1973)—the transformation criterion of education (Barrow and Woods, 1982). Aims express intentions and purposes rather than explicitly achievable ends. They are long term and generalized (Higginbottom, 1976).

This highlights a fourth significant feature in discussing aims as targets: the relationship between aims and the concept of education. It has been argued (Ryle, 1949) that the concept of education has to be regarded in both 'task' and 'achievement' senses. This has resonances with Passmore (1980) who discusses teaching as an 'attempt-word' and a 'success-word'; for example, teaching someone swimming is a 'task' or 'attempt' whereas actually teaching her or him to swim implies success or achievement, as in 'I taught him to swim' or 'I taught her to drive'.

If 'education' is taken is this 'achievement' sense then problems are raised, for though teachers' aims might be to educate children they might be unsuccessful (Peters, 1973). Indeed, it is suggested that difficulty and distance—their long-term nature—are endemic to notions of aims (Hirst and Peters, 1970), echoing the Plowden report's comments that statements of aims tend to be little more than expressions of benevolent aspirations. Alternatively, education can be regarded as a 'task' word, stressing the doing rather than necessarily the successful outcome—seeking as opposed to finding, educating as opposed to education—clearly a process view which has sympathy with the primary ethos.

There is a clear lesson here that education should be used in both 'attempt' the 'success' terms, 'task' and 'achievement' senses. A problem is raised in using 'education' as a 'task' word, in that this could betray a solely instrumental view of education (Langford, 1968), where education serves some extrinsic purpose or aim, for instance to produce a socialized adult or a suitable candidate for the labour market. This contention has been censured (Brubacher, 1962; Peters, 1966, 1973; Barrow and Woods, 1982), particularly with reference to the primary ethos, where education is regarded as intrinsically worthwhile, having no end beyond itself, being its own end. Hence from this perspective it is more fitting perhaps to discuss aims *in* education rather than aims *of* education.

If education is to comprehend both 'task' and 'achievement' senses; if it is to be predicated on intrinsic and extrinsic value, then there are four clear implications of this for curriculum planners. Initially, the notion of an aim as finite and achievable will have to be replaced by a version which regards aims as statements of desirable processes or criteria—coterminous with values (Ormell, 1980). Indeed, it is this sense that comes out clearly in statements of aims:

1. To acquire knowledge, skills and practical abilities, and the will to use them.
2. To develop qualities of mind, body, spirit, feeling and imagination.
3. To appreciate human achievements in art, music, science, technology and literature.
4. To acquire understanding of the social, economic and political order, and a reasoned set of attitudes, values and beliefs.
5. To prepare for their adult lives at home at work, at leisure and at large, as consumers and citizens.
6. To develop a sense of self-respect, the capacity to live as independent, self-motivated adults and the

ability to function as contributory members of co-operative groups.

(Schools Council, 1981; p. 16)

Education becomes an open-ended, ongoing, lifelong activity (Peters, 1966), and the curriculum and its aims must reflect that. Second, the curriculum planner will have to clarify the extent to which instrumental concerns are uppermost in designing the activity. Clearly an activity can serve extrinsic and intrinsic aims simultaneously for instance reading can be useful, fulfilling and enjoyable. In being clear on the instrumental or intrinsic value of the activity, the curriculum planner will be able to ensure breadth of the curriculum—breadth comprising breadth of justification and purpose as well as expression.

Third, the curriculum planner will have to clarify whether the planned activity lays emphasis on 'task' or 'achievement', for upon this rationale will hinge criteria for evaluation of pupils' learning. It would be inappropriate to condemn a child for an unacceptable product if the intention of the activity lay elsewhere. Finally, the effect of casting attention to the 'task' as well as the 'achievement' aspect of an activity is to reinforce the primary ethos, it is possible to discern a link between intrinsic value, processes, tasks and progressive ideology on the one hand, and a link between extrinsic value, achievements, instrumentalism and conservative ideologies on the other. Aims, then, can be regarded as general statements of long-term intentions, derived from value systems which may lie outside the immediate school context, being inexpressible in finite or achievable terms. Their appropriate and characteristic usage is to preface whole curriculum statements or courses or programmes of activities, for example:

1. To help pupils to develop lively, enquiring minds, the ability to question and argue rationally and to apply themselves to tasks, and physical skills.

2. To help pupils to acquire knowledge and skills relevant to adult life and employment in a fast-changing world.
3. To help pupils to use language and number effectively.
4. To instil respect for religious and moral values, and tolerance of other races, religions, and ways of life.
5. To help pupils to understand the world in which they live, and the interdependence of individuals, groups and nations.
6. To help pupils to appreciate human achievements and aspirations.

(DES, 1981; para. 11)

The Curriculum Development Centre (CDC, 1980) offers its own list of aims of education:

1. The nurturing and development of the powers of reasoning, reflective and critical thinking, imagining, feeling and communicating among and between persons.
2. The maintenance, development and renewal (and not merely the preservation) of the culture; that is of our forms and systems of thought, meaning and expression—such as scientific knowledge, the arts, language and technology.
3. The maintenance, development and renewal (and not merely preservation of) the social, economic and political order—including its underlying values, fundamental structures and institutions.
4. The promotion of mental, physical, spiritual and emotional health in all people.

(Curriculum Development Centre, 1980; p. 9)

TYPES OF AIMS

Aims vary according to their focus and to the concept of education held by curriculum planners. For example, if eduction is conceived of as training then the aims of the curriculum will emphasize the successful performance of a particular set of skills: if education is conceived of as instruction then successful retention of information might be stressed. However, if the concept of education is broader than this, emphasizing either induction into the thought systems of a culture and a society or initiation into social values and norms, then the parameters of the aims will be necessarily wider (Stenhouse, 1975). If this is so then one would expect to see perhaps conflicting discussions and conceptualizations of aims, particularly if the origins of aims are seen to reside in values and ideological systems. This reinforces the view of Hartnett and Naish (1976) that education is an 'essentially contested concept'. Value systems will represent a view of society, a view of culture, a view of knowledge, a view of the individual and a view of education. If one considers the potential for disagreement among value systems and their holders' aims for education, e.g. those of the DES, local education authorities (LEA), industrialists, employers, academics, parents, pupils and teachers, one would hardly be surprised to find conflicting statements and priorities (c.f. Lawton, 1984). Yet statements of educational aims are marked by consistency and consensus (e.g. DES, 1985b). This is scarcely surprising perhaps as, by their general nature, aims will bind together disparate values and interests:

> education has certain long-term goals. They are first, to enlarge a child's knowledge, experience and imaginative understanding, and thus his awareness of moral values and capacity for enjoyment; and second, to enable him to enter the world after formal education is over as an active participant in the society and a responsible contributor to it, capable of achieving as much independence as possible ... The purpose of education for all children is the same; the goals are the same. But the help that individual children need in progressing towards them will be different.
>
> (DES, 1978b; para. 14)

There are dangers in accepting this broad consensual view of aims (Whitty, 1985), for it may be that it suppresses the valuable debate about conflict; it conceals fundamentally conflicting ideologies, allowing perhaps the hegemony of the dominant ideology to suffuse the educational system unquestioned. It may be thus more productive to maintain difference rather than to swamp it in consensual terminology and statement.

How then can curriculum planners organize their thinking about aims? One common means is by discussing aims which refer to individual development and aims which refer to the needs of society (Ashton, Kneen, and Davies, 1975), acknowledging that they are not mutually exclusive (Central) Advisory Council for Education (CACE), 1967; (White, 1982b). However, the dichotomy is untenable and erroneous; education does not serve either one or the other; the child inextricably belongs to a culture, a society; children do not lose their individuality by serving society, indeed the opposite may be true. This latter point is well recognized by Plowden where the best preparation for a happy and useful life is seen as being founded on a fulfilled childhood.

Alternatively, Ashton, Kneen and Davies (1975) analyse aims through a matrix (Figure 4.1). The vertical axis relates to aspects of pupils' development, and the horizontal axis lists elements of learning. One can remark the admixture of process and content aims—'task' and 'achievement' conceptions of education. A similar matrix can be constructed out of the DES (1985b) conceptions of the organization of the curriculum.

Intellectual	Knowledge	Skill	Qualities
Physical			
Spiritual/religious			
Emotional/personal			
Social/moral			

Fig. 4.1: A classification matrix of aims of education.

What must be borne in mind when using these matrices is that they are essentially analytical models which are being used prescriptively (c.f. DES, 1985b). They do not describe actual channels of child development (Alexander, 1984) nor is any substantial justification for these conceptions preffered. In using them, then, the curriculum planner has to be aware that they do not reflect actual states of mind or lines of child development or curriculum plans, i.e. that development and education do not follow these discrete paths. The significance of this is to realize that they provide a helpful, if incomplete, framework for planners; they articulate the terms of the curriculum and educational debate. The framework must therefore be enabling and facilitating for planning rather than constricting or constraining; it must be a ladder rather than a case.

Areas of learning and experience \ Elements of learning	Knowledge	Concepts	Skill	Attitudes
Aesthetic and creative				
Human and social				
Linguistic and literary				
Mathematical				
Moral				
Physical				
Scientific				
Spiritual				
Technological				

Fig. 4.2: Interpreting HMI classification of aims.

The second important consideration for curriculum planners using these matrices is to ensure that every cell of the matrix is addressed. It is significant that in the Ashton, Kneen and Davies study (1975) there is an absence of 'skills' in the 'spiritual/religious' cell, and of 'knowledge' in the aesthetic development cell (c.f. Alexander, 1984); the question must be raised of the ideological taste betrayed by such omissions. If the models are to be used then perhaps they should be used in their entirety rather than partially.

In classifying aims the curriculum planner must ensure, then, that due weight is given to individual and societal needs, to comprehensiveness of coverage and expression; e.g. epistemological, ideological and psychological concerns, and to an articulation of the justification for the aims, the rationales on which they are premissed. Given that aims are fundamental building blocks of the curriculum, the values which underpin them must be thought through by curriculum planners and equally thoroughly expressed.

NATURE AND PURPOSE OF OBJECTIVES

In approaching the field of objectives, curriculum planners can define objectives as operational statements of the desired outcomes of curricula. Tyler (1949) argues for the necessity of having objectives in curriculum planning and improvement in that:

> if an educational program is to be planed and if efforts for continual improvement are to be made, it is very necessary to have some conception of the goals that are being aimed at. These educational objectives become the criteria by which materials are selected, content is outlined, instructional procedures are developed and tests and examinations are prepared.
>
> (Tyler, 1949; p. 3)

Objectives, then, are far more specific and purportedly unambiguous than aims. They translate aims into practice coherently rather than haphazardly; they offer more precise direction than aims; aims are insufficient guides for making specific decisions about specific curricula. Aims orientate, they are strategical; objectives implement, they are tactical (c.f. Davies, 1976).

Objectives are operational in that they describe what the teacher or the child will be doing, they can prescribe outcomes in their statements of what the child or teacher should have achieved or practised or covered by the end of a lesson or course. An example of a lesson objective might be: 'the object of this lesson is for the children to learn the words and music of *Country Gardens*', or 'the object of this lesson is to practise anaphoric and cataphoric reading cues in a piece of cloze procedure about hunting seals in the Arctic Circle'.

There are several claims for the purpose or value of planning the curriculum by objectives. Taba (1962), for example, suggests that they guide decisions on content selection and suitability of experiences to learn that content; they offer clarity in selecting from the vast areas of knowledge that which is necessary for the movement towards achieving aims; they clarify issues and thinking about purposes and intentions:

> the necessity for objectives is simply the necessity for us to know what it is we want children to learn if we are to be able to do our best to help them learn. Pupils must learn something, and how can we plan that they achieve that without being clear what it is.
>
> (Hirst, 1980; p. 9)

The thrust of the argument here then is that objectives clarify thinking and clarify and specify pathways through knowledge. They enable curriculum planners to decide which ways are beneficial to the achievement of ends and purposes. There are many ways of learning a concept; for example, if one wished to learn about the concept of flotation one could learn practically by experimenting, vicariously by reading about it or by listening to a teacher talking about it, iconically (Bruner, 1960) by watching a film or video programme or by drawing a picture about it or symbolically by writing about it. By being precise and specific in stating objectives, the curriculum planner can clarify the most apposite ways of attaining the objectives. Clarification, as has already been mentioned, is a critical quality of the reflective teacher.

Objectives facilitate evaluation, indeed they may predetermine evaluation criteria. Curriculum planners need to know their intentions for children's learning in order to judge how successfully the intentions have been achieved. It is quite ridiculous to argue that a course or a lesson went well if the criteria for that judgment were not clear; these criteria could be contained in the objectives. This has a twofold benefit: improvement of the curriculum is assisted if feedback on achievement is available and, second, it makes for better matching of tasks to children, setting realistic demands.

There are, however, problems with the notion of using objectives in the evaluation process, principally because they tend to lock evaluation into a certain mode—assessment and measurement rather than diagnosis and judgement. The problem is particularly acute in discussing behavioural objectives—to be reviewed later in the chapter.

The strongest justification for planning the curriculum by objectives lies in its appeal to rationality; that part of the meaning of an activity to be rational is that it should be directed to some clear goal or purpose. For the curriculum to be rational, then, it must state its purposes (Hirst, 1980):

> In curriculum decisions we are concerned with a programme of intentional, deliberately and consciously planned objectives...planned so that certain objectives will be reached, so that pupils will come to know certain things, have certain skills, will be able to appreciate certain things, have certain habits, patterns of emotional response and so on...curriculum activities are...the means to the intended ends.
>
> (Hirst, 1980; p. 9)

Education, as mentioned earlier, is an intentional activity. Hirst (1975) argues that rational planning must adhere to Mill's principles of defining ends and then means to achieving them, and to Oakeshott's (1976a; 1976b) principle that curriculum planners must look to the specific activity, the specific school and the specific curriculum as practised in that school ('the idiom of the activity') to ascertain the most appropriate objectives. In this sense curriculum planning can scarcely ever be wholesale, but piecemeal (c.f. Skilbeck, 1984):

> all action takes place within a specific context and a set of traditions. It is only within this that rational development can take place. The idea of *ab initio, carte blanche* planning is a megalomaniac delusion...Rational planning is not, and cannot be Utopian. It must be piecemeal development on the spot, using all the available understanding and knowledge.
>
> (Hirst, 1975; pp. 14-15)

Hirst, then, offers a provocative reassertion of the need for objectives and indeed their usefulness for curriculum planners, cast in a powerful justificatory language.

Curriculum planning embraces general and specific objectives. An example of a general objective might be: 'to introduce children to scientific experimentation' or 'to interest pupils in local history', i.e. the setting out of a field of study. An example of a less general objective in this science field might read: 'the ability to apply various methods of separating and purifying chemicals to the demands of an astronaut's life support system in a space craft' (Whitfield, 1980, p. 86), or in fine art it might be: 'to develop skill in mixing water colour' (ibid., p. 25). At a highly specific level it could be: 'to measure in kilometres per hour (kph) the speed of an articulated lorry travelling down Nonesuch hill with a full load', where an explicit task is set, the conditions in which that task is performed are clearly delineated (travelling downhill with a full load) and the criteria for successful performance indicated (measuring speed in kph).

The issue raised by different levels of objectives is significant, for it directs attention to the point that though objectives are more specific than aims, being operational, they are not necessarily solely highly specific ends written in narrow behavioural terms. Such recognition brings out the view that objectives can be short-term or long-term, though in reality argument tends to treat them as shorter rather than longer term ends. With this in mind it is possible to present a model showing how objectives are devised and who devises them (Figure 4.3).

The model is perhaps descriptive; its prescriptivity is highly questionable. The caution that must be exercised in examining this model concerns the discreteness of each level and type of decisions on objectives and courses, for it could be argued (Carson, 1984) that decisions on general aims and curriculum areas are not the preserve of the DES, LEA, or senior management levels of schools. In fact, for primary schools the opposite may be more pertinent. The danger of this model lies in the way that it might be seen to prescribe a bureaucratic, hierarchical structure of curriculum planning rather than a democratic, open structure. An alternative then could be presented (Figure 4.4).

In this model the concept of negotiation and interaction is presented, again requiring reflective thinking about education and the curriculum by teachers. It accords with professional autonomy and its concomitant responsibility to all major participants in the curriculum planning process. Teachers are agents in planning rather than simply recipients of others plans.

General ↓	Bodies	Form of objectives	Dicisions on courses
Level 1 ↓	DES LEA	Very generalized	Major areas of the curriculum defined
Level 2 ↓	School or deparment	Broad parameters and direction	Decisions on the framing of courses
Level 3 ↓	Teams of staff	More detailed objectives	Course content and seqence as a whole
Level 4 ↓ Specific	Teacher	Highly specific behaviours and content	Lesson content

Fig. 4.3: The range of curriculum objectives presented by levels of decision-makers.

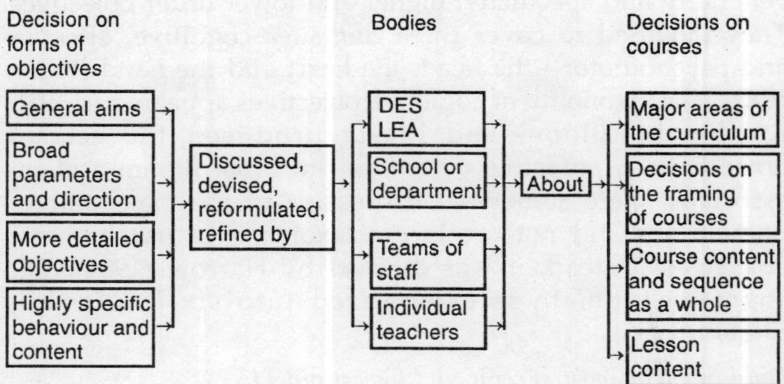

Fig. 4.4: A model of participatory decision-making in objectives-based planning.

CLASSIFICATION OF OBJECTIVES

Objectives need not simply be classified in terms of levels of generality—from general to specific, as mentioned in the previous section. What is required here is an analysis of types of objectives so that curriculum planners can identity scope for balance, coverage and breadth in planning. One useful form of classification finds five sorts of objectives (Taba, 1962):

1. Objectives concerning knowledge (facts, ideas, principles, concepts).
2. Objectives concerning reflective thinking (critical thinking, interpreting data, applying facts and principles, logical reasoning).
3. Objectives concerning values and attitudes.
4. Objectives concerning sensitivities and feelings.
5. Objectives concerning skills.

This has clear resonances with Scrimshaw's (1983) categorization of components of children's learning. Alternatively, a much publicized way of classifying objectives is taxonomically. Bloom and his associates (1956) developed taxonomies of educational objectives, specifying levels of generality and specificity, higher and lower order objectives. They intended to cover three domains: cognitive, affective and psychomotor—the head, the heart and the hand (Kelly, 1982). The taxonomy of cognitive objectives appeared in 1956; Krathwohl, Bloom and Masia produced the second taxonomy—of affective objectives—in 1956. Bloom and his associates were somewhat dismissive of the psychomotor domain and did not produce a taxonomy of psychomotor objectives; instead, it was devised by Harrow (1984). The cognitive domain is categorized into six levels thus (Bloom, 1956):

Level one (the most specific and lowest order)

> Knowledge—ability to recall specifics, universals, methods, processes, patterns, structures or settings (Bloom, 1956; p. 201).
>
> 1.10 Knowledge of specifics.
>
> 1.20 Knowledge of ways and means of dealing with specifics.
>
> 1.30 Knowledge of universals in a field.

Level two

> Comprehension—which requires knowledge, an ability to grasp what is being communicated to be able to use the material or idea without necessarily relating it to other material or seeing its fullest implications, (ibid., p. 204)
>
> 2.10 Translation.
>
> 2.20 Interpretation.
>
> 2.30 Extrapolation.

Level three

> Application—which requires knowledge and comprehension, an ability to use ideas, concepts or principles in particular and concrete situations (ibid., p. 205).

Level four

Analysis—which subsumes levels one to three, an ability to break down an idea or concept into its constituents parts and their interrelationship which clarify or illuminate the whole curriculum (ibid., p. 205).

4.10 Analysis of elements.

4.20 Analysis of relationships.

4.30 Analysis of organizational principles.

Level five

Synthesis—which subsumes levels one to four, an ability to assemble elements into a unified whole not clearly present initially (ibid., p. 206)

5.10 Production of unique communication.

5.20 Production of a plan or a proposed set of relations.

5.30 Derivation of a set of abstract relations.

Level Six

Evaluation—which subsumes levels one to five, an ability to appropriate criteria to judge the value of material and methods for given purposes (ibid., p. 207).

6.10 Judgement in terms of internal evidence.

6.20 Judgement in terms external criteria.

An example of a low-order objective might be: 'to list five types of defences for castles', whereas a high-order objective might be: 'to say why castle defence "x" is the most effective'. Low-order objectives make slight cognitive demand, e.g. 'to add two and two', 'to weigh five buckets of dry sand'; whereas high-order objectives involve applying many concepts and abstractions, e.g. 'to suggest why *The Shrinking of Treehorn* is a good book', or 'to appreciate the icy atmosphere depicted in Vaughan Williams's *Sinfonia Antarctica*'. One can construct a chart to graph the twin continua of low to high order and specific to general objectives.

An example of low-order, general objective (the top left-hand quadrant) might be: 'to know that many trees shed their leaves in autumn'. The significant phrase here is 'know that'—a fact, rather than 'knowing how'—an understanding.

Examples of high-order, general objectives (the top right-hand quandrant) might be: 'to understand the principles of capitalism', or 'to appreciate the need for ecological interdependence', where both understanding and a valuative perspective on that understanding are required. An example of a low-order, specific objective (the bottom left-hand quadrant) might read: 'to colour in three printed houses'; whereas examples of high-order, specific objectives might be: 'to write a critical commentary on *The Wild Swans of Coole*', or 'to appreciate the need for vitamins in the human body'.

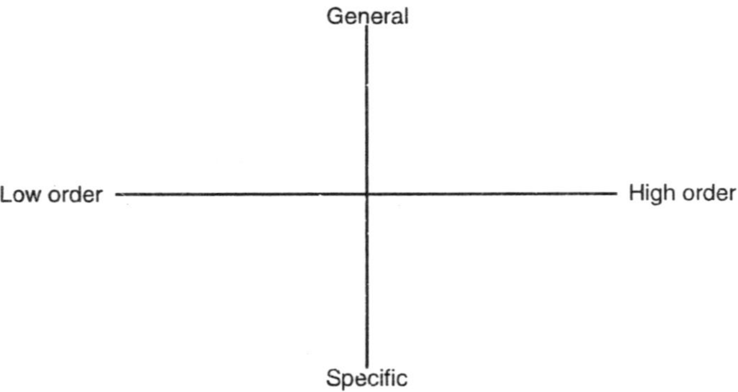

Fig. 4.5: Two dimensions of curriculum objectives.

In the affective domain five levels are identified:

Level one

Receiving—attending to, being sensitized to the existence of certain phenomena and stimuli (Krathwohl *et al.*, 1956; p. 176).

1.1. Awareness.

1.2 Willingness to receive.

1.3 Controlled or selected attention.

Level two

Responding—which subsumes level one, actively attending and interested (ibid., p. 178).

2.1 Acquiescence in responding.

2.2 Willingness to respond.

2.3 Satisfaction in response.

Level three

Valuing—which subsumes levels one and two, judging worth and internalizing values, developing conscience (ibid., p. 180).

3.1 Acceptance of a value.

3.2 Preference for a value.

3.3 Commitment (conviction).

Level four

Organization—which subsumes levels one to three, organizing and adapting values, determining their interrelationships and prioritizing them (ibid., p. 182).

4.1 Conceptualization of a value.

4.2 Organization of a value system.

Level five

Characterization by a value or value complex—which subsumes levels one to four, generalizing and integrating values into a coherent, consistent system (ibid., p. 184).

5.1 Generalized set.

5.2 Characterization.

Krathwohl *et al.* (1956) acknowledge the arbitrary separation of cognitive and affective domains, arguing that it is done in the interest of analytical clarity, and has heuristic value only; indeed, they parallel the two taxonomies.

Cognitive domain	Affective domain
knowledge	receiving
comprehension	responding
application	valuing
analysis	conceptualization
synthesis	conceptualization
evaluation	organization and characterization

Fig 4.6: Matching two taxonomies.

In the psychomotor domain, Harrow (1974) delineates four levels of behaviour:

Level one

Observing—where the child observes the techniques and processes of a behaviour.

Level two

Imitating—which subsumes level one, where the child practises and performs given movements cautiously.

Level three

Practising—subsuming levels one and two, where movements become habitual, unconscious and smooth.

Level four

Adapting—subsuming levels one to three, where the child adapts routines and processes to suit her or his own purposes.

The claimed advantages of using taxonomies for devising curriculum objectives lie in their hierarchical classification systems and their clarity (Cave, 1971). They offer curriculum planners a checklist for achieving comprehensiveness in the curriculum (Bloom, 1956), knowing which domain and level of the curriculum assets analysis and coverage of the curriculum. Second, they facilitate communication of intentions and purposes between curriculum planners by offering a common referent. Third, they assist in pitching test items at an appropriate level and are useful for evaluation purposes. Fourth has claimed that they should stimulate thought about educational programs. Finally, their authors contend that the taxonomic approach is seen as a useful and effective tool for devising objectives.

Against these points are arranged several powerful arguments. It is suggested (Sockett, 1976) that Bloom's taxonomies demonstrate a lack of epistemological coherence, assuming that different areas of understanding and learning will have a similar structure; for example, that the structuring of aesthetic understandings will be similar to the structuring of understandings in the physical sciences, or maths or morals, or that problem-solving in mathematics will be the same as problem-solving in physics, or art, or music.

Just as the taxonomies artificially separate behaviours into domains, a fact which is acknowledged by the compilers (Krathwohl *et al.,* 1956), so within each taxonomy behaviour is separated artificially. For example, knowledge entails comprehension, recall and application simultaneously; knowledge does not equate solely with recall.

The thrust of this criticism is twofold. It acknowledges the undesirability of attempting to categorize behaviour too tightly as this reflects poorly the actuality of both epistemology and the learning child; behaviours cannot be pigeon-holed into single, discrete units. There is a suggestion in the compilation of the taxonomies that, even though each successive level subsumes the lower levels, there is no clear or immediate relationship between levels (Davies, 1976), which is epistemologically fallacious.

The second implication of attempting to separate behaviours for which taxonomies have been criticized (Hirst, 1975) is that they reduce the complexity of the curriculum and of learning to a level of simplicity which renders them both meaningless and fruitless, neglecting the complex interrelationships of skills, concepts, values, attitudes and perceptions (Hirst, 1975). The effort required to do justice to that complexity would be both time-consuming and, from the preceding argument, wasted.

As a model for primary curriculum planning, which celebrates unity of knowledge and experiences, the taxonomic approach, which separates behaviours rather than integrates them, is perhaps inappropriate. One can nevertheless look to taxonomies not necessarily as they have been interpreted, but as they were intended to be used—as tools to stimulate thought (Bloom 1956)—however flawed or incomplete they may be, a fact acknowledged by their authors. If they serve to promote discussion, debate, reflective thinking and teaching, then there must surely be a place for them in the curriculum planner's repertoire. One has to remark on the considerable currency commanded by taxonomic approaches to devising curricula: witness the Barrett taxonomy of reading comprehension (1972) and the hostility provoked to taxonomic planning (c.f. Smith, 1971; Morrison, 1984), to realize that as conceptual aids to debate they are perhaps useful.

Objectives have been classified according to Taba's (1962) scheme and to taxonomic schemes initiated by Bloom and others. A third classification exists which sorts objectives into types, principally three:

1. Specific statements of intent.
2. Behavioural objectives.
3. Expressive objectives.

The first of these has already been discussed, the others will be discussed in order.

BEHAVIOURAL OBJECTIVES

Behavioural objectives—sometimes called instructional objectives—are statements which prescribe the behavioural outcomes of a program. They specify intended learner or learned behaviour as a result of a lesson or course: these behaviours are observable and measurable (Tyler, 1949). For an objective to be behavioural it must satisfy three conditions (Mager, 1962):

1. It must identify intended terminal behaviour which demonstrates that learning has taken place.
2. It must describe the important conditions under which that behaviour is to occur.
3. It must specify the criteria of acceptable performance.

Wiles and Bondi (1984) name this the ABCD rule: the behavioural objective specifies the Audience of the objective (who will be displaying the behaviour); the Behaviour which will be displayed (the task); the condition, the Context of the behaviour (what material or resources will be used); the Degree of completion, how the performance of the behaviour will be assessed, what the criteria are for successful performance.

An example of a behavioural objective which fulfils the ABCD rule would be: 'at the end of this lesson the children will be able to draw a dinosaur on stiff card and cut it out carefully'. Here:

A = the children

B = drawing a dinosaur and cutting it out

C = on stiff card

D = carefully

Another example would be: 'by the end of the lesson the children will have successfully made a ten-page booklet which illustrates seventeenth century clothing fashions in England'. Here:

A = the children

B = making a book illustrating seventeenth century English clothing fashions

C = a ten-page booklet

D = successfully made.

Significantly, then, the behavioural objective must specify both the content and the process (Tyler, 1949): the knowledge and information and how it is to be acquired, utilized or practised; what it is and what will be done with it. Clearly, the success of a behavioural objective lies in its ability to describe a behaviour explicitly and unambiguously.

Fashions dictate the support or resistance offered to behavioural objectives, and there are significant arguments for and against their use. Interestingly, many arguments advanced in their favour are also used against them, revealing the ideological bases and conflicts in the debate. In their support are ranked several important considerations. They can be claimed to constitute the most fully worked out expression of rational planning outlined earlier, and have a curriculum pedigree which can be traced back to the early part of the century (Bobbitt, 1918; Charters, 1924). They have internal consistency with major models of curriculum planning (Tyler, 1949; Taba, 1962; Wheeler, 1967).

Such a pedigree claims the respectability of the behavioural tradition and scientific methodology employed in earlier curriculum writings. In this view their predetermination of children's terminal behaviour is seen as a merit. It is claimed that they facilitate curriculum organization in a means-end style by focusing many variables and problems into a chronologically linear sequence. On a practical level they can clarify thinking and resolve ambiguities (Popham, 1975), exposing the trivial and yet enabling planning in detail to be promoted. As with arguments in favour of taxonomic detailing of objectives, so in behavioural objectives a strength is claimed in their communicability to teachers and, importantly, to learners, reducing learner anxiety about the future and the requirements laid on them.

From a conservative ideology they can be said to concern the acquisition of the 'know'—a received curriculum—the corollary of which is to cast the teacher into the role of an expert or controller. This can be extended beyond the teacher's control to suggest that curriculum planners beginning from a statement of behavioural objectives can produce 'teacher-proof' materials and curricula, with instructions, goals or objectives so unambiguously formulated as to render teacher intervention or modification unnecessary. The teacher simply carries out the prescriptions.

This is seen positively as a means of supporting anxious teachers and ensuring that a sound education is provided even by inadequate teachers. At the level of evaluation it is claimed that behavioural objectives lead logically to evaluation, suggesting explicitly what has to be evaluated and the criteria for that evaluation, i.e. that evaluation is meaningful rather than being an imposed evaluation which may not be completely relevant (for example, nationally standardized tests of performance). Being measurable and testable in behaviour, behavioural objectives are useful fuel in the accountability debate.

Against these arguments are several key questions and doubts, many of which express the uncertainty of using behavioural objectives as the basis for planning the curriculum in general, and the primary curriculum in particular, notably their incompatability with the primary ethos. Arguments against the use of behavioural objectives present themselves at various levels. At an ideological level the notion of behaviourism is suspect in that it supports an instrumental or utilitarian view of education rather than regarding education as intrinsically worthwhile. This casts learners in a very passive, accepting role rather than as agents of their own learning—a view on which the primary ethos is predicated. Similarly, it casts teachers in given roles as experts, managers, technicians and controllers rather than co-learners, guides, chairpersons, facilitators, catalysts, denying perhaps their autonomy (Pring, 1973), their agency (Giroux, 1983). Such a view restricts the fluidity and breadth of teacher—pupil interaction and relationships which is one of the cornerstones of the primary ethos.

In this light the development of 'teacher-proof' materials is a weakness, a disadvantage rather than a strength. The concept of education supported by behavioural objectives suggests fixity and certainty whereas the concept of education suggests unpredictable outcomes (Stenhouse, 1975). The process of education is replaced by output dependence. That output might well be a set of unconnected skills rather than an uneducated person. In this vein MacDonald-Ross (1975) contends that behavioural objectives are constricting in the sense of neglecting the value of 'voyages of exploration'—opportunistic learning and teaching, shared discovery learning, the unanticipated class events and interests—this despite Popham's (1975) assertion that opportunism is to be welcomed as long as it contributes to the attainment of worthwhile objectives, and Pope's (1983) assertion that teachers embarkings on 'voyages of exploration' should have clearly addressed the question of accountability for their actions.

In sympathy with this approach, James (1968) argues that using objective does not ensure understanding; children may go through the motions of an activity without really understanding it. In the primary curriculum, as with the curriculum of the later years, the emphasis on understanding renders this criticism noteworthy. A critical educational and ideological argument against behaviourism is advanced by Hirst (1975), who holds that the central features of education (internalized processes, thoughts, values) are not reducible to the observable states which behavioural objectives require to be demonstrated, i.e. that behaviourism at root is an inappropriate conception of education (MacDonald-Ross, 1975; Stenhouse, 1975).

At an epistemological level, it is argued that behavioural objectives mistake the nature of knowledge, seeing it as purely in a product version, rather than product and process together. Thus it leans towards a 'facts'—based curriculum which maybe acceptable to conservative ideologies, but which unfairly represents the central tenets of the primary ethos which are founded on empiricist views as well as rationalist views of knowledge.

At a curriculum level behavioural objectives, it is suggested, are unsuitable for vast areas of the curriculum. For example, in science the principle of falsifiability is violated if outcomes are specified (Sockett, 1976), in the humanities and aesthetic education important outcomes, e.g. appreciation, are pushed aside (Eisner, 1975). Eisner suggests that it is not possible to prespecify outcomes of appreciation except at the level of banality; that it is undesirable to specify the content of appreciation, indeed using behavioural objectives could easily diminish creativity. Eisner is arguing that the subject-matter of education necessarily affects the applicability of planning by behavioural objectives—that whereas they may be useful in planning for highly specific skills to be trained, e.g. stripping down a car engine, or 'handwriting', they are unsuitable for areas of the curriculum which do not fit comfortably into being so tightly specified; major areas of the curriculum are not susceptible to planning by this form of objectives. Behavioural objectives predetermine only one pathway through curricular knowledge (MacDonald-Ross, 1975) which may be inappropriate for many areas of the curriculum and many learners (though Pope, 1983, offers a rejoinder to this, commenting that some paths through knowledge are less effective than others and that in the interests of economic teaching efforts must be made to establish those ways which are most effective).

At a practical level there are several inadequacies in planning by behavioural objectives. As with taxonomies, so behavioural objectives miss the complexity of the curriculum the ramifications of this are several. Either curriculum planners have to amass an inordinately long and unworkable list of objectives (MacDonald-Ross, 1975) to do justice to the complexity of the curriculum, or they concern themselves with that which can be easily expressed and operationalized. If one opts for the former then, apart from the considerable time needed to write lengthy lists of unambiguous objectives, there is no guarantee that teachers will either refer to them

(Taylor, 1970) or in fact need to refer to them. Witness the neglect of the pages of objectives reproduced at the end of every *Science 5-13* book; teachers teach efficiently without them, and there is little reason to suspect that inattention to behavioural objectives has been detrimental to their teaching (Stenhouse, 1975).

If one opts for the latter then teachers may well be dealing only in trivial and low-level processes. Popham (1975) would argue that a measure of this is acceptable, for in exposing the trivial the planner can see more clearly the significant issues, and plan those more carefully.

This is perhaps a slur on the expertise of teaches as planners. It also presupposes that behavioural objectives can be written in unambiguous terms, which is questionable (Mac-Donald-Ross, 1975; Sockett, 1976) as words themselves have different meanings according to contexts and users' frames of reference. For example, what is unambiguous to one person may be ambiguous or unintelligible to a child or another person. Even acknowledging Pope's (1983) valid point that difficulty in reducing ambiguity may be due to lack of clarity in the planner's mind, it nevertheless remains a serious problem which semantic analysis exacerbates rather than solves. At a practical level the argument that behavioural objectives are necessary for clear evaluation is fictitious; one might require objectives, certainly, but these need not be behaviourally expressed. Similarly, casting evaluation at the end of an educational program presupposes only a terminal, summative form of evaluation, whereas perhaps evaluation should be continual and formative. It also presupposes a particular form of terminal evaluation—achievement measurement—which is limiting and perhaps ideologically unsuited to the primary ethos.

Finally, at a curriculum development level, behavioural objectives offer little guidance to planners, for they do not address the question of the origin of the objectives. This renders their claimed value of neutrality a weakness rather than a strength. They presuppose, perhaps, consensus where there is conflict over moral choices about aims and goals. Unless curriculum planners are apprised of aims and values upon which the behavioural, objectives are based, there can be little useful discourse about new directions in curriculum planning. The results of such neglect could be an inability to take forward the curriculum to match societal and cultural change; it would present a static rather than regenerative curriculum.

Thus the picture of behavioural objectives is cloudy; the curriculum planner, while conceding that there are times when they may be useful, has to recognize their limitations and the difficulty of writing them. Are they so difficult to write that only 'experts' can devise them—in which case they can be a dangerous tool in curriculum direction and control, or should teachers be versed in their devising and utilization?

EXPRESSIVE OBJECTIVES

Expressive objectives can be seen as an attempt to preserve a measure of rigour in curriculum planning but to avoid the unpalatable excesses of the behavioural objectives model. They derive from Eisner (1975); their purpose is to describe learning situations which are intended to evoke personal responses from pupils rather than prespecifying a specific or uniform response or outcome. Hence their expression is gentler than that of behavioural objectives. They specify an activity, experience or encounter in which learners engage but drawback from specifying an intended learning outcome; they are evocative rather than prescriptive. Examples of expressive objectives might be: 'to visit a church and discuss what was interesting' or 'to depict, in any medium, the story of Rama and Sita'.

One can detect in expressive objectives three key features. First, they are apposite in planning in the aesthetic and humanities areas of the curriculum, where a personal response is a central aim. Second, by dint of that intention to evince a personal response, they are necessarily open-ended: they focus on processes as well as content. Third, they refer directly to the classroom learning model, where the key features—experience, observation, transformation, communication, incubation and accommodation—are key features also of expressive objectives. That model is premissed on the primary ethos. The intention of expressive objectives is to seek diversity rather than homogeneity of response, uniqueness rather than similarity; this accords well with the central features of progressive ideology.

EVALUATING AIMS AND OBJECTIVES

In evaluating aims and objectives, curriculum planners may address a range of questions which seek to examine their place and usefulness in building the curriculum:

- How worthwhile are the aims and objectives?
- How well and how comprehensively do the aims reflect the philosophies, contexts of and constraints on the curriculum and its planning?
- What are the ideological commitments of these aims and objectives?
- How clearly do the objectives follow from the aims?
- How well and how comprehensively do the objectives serve the aims?
- How practical and practicable are the objectives?
- How well do the objectives express different levels of cognitive, affective and psychomotor demand?
- How far do the objectives steer a middle course between necessary and unnecessary specificity?
- How are the aims and objectives decided, and by whom?
- How completely do the objectives address knowledge, concepts, skills, qualities, attitudes, personal and social development?
- How can taxonomies be used effectively in curriculum planning?

- How clearly stated are the aims and objectives?
- How appropriate are the aims and objectives to the children's individual needs, interests, and abilities?
- How can these objectives be developed and formulated?
- What alterations to existing philosophies, practices, organizations and managements are suggested by aims for a new piece of the planned curriculum?
- How will these aims and objectives assist in planning content, pedagogy and evaluation?
- How appropriate is the differentiation of aims and objectives in planning?
- How well do the aims and objectives cover issues which permeate the curriculum e.g. multi-cultural education, equal opportunities, health education, information technology, political education?
- How will aims and objectives for the curriculum be discussed, negotiated and decided?
- How will disagreement on the formulation and the content of the aims and objectives be managed?
- Who will decide the aims and objectives?

While the list is by no means exhaustive, it attempts to draw together the range of issues raised through the book so far. This involves looking at the stages and levels of curriculum planning, the managerial aspects of the curriculum debate and the structuring of the curriculum. Aims and objectives should embody and reflect such a range. Discussion of aims and objectives is ongoing just as the curriculum debate is never static.

CONCLUSION

In conclusion there are four main points which merit attention by curriculum planners considering aims and objectives. First, despite the many and significant problems associated with the employment of behavioural objectives, they need not necessarily be totally disregarded in planning the curriculum. Skilbeck (1984) offers a strong argument for their retention, suggesting that curriculum planning ought to attempt to identify desirable and desired learning outcomes in children, that the implausibility and undesirability of predicting outcomes in certain curriculum areas should not blind planners to the need for anticipating outcomes in others.

Second, if it is accepted that objectives need not be behavioural, then there remains a very powerful argument in favour of teachers planning by objectives (Hirst, 1980), that using objectives does not necessarily mean predicting highly specific outcomes. If knowledge is tentative and provisional then the objective can be written to reflect and incorporate this. This reduces the need to regard objectives as having to conform to taxonomic structures (Hirst, 1975); taxonomies are tools for thought, not necessarily prescriptive guidelines. Third, linked to this is the notion that objectives cover a wide field—knowledge, products, processes, concepts, skills, attitudes and values, organizations, activities and experiences (c.f. Carter and Hooley, 1983). Which type of objective curriculum planners may use is determined by ideology, epistemology, psychology, cultural and sociological pressures and constraints.

This issue of appropriacy engages the final point of fundamentally questioning the desirability of objectives. While one might accept the need for, and the desirability of, expressing aims and very general objectives and goals, it is the thin end of a wedge whose predetermining force at the specific and detailed end of curriculum planning is to stultify development and curriculum change, to minimize teacher and pupil autonomy, and to foreswear commitment to the ethos of primary education. Between these poles of commitment and abandonment of aims and detailed prescriptive objectives there is ample room for manoeuvre by curriculum planners.

5
Curriculum Content

In taking the discussion to issues of curriculum content, several critical questions are raised. Given that not everything can or should go into the curriculum, planners will have to be selective and to justify their selection. The issues here have been whether one wishes to serve society, preserve traditional and perhaps arcane knowledge, to anticipate future society and cultures, or to concentrate on child-centredness. Attempts have been made to serve all interests (Lawton, 1983; DES, 1985b; Hewlett, 1986; Lawton 1986), though they are not all without criticism.

The value of Lawton's 'cultural analysis' model has been questioned (Whitty, 1985) on four counts: first, for glossing over the role and importance of conflict in society in preference to a curriculum statement which is bland and which seeks a consensus which may be counterproductive; second, for providing an inadequate analysis of issues and conceptions of class; third, for an inadequate analysis of the relationship between education and equality in society; finally, for failing to offer suggestions which will break down inequality in society through education.

Similarly, the HMI 'areas of experience' have attracted criticism (University of Leeds, 1985; Hewlett, 1986; Morrison, 1987) on six counts: initially for reinforcing traditional curricula, schooling and curriculum debate; second, for striving for consensus at the expense of the value of conflict and difference; third, for accepting DES centralism as a *fait accompli;* fourth, for being unclear on its philosophical and sociological origins and justifications; fifth, for elevating the importance of technology too highly; finally, for operating at a level of generality which offers little real assistance to curriculum planners.

The impact and implications of these criticisms can be addressed by curriculum planners on three levels. Initially they may point to the need for a radical redrafting of the curriculum. Such a proposition has been addressed by Hewlett (1986) who discusses 'regions of application' to replace 'areas of experience', focusing on the social utility of children's knowledge: the domestic sphere; the world of work; leisure; continuing education research and exploration; neighbourhood and community education; education about the wider social world—social, political, economic and physical; education about the family; personal relationships in formal and informal spheres; self/personal relationships, the spiritual dimension.

Second, they point to the need to regard any prescriptions as tentative, incomplete and in need of further refinement and extension. Third, this reflects a major theme of this book, that curriculum planning is an ongoing debate rather than a production of a final and unchangeable plan; it is negotiable and subject to scrutiny. Hence the discussion on issues involved in planning curriculum content which follows should serve that notion of a curriculum plan as a proposal. In looking at issues in deciding curriculum content there are many process factors which have to be considered.

COMMONALITY AND INDIVIDUALISM

The same set of constraints and contexts in the curriculum debate can give rise to diverse practices; indeed, such variety is the embodiment of the primary ethos at individual teacher and child levels. The question then is raised for curriculum planners of whether, in the face of such potential variety, a measure of commonality in decision-making about curriculum content across schools, teachers and pupils can and ought to exist. If it can exist then at what level ought it to operate: commonality of aims, concepts, skills, pedagogy, attitudes, areas of knowledge, or organizations of knowledge? Therefore, in planing curriculum content the balances between consistency, commonality and individualism have to be struck.

At the level of knowledge planners will have to ask, for example, how acceptable it is for a child in school A to study a topic on 'railways' while a child in school B does not, or whether a ten-year-old one year will study something different from a ten-years-old in the following year. The debate is ideological—how far child-centredness can tolerate such differences and whether in the long run teachers do children a service by allowing such flexibility.

Educational aims such as those expressed in Chapter 3 can endure over the years, while knowledge, practices, skills and pedagogy may change. At an epistemological level, too, only limited solace can be found for curriculum planners anxious to secure an identifiable delineation of content from the classifications of knowledge, for while they are marked by similarity of title this can conceal a wide variety of expressions in practice both within and between titles. For example, the aesthetic and creative areas of the curriculum could be totally different in two schools or two classrooms; the 'back to basics' conservatism of one teacher could support mathematical practices which are anathema to a more open-ended, progressivist ideology of another mathematics teacher; one teacher's topic on 'ourselves' may be completely different from another's; the language curriculum of one class may appear on a formal timetable where in another class it does not appear *per se* but has permeated the curriculum.

The management question for the school is to decide on the degree and level of commonality or variety of the curriculum content. In practice there may be a high level of consensus at the levels of aims and definitions of the area of

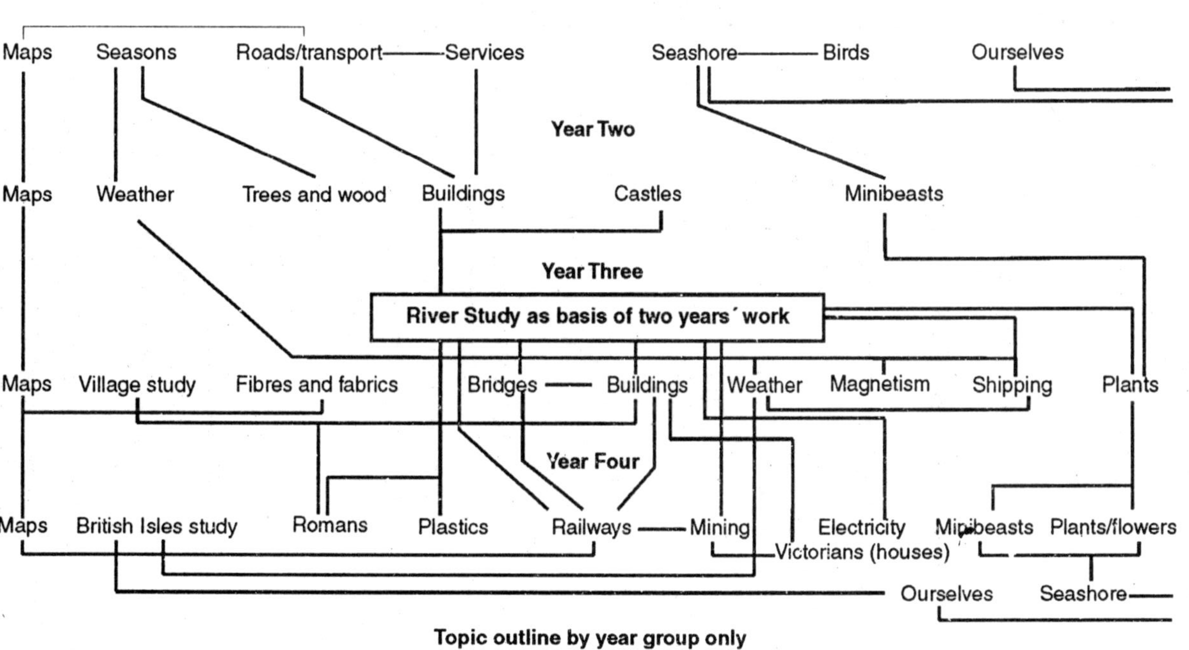

Fig. 5.1: Curriculum devised in content terms for a junior department.

learning (Ashton *et al.*, 1975; Wicksteed and Hill, 1979), but such consensus ought not perhaps to be left to fortune. Curriculum planners have to resolve questions of individual teachers' freedoms, collegially taken decision, curriculum responsibility posts and power structures which may coexist in tension rather than consensus.

In some areas of the school there may well be curriculum commonality which is determined by resources—e.g. the mathematics or reading schemes for the whole school, specialist teachers for music or PE, materials for art, craft and design, computing facilities. In other areas the problem at the level of knowledge is less tractable, for the art of teaching and the primary ethos supports the value of individual teachers being free to decide and interpret curricular guidelines. This is problematic, for the inclusion and exclusion of knowledge has to be justified. The realm of 'topic work' is notoriously difficult here, for without whole school planning it could become fragmented, superficial and repetitive over the primary years (Blyth *et al.*, 1976; DES, 1978a, 1982b).

However, even if one does produce curricula on content terms to avoid this, one still cannot guarantee that the problems of teacher interpretation and choice destroying commonality will be overcome. One teacher's work on 'castles' (year two) may be totally a book study, while another teacher's may be largely observational and practical. Similarly, providing choice from the range of topics each year in the example involves justifying inclusion and exclusion. Listing content by title, then, is difficult and perhaps inadequate for planning (DES, 1982b) for while it accords teachers the autonomy which the primary ethos celebrates, it risks neglecting continuity and progression (DES, 1982b).

Attempts to meet this problem in social studies have been addressed through the notion of 'key concepts' and skills (Taba, 1962; Schools Council, 1973; Blyth *et al.*, 1976; Lancashire County Council 1981; Waters, 1982), as presented in Table. 5.1. The principles of working from key concepts and skills can be applied to other curriculum areas, of course. What can be drawn from the discussion are the notions:

1. That commonality has to be planned and negotiated so that teachers are not merely recipients or agents of other planners' ideas.
2. That commonality exists at the levels of both content and process.
3. That content and process exist symbiotically in a context, e.g. that observation in science is *scientific* observation rather than artistic observation (Jenkins, 1987), and classification in history is qualitatively different from classification in science or mathematics.

The notion of commonality is well represented by the CDC (1980). At a philosophical level curriculum planners are not necessarily presented with an 'either/or' situation—*either* commonality *or* the principles of the primary ethos which support individuality and autonomy. Individuals can contribute to collective collegial decision-making; discovery methods and practical activity can be well served on pre-planned curricula. Commonality implies sharing at all levels—one of the key tenets of the primary ethos.

Missing from the model and the discussion so far is the question of whether the notion of commonality should extend beyond aims, knowledge, concepts and skills to cover pedagogy and evaluation—its principles, purposes, criteria, foci and methods. Teachers may well see such an extension as being the final erosion into their authority and professionality, as setting the seal of approval on the 'teacher-proof' curriculum so questionable in the 1970s, as being thorough in planning to the point of pedantry, or as being unnecessary. Alternatively, a measure of agreement on pedagogy and evaluation at the level of principle must be unavoidable. For example, if an environmental studies

Table 5.1
Key concepts and skills for topic work

Taba (1962)	*Schools Council (1973)*	*Blyth et al. (1976)*
Causality Conflict Co-operation Cultural change Difference Interdependence Modification Power Societal control Traditions Values	Developing interests, attitudes and aesthetic awareness Observing, exploring, and ordering observations Developing basic concepts and logical thinking Posing questions and devising experiments or investigations to answer them Acquiring knowledge and skills Communicating Appreciating patterns and relationships Interpreting findings critically	Communication Power Values and beliefs Conflict/consensus Similarity/differences Continuity/change Cause and consequence

Lancashire County Council (1981)

1. Learning about living things:
   plants, seeds, trees, mosses, fungi, seaweeds, animals, insects, fish, birds
2. Learning about ourselves:
   body, food, looking after ourselves (health), social behaviour, reproduction
3. Learning about the immediate environment:
   buildings, transport, services, pollution
4. Learning about the weather and seasons
5. Learning about energy:
   sound, magnetism, electricity, water, heat, air, light, mechanics, conservation of energy
6. Learning about the properties of materials:
   structure, appearance, strength, change, flexibility, effect of water, magnetism, effect of light, effect of sound, electrical conductance, heat conductance

Waters (1982)

Investigative skills
Study skills
Manipulative skills
Creative skills
Communication skills
Personal and social development

curriculum is predicated on frequent use of the locality—using more than one teacher—then the relative merits of this form of learning will have to be debated; or if team teaching or subject specialist teaching is envisaged then this, too, will need to be discussed and planned. Similarly, if curriculum continuity is to be taken beyond the level of summary epithets and thumbnail sketech then evaluation will have to be planned and agreed.

INTEGRATION AND FRAGMENTATION

Curriculum planners have to decide on the extent of, and relationship between, an integrated and a subject-separate curriculum. The primary ethos has been seen to support an integrated curriculum for various reasons:

1. It accords with the way in which children view the world (Waters, 1982).
2. Children unify rather than atomize knowledge in their minds by as similating new knowledge to existing knowledge (Wheeler, 1967).
3. The 'whole personality' is best served by a holistic approach to the curriculum.
4. It opens up channels of investigation which subject specialist curriculum boundaries may close.
5. It facilitates a rhythm of learning so that individual rates and types of learning are not strangled by constantly switching subjects (Pring, 1976).
6. Knowledge is unfairly represented as discrete packages—relationships are implicit between areas and dimensions of knowledge (CACF, 1967).
7. Children are given power to decide and pursue their own learning paths (Schools Council, 1972).
8. It facilitates the study of complex human issues (ibid.).
9. Key concepts can straddle subject boundaries (Taba, 1962; CACF, 1967).

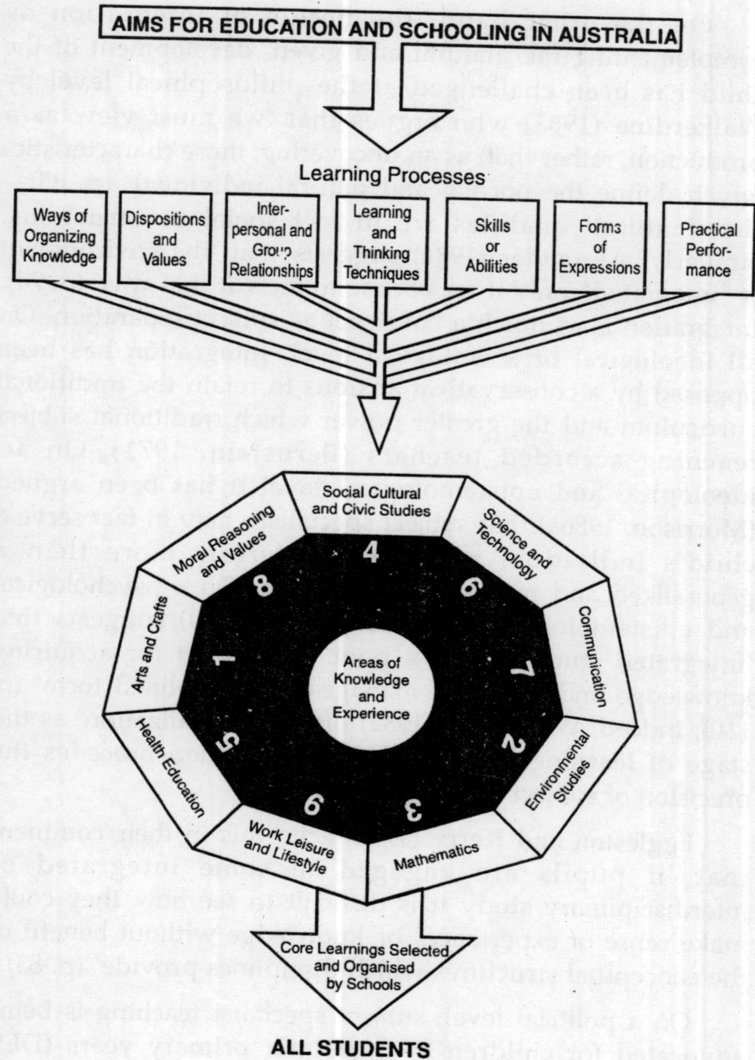

(*Source*: CDC (1980) *Core Curriculum for Australian Schools*, Canberra, p. 20]

Fig. 5.2: A core curriculum for Australian schools.

On the other hand, the notion of integration as complementing the 'natural and given' development of the child has been challenged at the philosophical level by Walkerdine (1983) who argues that 'we must view as a production, rather than as an uncovering, those characteristics which define the normal and natural individual' (p. 85)—that 'natural' qualities are in fact social constructions. Similarly, Alexander (1984) suggests that 'the environment is "integrated" only if we choose to view it that was' (p. 70). Integration is as much a construct as subject separation. On all ideological or sociological level, integration has been opposed by a conservatism anxious to retain the traditional curriculum and the greater power which traditional subject teaching accorded teachers (Bernstein, 1971). On an ideological and epistemological level it has been argued (Morrison, 1986a) that subject specialism may in fact serve a child's individual needs and interests more than a generalized and integrated curriculum. On a psychological and epistemological level, Entwistle (1970) suggests that 'integrated studies seem a poor instrument for acquiring knowledge and skill in a manageable, disciplined form' (p. 110). Indeed, Whitehead (1932) offers 'generalization' as the stage of learning which follows rather then precedes the precision of subject teaching.

Eggleston and Kerry (1985) echo this in their comment that 'if pupils are engaged in some integrated or interdisciplinary study it is difficult to see how they could make sense of experiences or knowledge without benefit of the conceptual structures which disciplines provide' (p. 83).

On a political level, subject specialist teaching is being advocated for children in their later primary years (DES, 1978a, 1983, 1985c) as an attempt to bring depth of study into the curriculum. Curriculum planning and decision-making will have to resolve the relationship between subject teaching and integrated curricula: whether they can complement each other rather than being alternatives

(Entwistle, 1970) or whether the two are in a relationship of tension (Morrison, 1985). The primary ethos supports teacher and child autonomy, individual needs, interests, expertise and intrinsic motivation. This may best be realized through subject-centred teaching (Morrison 1986a) as well as through an integrated curriculum. While subject teaching may embody the principles of the disciplined enquiry, it should not be allowed to sacrifice the principles of the primary ethos—flexibility, originality, diversity—to uniformity and outworn subject matter (ibid.). If subject teaching is to operate (which may well be the case) then clear links between subjects will have to be drawn where possible, requiring teachers to discuss, negotiate and plan corporately (Morrison, 1985), key elements of a healthy school climate.

Content and process can come together in subject teaching through the notion of guided discovery, for in the hands of specialist teachers such learning can be more exciting for children than an integrated curriculum taught by generalists. The limitations of this approach start where child-centredness is equated with a child-chosen curriculum, for children may select work which does not fall comfortably into a specialist's domain. Here perhaps the notion of generalist teachers with specific expertise which can be tapped by both pupils and teachers is useful—a far more open utilization of staff than in many traditional classrooms. Curriculum planners will have to decide how to implement such principles to best advantage.

Constructing a Matrix

One way of planning within a subject is by constructing a matrix. In art education, for example, a matrix to ensure comprehensive coverage at the planning stage could be presented as in Figure 5.3 (DES, 1983b). In matrix planning for subjects it may be useful to list the content in the columns and the intellectual and affective skills in the rows. For example in science one can construct a matrix from Table 5.1 and present it for planning purposes as in Figure 5.4.

If an integrated curriculum is being planned then the 'integrative threads' (Taba, 1962) for that curriculum have to be decided. What is the common focus through which various curriculum elements are brought together? There are a variety of 'threads' available: key concepts can be set and defined and returned to at ever increasing levels of complexity and abstraction in a 'spiral curriculum' (Bruner, 1960).

Second, there is the integration of learning and experience provided by resources, e.g. the home corner, the painting area, the library. Third, integration can be reached through the notion of an activity or group of activities, e.g. growing plants in different environments, visiting a farm, where a range of skills and forms of representation are brought to focus on the activity (Figure 5.6).

Fourth, a problem-centred approach (Waters, 1982) can be an integrating principle where children learn to 'approach social problems from a number of different angles and to see experience from as many relevant facets as possible, so that they resist prejudiced conclusions or simple solutions' (Entwistle, 1970; p. 110).

Fifth, on a smaller scale, centres of interest can be used to integrate experiences, where for example by careful questioning, discussion, display and addition of children's work, a collection of shells or leaves can provide a stimulating environment for children—one of the features of the primary ethos.

Sixth, the notion of integration can extend to cross-curricular planning, e.g. language or mathematics across the curriculum (DES, 1974, 1982b). Curriculum planners can approach this conceptually through matrix planning (Figure 5.7), where, for example, mathematics across the areas of experience can be ascertained by reading across the mathematics row, or where for instance the relationship of the 'aesthetic and creative' area to the other areas can be planned. This can be taken further, where each area is broken

	Creating, making	Appreciating, evaluating	Practising	Introducing, knowledge of	Synthesizing	Co-operating
Experience of terms colour line shape texture form tone spatial relations						
Experience of media oil water chalk crayon clay plaster wood fabric paper card thread linoleum plasticene wire metal plastic						
Manipulative skills cutting glueing sewing knitting weaving printing dyeing painting drawing shaping enamelling firing glazing						

Fig. 5.3: Matrix planning for an art curriculum.

	Developing interests, attitudes and aesthetic awareness	Observing, exploring, ordering observations	Developing basic concepts and logical thinking	Posing questions and devising experiments or investigations to answer them	Acquiring knowledge and skills	Communicating	Appreciating patterns and relationships	Interpre findings critically
Living things								
Ourselves								
Immediate environment								
Weather and seasons								
Energy								
Properties of materials								

Fig. 5.4: Matrix planning in a science curriculum.

down into its constituent parts. For example, in language work a matrix could be set out as in Table 5.2. The principle can be applied to other areas of the curriculum.

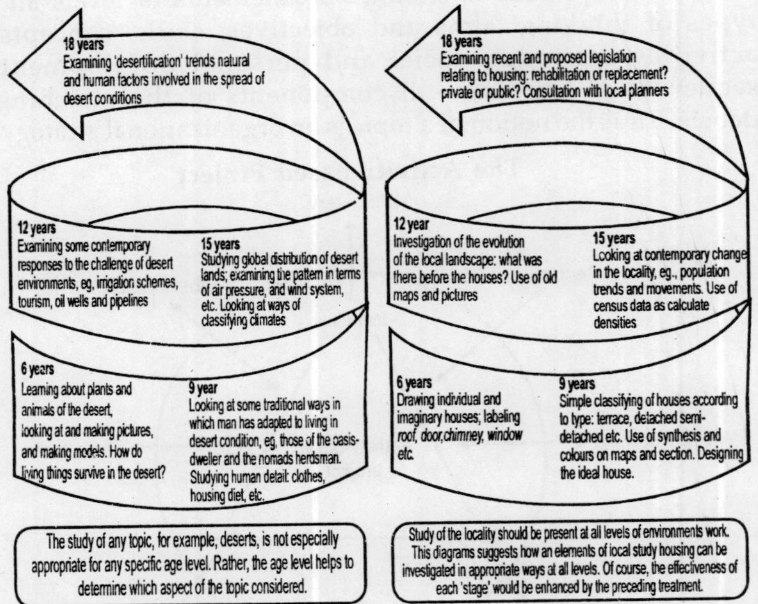

(*Source*: Inner London Education Authority (1981) *The Study of Places in the Primary School*, p. 4.]

Fig. 5.5: A spiral curriculum approach to curriculum planning.

There are further 'essential issues' which DES (1985b) suggest should cross the curriculum even though they pay relatively scant attention to them throughout the document (Morrison, 1987). These then can become the basis for matrix planning (Table 5.3). The principle of establishing cross-curricular links or issues which permeate the curriculum is vital at the planning stage otherwise it risks being lost or neglected in the practical implementation of the curriculum.

Seventh, integration can be achieved through the multidisciplinary 'topic' or 'project' (e.g. trees, the locality, ourselves) where the topic draws on several areas of the curriculum (see Figure 5.8). Here the planning draws comprehensively on the discussion already on tactical levels of planning, for additional to the 'areas of experience' upon which the topic draws should be statements of levels and types of thinking: aims and objectives, skills, concepts, activities, attitudes, social and personal development, sequences of learning—all components of the matching debate. Thus the notion of a topic is an organizational strategy.

The Activity-based Project

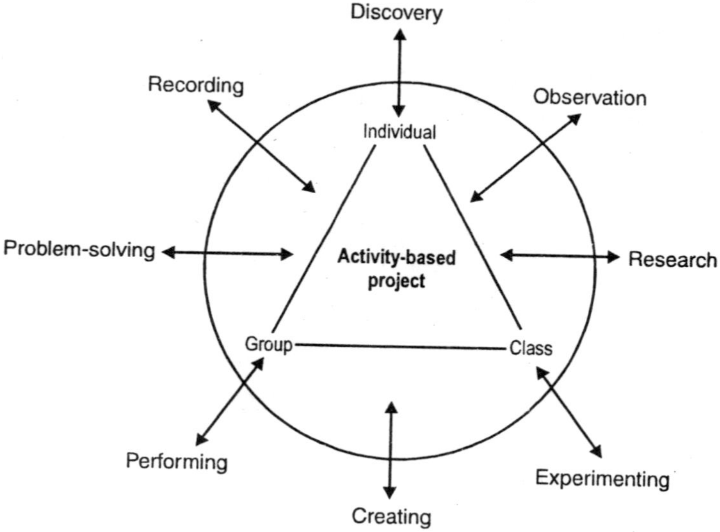

(*Source:* Waters, 1982, *Primary School Projects: Planning and Development* p. 21).

Fig. 5.6: Activity-based curriculum planning.

Curriculum planners will have to decide where an integrated approach fits most comfortably, for to try to integrate artificially or to press all areas of the curriculum unthinkingly or at whatever cost into the service of spurious integration is a recipe for a poor curriculum at both theoretical and practical levels. Integration must be appropriate to the aims, curriculum content and components in the matching debate rather than contrived. In decision-making about the

	Aesthetic and creative	Human and social	Linguistic and literary	Mathematical	Moral	Physical	Scientific	Spiritual	Technological
Aesthetic and creative									
Human and social									
Linguistic and literary									
Mathematical									
Moral									
Physical									
Scientific									
Spiritual									
Technological									

Fig. 5.7: Matrix planning from HMI areas of experience.

Table 5.2
Areas of a language curriculum which could be put into matrix form across the HMI areas of experience (DES, 1985a)

Reading

Reading to gain an overall impression of a single passage or chapter

Reading to select information relevant to a particular topic

Reading to expand on information previously supplied

Reading to follow a sequence of instructions

Reading to identify answers to questions by direct reference to a given text

Reading to detect information implied in a given passage

Reading to interpret and evaluate a writer's assumptions, intentions, to show awareness of characteristics of different kinds of writing

Reading for pleasure

Reading different types of literature

Writing

Describing	Explaining
Narrating	Expounding
Recording	Planning
Reporting	Eliciting
Persuading	
writing for various audiences	
writing in various forms	

Speaking

Questioning	Describing	Clarifying
Expressing	Instructing	Dramatically presenting
Directing	Informing	Discussing
Expounding	Narrating	Explaining
Arguing	Presenting	
Conversing	Recalling	

Listening

Carrying out instructions

Comprehending ideas and expanding on them

Participating in discussions ('active listening')

Maintaining listening span

Following plot and line of argument

Listening responsively to a story and to poetry

organization and structure of the curriculum content, then, planners, are driven again to weigh theoretical, epistemological, ideological and practical issues. On a management level curriculum planners will need to decide how resources of time, staff, money, space and materials are to be best deployed if an integrated or separated curriculum is to operate.

CHARACTERISTICS OF THE CURRICULUM

The planning of the content of the primary curriculum will need to bear certain hallmarks or characteristics. While many of these have been addressed already, there are several other current 'catchwords' which can be used as referents in the curriculum debate, notably provided by HMI (DES, 1985b): breadth, balance, relevance, differentiation, progression and continuity.

Table 5.3

HMI essential issues which permeate the areas of experience

Environmental education
Health education
Information technology
Political education
Education in economic understanding
Preparation for the world of work
Careers education
Equal opportunities
Education of ethnic minority children

Breadth

While much of this discussion has been rehearsed in the section on commonality and individualism, there are additional issue which can be raised. DES (1985b) suggest that breadth should obtain cross and within all areas of experience, elements of learning and essential issues in the curriculum. The problem of interpretation of these terms has already been met, asking what mathematics, what art and design, what history, etc. Additionally, breadth can be extended to cover pedagogic styles, classroom organization, learning processes, assessment techniques, aims and objectives, ideologies and epistemologies.

Given such a wide field of application of the term, curriculum planners are driven again to decide the dimensions in which breadth of curriculum operates; to consider the selection of content which they make for the curriculum; and to decide on minimum levels of content and dimensions beyond which breadth is lost.

The concept of breadth suggests both a broadening of the notion of 'basic skills' to incorporate more than the 'three Rs' and the view that the 'three Rs' can be taught through a wide curriculum (DES, 1978a). Planners will have to decide whether breadth of the curriculum is best achieved through subject teaching or by integration, through specialist or generalist teachers.

Apart from the notion that breadth should not be sacrificed to depth, there is an added difficulty in the term 'breadth', as there is with many of the terms here from HMI, for it may lie uncomfortably with the notions of individual needs, differences and interests encapsulated in the primary ethos. The question arises of whether a child's individuality may be better served by a broad or a narrow curriculum. Hence the notion of breadth may be disjunctive with 'relevance' or 'differentiation'; the issues may exist in tension rather than harmony.

In evaluating breadth in the curriculum, planners can address the following questions; these are arranged for convenience into management and curricular issues.

Management Issues

1. Who will take the decisions on breadth?
2. How will breadth be planned, managed, implemented, realized, monitored, recorded and evaluated?

Key ideas: Wheels — how they work, axles
— their use in machines
— wheels as on of a set of circular objects

Events, visits — one or two of the following:
Garage/seeing wheel change
Farm or farming museum
Railway station or railway museum
— a display of wheels would be set up

WHEELS

LINGUISTIC AND LITERACY

Stories—some taped for individual listening

Development of vocabulary
Writing—bus ticket

HUMAN AND SOCIAL

Wheels used to help us—transport, simple machines

Wheels in old vehicles (farm carts, etc.)

Working with wheels (potter, miller)

MATHEMATICS

Shape—circles, pattern work
Timetable—bus play
Money

Ideas of sequence—steps in changing a wheel

Number of wheels on a vehicle

AESTHETIC AND CREATIVE

Representations of wheeled vehicles in two and three dimensions

Pattern making/printing—circles
Poems

Songs, action songs, listening to sounds

MORAL

Co-operation in play—bus play
Road safety—devising rules

TECHNOLOGY

Layouts for vehicles (cars/trains)
Route for wheeled toy traffic—outdoor
Construction work (various challenges to make wheeled toys, etc.)
Examine simple machines—egg whisk, hand drill, wheels on tricycle

PHYSICAL

Through all art/craft work, making and modelling activities
Ability to steer, turn a vehicle
Play with hoops
Large scale construction—bus, train

SPIRITUAL

Use of natural forces—wind/windmill, water/waterwheel

SCIENCE

Wheels—simple inclined plane or chute
Energy—power that causes toy cars to move—push, friction, clockwork, twisted elastic, battery
Cooking—use of whisk

Fig. 5.8: A topic web for a nursery class.

3. What preparations are necessary before staff can discuss breadth? How can the climate for such discussion be set?
4. How will breadth be ensured across the year/school/schools?
5. How will subject teaching and subject specialist teaching be managed to ensure breadth?
6. In whose terms will breadth be discussed and decided?

Curriculum Issues

1. How far is breadth a desirable aim of the curriculum?
2. In what terms will breadth the discussed (e.g. epistemological, ideological, cultural, pedagogical, knowledge, concepts skills, attitudes, areas of experience, regions of application, subjects)?
3. How will the constituents of breadth be decided and prioritized?
4. How will consistency of breadth be ensured?
5. What is the relationship of breadth and depth?
6. How will breadth be ensured in the child's mind?
7. What is the relationship of breadth and differentiation for individual needs and interests, generalism and specialism?

Balance

While the curriculum is to be broad it is also to be balanced. Initially, this entails a realization that balancing a curriculum does not necessarily entail giving equal amounts, both in quantity and time, for each area of experience, element of learning or essential issues. Just as a balanced diet involves eating different amounts of different types of food, the analogy can be extended to the curriculum and its components (Kelly, 1986). Who will decide on the ingredients of the curriculum cake? The further difficulty for the curriculum is to decide the constituents and the relative amounts of curriculum components.

To compound the difficulty the primary ethos, with its notions of individual needs and differences, suggests that children and teachers all have different dietary needs and interests (Kelly 1986, pp. 149-50). One child's balance is another child's imbalance; balance and commonality do not always go together. The problem is not solely theoretical. The teacher is constantly faced with the ideological problem of how much latitude to give to children's choice, e.g. in a reception class why should the teacher intervene to move a child on from one type of learning experience to another—the wet area to the jigsaw puzzles—when the child is not interested in jigsaws at that time? How can teachers be certain that a child is covering the range of the curriculum areas of experience when that child follows activities in ways not fully envisaged by the teacher?

The problem here is that of ensuring that the curriculum as planned becomes the curriculum as practised by the children. Balance must exist in the child's mind as well as with the teacher. Thus either balance needs to be tempered by individualization or perhaps balance in the curriculum needs to be seen as only achievable through seeking the lowest common denominator of curriculum components. If this latter is the case then the concept of balance may lead to a bland, undifferentiated and perhaps irrelevant curriculum. Again this reinforces a tension between balance and relevance and differentiation. There has to be a balance between need and content area. The constituents of the 'appropriate' balance for each child are problematic.

HMI (DES, 1985b) provides little assistance in resolving this problem, for its recommendations that balance is achieved through "appropriate attention to, and sufficient time on, each area, or through each area being 'fully developed'" (para, 112) offer little to guide planners anxious to ascertain what 'appropriate attention' or 'sufficient time' is or what it is to be 'fully developed'. In one sense—fortuitously perhaps—HMI is suggesting that these terms have to be negotiated and debated, one of the main features of primary curriculum planning.

In deciding what has to be balanced one cannot remain solely with the terms provided by HMI—areas of experience, elements of learning and characteristics of the curriculum; there are additional factors. The discussion throughout the book has suggested that balances must be struck between ideologies—individual and societal needs—epistemologies (rationalism and empiricism), process and content, breadth and depth, theory and practice (Kelly, 1986), types and levels of skills, subject-bound and integrated curricula, specialism and generalism, the curriculum as derived from forms of knowledge (Hirst, 1965) and cultural analysis (Lawton, 1983), working class and middle class curricula, representations of subcultures, cognitive and affective demands, commonality and individuality, pedagogic styles, organizational practices, autocratic and collegial planning.

This takes the curriculum planner back to reviewing the whole concept of 'match'. It raises too the question of how far the demand for balance is a demand for compromise—ideological, epistemological, cultural, managerial, curricular—and how far such compromise is necessary or desirable. The notion of balance is integrative; it runs through the discussion of the other characteristics of the curriculum.

In evaluating balance in the curriculum, planners could address the following questions, again for convenience arranged by management and curriculum issues.

Management Issues

1. How will balance be ensured across the year/school/schools?
2. How will the ground be laid to discuss balance among staff?

3. How will balance be planned, managed, implemented, realized, monitored, recorded and evaluated?
4. Who will decide on the terms and nature of the balance(s)?
5. In whose terms will the concept of balance be discussed and decided?

Curriculum Issues

1. How far is balance a desirable aim of the curriculum?
2. How will the balance be struck between integrated and subject-bound knowledge?
3. What are the terms for discussing balance (e.g. knowledge, concepts, skills, attitudes, elements of learning, areas of experience, regions of application, discipline, experiences, ideologies, epistemologies, pedagogies, organizations)?
4. In what terms will the balance(s) be struck between relevance, differentiation, individual needs and interests and abilities, received and reflexive curricula, types of task (incremental, practice, revision, application, enrichment, problem-solving, investigational), teacher decision and pupil choice?
5. In what terms will the balance be struck between innovation and existing practice (e.g. ideologies, ideas, epistemologies, curriculum structures, organizations, managements, pedagogies, continuity and discontinuity, content and process, processes and outcomes, breadth and depth)?
6. How will planners ensure that balance avoids resulting in low-level confusion of practices and epistemologies?

Relevance

The concept of relevance accords with the notion of matching, as the answer to the questions 'relevant to what?' and 'relevant to whom?' will demonstrate. While HMI (DES, 1985b) veils its discussion in generalities [e.g. 'relevant in the sense that it is seen by pupils to meet their present and prospective needs' (para. 116)], curriculum planners require more than this. One can suggest that curriculum content ought to be relevant to:

- Individual and social needs (not necessarily discrete areas).
- School ethos, aims, organization, staff education and vocationalism.
- Ideologies and epistemologies.
- Building motivation and self-concept in children.

The primary ethos, underscoring the notion of relevance, suggests the need to meet individual needs and abilities. However, this raises the problem that what constitutes relevance for one child could well be totally irrelevant to another's needs, interests or abilities. Who is to be the arbiter in such a problem—the child, the teacher, the planner? Will the decision be taken for the child? Will the ideology of the child-chosen curriculum have to be replaced with a curriculum planned in their interests (Peters, 1967)? Do teachers allow the child the choice of not to follow a curriculum, to move out of the frame of reference? Further, how will the problem be resolved if the planner sees that providing a relevant curriculum for each child means providing an unbalanced or narrow curriculum? As with other notions the concept of relevance is seen to run uneasily with differentiation; the HMI terms may coexist in tension.

In evaluating the notion of relevance in the curriculum, planners can address the following questions, arranged in management and curriculum issues.

Management Issues

1. How will relevance be ensured across the year/school/schools?
2. How will relevance be planned, managed, implemented, realized, recorded, monitored and evaluated?
3. In whose terms will relevance be discussed and decided?
4. How will discussions of relevance be managed?
5. How will the ground be laid for such discussion?

Curriculum Issues

1. How up-to-date must the knowledge be in different areas of the curriculum?
2. How practical must the work be to ensure relevance?
3. In what terms will relevance be discussed (e.g. knowledge, concepts, skills, attitudes, areas of experience, regions of application, disciplines, subjects, pedagogies, ideologies, epistemologies, sociologies, organizations, school locations)?
4. How will the relationship be achieved between the logical structures of knowledge and the psychological frameworks of children's learning?
5. To whom, and to what must the content be relevant?
6. In what terms will relevance be achieved across and through the school?
7. How will children be motivated?
8. How will relevance be balanced to differentiation?
9. How will relevance be decided in teacher-chosen and child-chosen curricula?

10. How will relevance enter the discussion of breadth and depth in curricula in relation to individual needs, interests and abilities?
11. How will relevance enter the discussion of balanced and unbalanced curricula?
12. How will knowledge be structured so that it is readily assimilated by children?
13. How specific or immediate to the school situation ought the curriculum content to be?
14. How will children's perceptions of relevance be ensured?

Differentiation

This notion encapsulates a central feature of primary education—its emphasis on the individual. For curriculum planners there are two main implications of this term. Either it can mean children learning and progressing at their own rates and in their own ways on predetermined tasks [where teachers operate from individual levels of demand, expectation and pedagogic styles (DES, 1985e)], or it can mean a child-chosen curriculum or part of a curriculum. Though HMI does not reach a decision on the alternatives, curriculum planners will have to address the issue, which has both ideological and organizational ramifications.

Planners will have to consider the relationship or balance between differentiation and the other terms from HMI, to decide how much increasing differentiation will decrease balance and breadth, how far the system can tolerate differentiation in children with special educational needs in mainstream classes or how far differentiation will lead to separation, and at what levels curriculum differentiation will apply—aims, objectives, content, pedagogy, evaluation criteria, and resources.

In evaluation the curriculum for differentiation planners could address the following questions.

Management Issues

1. At what stages of planning should notions of differentiation enter the discussion?
2. How can teachers be prepared to observe and plan for differentiation?
3. How will differentiation be ensured across the year/school/schools?
4. How will differentiation be planned, managed, realized, recorded, implemented, monitored and evaluated?
5. In whose terms will discussions of differentiation be treated and decided?
6. How will notions of differentiation enter whole school discussion?

Curriculum Issues

1. In what terms can differentiation be discussed (e.g. rates of learning, abilities of children, types of task—incremental, practice, revision, application, enrichment, problem-solving, investigational—interests and relevance, pedagogies, areas of experience, regions of application, disciplines of knowledge, subjects, ideologies, epistemologies, levels of thinking (low to high order), organizations and structures of the curriculum)?
2. Where should differentiation be sought?
3. How desirable an aim is differentiation?
4. What is the relationship of differentiation and common curricula?
5. How will the content be planned to ensure that it is interesting, stimulating, and motivating to children?
6. How will individual learning styles be accommodated?

7. How does the content embody the principles of the primary ethos?
8. How will planners ensure that the child perceives and appreciates differentiation?
9. How will the balance be struck between differentiation and uniformity?
10. How does the content develop types and levels of thinking—the cognitive demand on children?
11. How will the knowledge be structured and approached so that it is readily learnt by children?
12. In what terms will pupils' age, grasp and development of the content be assessed and evaluated?

Progression

Curriculum planning for progression will have to be approached at both a theoretical and a practical level. At a theoretical level planners will have to decide on the criteria for progression—what progression in knowledge, concepts, skills and attitudes really means; whether progression is quantitative, qualitative or both. While this may be comparatively straightforward in subject-based curricula or in areas where logical developments are clear (Mathematics, for example), it is infinitely more difficult in integrated organizations or curricula or in skills-based teaching. How far, for example, can one plan for progression in topic work or study skills? Is progression simply the accretion of a number of skills, of should it be thought of in terms of levels of difficulty?

The problem with this latter criterion is that difficulty is specific to individuals. It is perhaps impossible to define levels of difficulty objectively (e.g. Goldstein's criticisms of the Rasch model for APU testing, in Lacey and Lawton, 1981). Similarly patters of progression may vary for each child. Thus planning for progression involves planning for development at norm-related and individual-related levels. One can progress in many ways (Bloom, 1956; Wheeler, 1967; Waters, 1982; Wilson, 1983; DES 1985e):

- simple to complex;
- singular factor to multiple factors;
- generality to specific details;
- low order to high order;
- unique instance to overarching principle;
- specific to general;
- concrete to abstract;
- familiar to unfamiliar;
- contemporary to past and future;
- near to distant;
- abstract to concrete.

Many of these sequences are almost polar opposites; there being no single way of proceeding, planners have to debate and decide on the most appropriate ways of achieving progression, building on previous knowledge, concepts, skills and attitudes perhaps through the notion of the 'spiral curriculum' discussed earlier.

In evaluating progression, planners could address the following questions, arranged by management and curriculum issues.

Management Issues

1. In whose terms will discussions of progression operate?
2. How will progression be planned, managed, realized, implemented, monitored, recorded and evaluated?
3. How will progression influence curriculum structure and staff deployment, e.g. generalism and subject specialist teaching?
4. How will the ground be laid for discussions of progression?

Curriculum Issues

1. How will progression in integrated curricula be discussed?
2. In what terms will progression be discussed [e.g. elements of learning, areas of experience, regions of applications, disciplines of knowledge, subjects, types of task (incremental, practice, revision, application, enrichment, problem-solving, investigational), rates of learning, levels of demand, low-order facts to high-order principle, quantitative and qualitative types of development]?
3. What are the constituents of progression in each curriculum area?
4. How far is progression quantitative (cumulative) or qualitative?
5. How can progression be systematized, sequenced and structured?
6. What is the relationship between logical sequences of content and psychological sequences in progression?
7. What is the relationship of progression and continuity?
8. What is the relationship of progression and differentiation?
9. How will planners ensure that the child perceives progression?

Continuity

Continuity is not concerned solely with transition periods, i.e. infant to junior, junior to secondary, first to middle, middle to upper; it is a concept which pervades the day-to-day implementation of the curriculum. Planners can strive for continuity in many forms; e.g. continuity of

- experience
- skills
- concepts
- knowledge
- attitudes
- in-school and out-of-school experiences
- pedagogy (across curriculum areas and through the school—vertical and lateral)
- organizations
- aims
- management styles
- ethos
- ideologies
- epistemologies
- key concepts
- assessment criteria and methods
- social experiences

At one level continuity of experiences can simply mean planning for flexible time boundaries so that children can work at their own rates until a task is completed. This is the principle embodied in the 'integrated day' form of organization, implementing the primary ethos very clearly. This reinforces the notion that continuity, like balance, must be perceived by the child as well as the planner.

At another level it involves planners in debating the areas in which continuity is to take place: how it will be implemented and monitored; what information will be passed and in what forms; what the relationship is between continuity and progression; whether there is a 'core' of areas in which continuity must be ensured; what the relationship is between continuity and common curricula; and how much continuity is desirable—whether times of 'planned discontinuity' (Tickle, 1985) might not have more merits than total continuity.

This latter point relates back to the discussion of commonality and individualism in curriculum planning and practice, to ask how far continuity reduces teacher autonomy and individuality. There is also the question of how far continuity will imply uniformity. It may be that children respond to—and look forward to—change, both in styles of teaching and organizations of curricula both across and through the curriculum (vertical and horizontal continuity, Blyth and Derricot, 1985). For example, at the time of primary to secondary transition, children may be seeking the different organizations of secondary schools. Primary schools can prepare children for this by some subject and specialist teaching for the older junior age range (Tickle, 1985). Teachers of top junior and early secondary children might also share the teaching in both schools, perhaps on a two-yearly cycle. The question then of the desirability of continuity is raised; at what point might conflict and discontinuity be more challenging and beneficial than continuity and total consensus?

By focusing on the issue of continuity, curriculum planners will have to address: the notions of coherence and consistency; the reduction of repetition of content (CACE, 1967); the need for whole school curriculum planning and policy making; the form, use and extent of formal record keeping; the problems of transition and liaison with other schools; the organization of knowledge; the problems of moving from integrated to separated curricula; and the dimensions of the curriculum along which it is to operate. It requires planners to identify and overcome barriers to continuity, which will involve the issues in the management of curriculum change (Dalin, 1978).

Continuity need not threaten individualism and autonomy; indeed, it may respect and build on it. Whole school planning and autonomy are not mutually exclusive.

Evaluation Questions for Addressing Continuity

In attempting to evaluate the curriculum in terms of the continuity issue raised, planners could address the following questions which, for each characteristic, are grouped according to management and curricular issues.

Management Issues

1. How will continuity be ensured across the year/school/schools?
2. What is the relation of continuity and teacher autonomy?
3. Who decides, and how is the decision reached, on where continuity will be?
4. How will continuity be planned, managed, realized, implemented, monitored, recorded-and evaluated?
5. How will barriers to continuity be identified and overcome?
6. How will liaison and communication be ensured in discussions of continuity?
7. How will the climate of the school be set up and built so that discussions of continuity can proceed?
8. In whose terms will continuity be discussed and decided?
9. How far does continuity imply conformity and uniformity of beliefs and practices by teachers and pupils?

Curriculum Issues

1. How much continuity is desirable?
2. Where is continuity desirable and undesirable?
3. In what terms will continuity be expressed (e.g. knowledge, concepts, skills, attitudes, experience, aims, ideologies, epistemologies, pedagogies, sociologies, in-school and out-of-school experiences, areas of experience, disciplines of knowledge, regions of application, subjects, organizations, management styles)?

General

1. Select topic—criteria of relevance, integrative potential, declaration of curricular emphasis, non-contrivance, concrete
2. Brainstorm/read around/investigate
3. Organize by curriculum areas and cross-curriculum areas.
4. Note knowledge, concepts, skills, attitudes, activities for each area—at a general level
5. Sequence—a flow diagram—single or multistranded. Plan continuity, progression. Continuity of what? Progression of what? Decide criteria for the sequence
   - —logical
   - —specific to general
   - —near to far
   - —concrete to abstract
   - —level of cognitive demand
   - —type of activity
6. Differentiate—what to differentiate
   - —how to differentiate

   Matching
   - —type of demand
   - —type of task
   - —level of demand
7. Decide appropriate teaching and learning styles for activities, children, stages of session:
   - —group, class, individual learning
   - —problem solving, investigational, didactic, informal
8. Decide resources—first hand/second hand
   - —materials
   - —time
   - —space
   - —display
   - —internal/external environment
   - —staff
9. Plan how to introduce/develop-conclude/evaluate
10. How to set out in writing the individual sessions, specificity of detail, link of planning to evaluation.

Specific

Fig. 5.9: A curriculum planning sequence.

4. What is the relationship of continuity and consensus?
5. What is the relationship of continuity and common curricula?
6. How will content be structured to ensure continuity and progression?
7. How will continuity be ensured in the child's mind?

CONCLUSION

The discussion of the characteristics of the curriculum has shown that both within and between them there are tensions and conflicts which are exposed by considering the principles which make up the primary ethos. Curriculum planning for the selection and organization of content will need to resolve those tensions collegially, deciding on the paths to be taken through them. It points to the need for curriculum planning to be considered at a whole school level in a way which preserves the best of individualism; Figure 5.9 shows a curriculum planning sequence.

Autonomy and whole school planning are not mutually exclusive. In evaluating curriculum content, planners will have to bring to the debate the full range of issues and contexts brought out through the book. The content is the outcome of those discussions. The curriculum is what each child takes away—should remind planners that curriculum content must balance with the psychological make-up and learning styles of each child. The balancing of flexibility and novelty exacts a price; the curriculum planner and decision-maker must be constantly and acutely aware of the responsibility to provide a coherent, comprehensive, interesting and developed curriculum.

6

Curriculum Evaluation

In planning the curriculum, decision-makers will have to address the notion of evaluation; evaluation must be planned, for too often it is arbitrary, incidental or simply absent from the curriculum debate. While criteria for evaluating issues in the curriculum have been discussed as they appear throughout the book, planners will need to address the issues of evaluation *per se*. This chapter raises such issues and attempts to offer guidelines for planning the evaluation components of a curriculum. To do so the chapter will consider a variety of issues involved in planning an evaluation.

DEFINING EVALUATION

At a definitional level evaluation subsumes judgement, decision-making, assessment, appraisal and review—and yet is more than the sum of these parts. The differences can be teased out further.

'Review' indicates a retrospective examination or reflection on a curriculum or practice (Skilbeck, 1984; DES, 1985g) and participants' perspectives on it. 'Assessment' is a 'process of determining and passing judgements on students' learning potential and performance' (Skilbeck, 1984, p. 238); it involves measuring or grading students according to some agreed criteria; it assumes comparison of pupils either with each other (norm-referenced assessment) or individually with a specific standard (criterion-referenced assessment). On the other hand, 'appraisal' is less quantitatively or comparison-based; it leans towards qualitative judgements about the worth or value of an activity, organization or curriculum (DES, 1985g).

Evaluation has many interpretations which draw on review, assessment and appraisal. It can be seen as the 'collection and use of information to make decisions about the educational programme' (Cronbach, 1963); alternatively, a clearer valuative tone is struck by Cooper (1976) and Simons (1984): 'curriculum evaluation is the collection and provision of evidence, on the basis of which decisions can be taken about the feasibility, effectiveness and educational value of curricula' (p. 51). Evaluation, then, is about judgments of value on the basis of evidence. It also implies in its notions of valuing the need for debate, a point reinforced by Kemmis (1982), which underlines one of the central themes of planning which runs through the book: 'evaluation is the process of marshalling information and arguments which enable interested individuals and groups to participate in the critical debate about a specific programme' (p. 221).

In approaching evaluation and evaluating curriculum planning there are several issues which have to be resolved, regardless of the level of the evaluation—from national to institutional, and from internal to external, formal to informal, institutional to individual, evaluation by others to self-evaluation.

METAPHORS OF EVALUATION

When considering evaluation of the curriculum it is useful to consider the metaphors which planners and teachers use in describing the curriculum, for it reveals the ways in which that curriculum is perceived (House, 1986). Curricula may be perceived as machines, each element designed to fit with another to produce a pre-ordained outcome. Thus evaluation becomes a question of making the machine more efficient—altering the parts, oiling the workings and assessing the outcomes. Evaluation does not produce a radically new machine, hence the ideological commitment of this curriculum and evaluation is conservative and revisionist rather than reconstructionist.

Alternatively, curricula may be perceived as buildings (House, 1986) where a firm foundation has to be laid, where the construction has to be firmly planned, where the design has to be interesting and where cost analysis figures importantly. Evaluations thus are expected to be solid, well constructed (ibid.) and to yield information about the design, construction, utility, cost-effectiveness, aesthetic appeal, sequence and structure of the curriculum. Third, if one thinks of curricula as pipelines (ibid.) laid between aims and outputs, then importance attaches to their effectiveness in bringing about outcomes. How does the input lead to the outcomes? What contaminating or purifying curricular interventions occur during the course of the pipeline to produce the outcome? How can the pipeline be improved so that the outcomes do derive from the aims and objectives of the curriculum? How one thinks of evaluation affects the focus, purpose, methods and criteria for evaluating.

PURPOSE OF THE EVALUATION

Because of the many facets of evaluation at a conceptual level, any evaluation must be clear on its purposes as this will affect the sort of information sought, the judgements made, and the methods employed. In posing the question 'why evaluate?' two sorts of answers may be given. The question 'why?' is ambiguous, focusing on causes of evaluation and intentions of evaluation. Causes of evaluation may lie in economic funding decisions, accountability and political expediency; intentions of evaluation may be broader and more professionally oriented.

Eraut (1984) classifies purposes in a threefold manner: extrinsic, intrinsic purposes and value judgements. In 'extrinsic purposes' evaluation serves decision-making, accountability and assessment of learning; in 'intrinsic purposes' it examines the relation between intention and realization, it interprets what is happening, it ascribes value to intentions, actions and activities; in 'value judgements' evaluation concerns what is good, what has priority, and what is reasonable. More fully perhaps it is possible to itemize purposes of evaluation, some of which have already been introduced:

- to answer questions of selection, adoption and value of curricula and activities (Glass, 1975);
- to compare courses (Pope, 1983);
- to monitor standards (Taylor and Richards, 1979);
- to check progress (ibid.);
- to inform decision-making for course improvement (Cronbach, 1963);
- to demonstrate a promotion seeker's competence (Walker, 1981);
- to inform a funding decision (Taylor, 1976);
- to act as a public relations exercise (McCormick and James, 1983);
- to clarify roles and role relationships (Whitaker, 1983);
- to revitalize the institution and release energy for development (Nuttall, 1981);
- to clarify a school's philosophy and policy (ibid.);
- to maintain morale (ibid.);
- to facilitate informed comparison between schools (ibid.);
- to provide information for LEA and governors (ibid.);
- to clarify leadership patterns (Whitaker, 1983);
- to aid professional development (McCormick and James, 1983);

- to diagnose—to obtain feedback on curricula, teaching, students, activities, strengths and weaknesses (Eisner, 1979);
- to compare—programmes, teaching, school organization (ibid.);
- to improve school quality (ibid.);
- to anticipate educational needs (ibid.);
- to determine whether, and to what extent, objectives have been achieved (ibid.);
- to diagnose the initial state of the curriculum, pupils, teachers and organization (Glaser, 1977);
- to ascertain weaknesses in course provision (Pope, 1983);
- to meet accountability demands (McCormick and James 1983);
- to determine the effectiveness of courses (Pope, 1983).

The purposes of the evaluation will illuminate the scope of the evaluation which can range from national levels (e.g. DES, 1974, 1978a, 1982b) to regional or school levels, from vast areas of the curriculum at a national level to education systems or whole school evaluation which cut across subject boundaries into policies and philosophies.

DEMAND FOR, AND AUDIENCES OF, EVALUATION

In considering the purposes of evaluation, the question has to be posed 'whose purposes does the evaluation serve?'; the origins of the demand for evaluation must be identified. House (1976), for example, contends

> the context of the valuation involves the basic slant derived from the genesis of the evaluation, and includes all those motivations, biases, values, attitudes and pressures from which the evaluation arose...[and involves] problems of trying to determine the social

worth of educational programs; valuation, justification, persuasion, values, thought, action, morality, knowledge, power.

(House, 1976, p. 12)

The identification of the origin of the demand for evaluation will involve ascertaining the reasons which the originators have for wanting the evaluation to be done (Harlen and Elliott, 1982). It will also denote the possible audiences of the evaluation (ibid.), e.g. LEA, parents, critics, governors, HMI, colleagues, course directors, planners, headteachers and other schools. The significance of these two factors lies in their ability to determine the level and type of information sought, the degree of involvement, exposure or honesty on the part of those being evaluated or participating in the evaluation, the formality or style of the report, and the credibility of the evaluation.

Eisner (1979) discusses such problems of writing evaluation reports as those of communicability—that the form of the report must be appropriate to the audience. For example, the demand from an adviser to produce an evaluation document on science teaching in a school for receipt by parents, governors and LEA, will very likely produce a different report from an evaluation of science teaching instigated by a non-scientist colleague wishing to find out how she or he can improve their own science teaching.

One may be factual, stating staffing, qualifications, curricula in their broadest sense, resources and perhaps examination results, whereas the other, if it is in report form at all, may contain analysis of strengths and weaknesses of the curriculum, its teaching strengths and weaknesses, unsupported opinion and judgement, and perhaps proposals to improve the quality of the curriculum and teaching. The former may be self-justificatory or bland, the latter—with a highly restricted audience and specific purpose—may be critical, honest and perhaps speculative.

The recipients of the evaluation will determine both what is included and how it is written up, for different audiences will have different backgrounds, perceptions, constraints on them and power to take action. This will influence the format of the report, from highly formal to informal. A highly formal report will be pitched at influential groups and the academic community (Walker, 1981), and adopt a weighty and academic style, with sophisticated evaluation instruments and clearly defined methodology. An informal report—pitched for a more general readership—will be written in everyday language, making no pretensions to a 'scientific' approach, and involving limited measurement techniques. At a level of medium formality, between the two extremes, a planned evaluation, aimed at interested parties and specified audiences, will use some data collection and treatment techniques even though these are relatively unsophisticated.

There is clearly a political aspect to the issue of the audiences of the evaluation; the evaluators and those evaluated will have to choose their allegiances or clarify the terms of reference unambiguously and unequivocally (MacDonald, 1982), recognize the limits to their autonomy, and recognize the potential threat to teachers which evaluation can pose (Adelman, 1984). Evaluation has a concomitant political dimension. In this respect MacDonald (1976) has outlined three forms of evaluation—bureaucratic, autocratic and democratic. The three characterizations hinge on the power of the evaluator and the power of the recipients of the evaluation to take action and decisions.

In bureaucratic evaluation the evaluators unconditionally serve those demanding the evaluation, providing information or recommendations which, once given, are out of their control or ownership—who pays the piper calls the tune. The controlling power demanding the evaluation can use the information as it wishes, and can accept or reject any recommendations made by the evaluators or the evaluation. In autocratic evaluation conditional service is given by the evaluator. Information and recommendations are made with which the receiving authority must comply; hence a measure of power and independence is controlled by the evaluator. In democratic evaluation the audience is wide, the evaluator is providing the whole community, however defined, with information; the report does not make recommendations or judgements, the community decides.

These three characterizations typify perhaps the proactive and reactive power that audiences of evaluation can have on the nature of the report. If teachers regard evaluation as a threat, inviting them to reveal their weaknesses, then natural reluctance in this respect is inevitable, particularly if the audiences could be condemnatory, powerful in determining career prospects or significant decision-makers on funding, resources and policies. For example, teachers will understandably be unwilling to divulge what they perceive to be their own weaknesses to a head-teacher or adviser who a week later might be interviewing them for promotion or for filling a vacancy in a particular school or curriculum area. Certain types of information, then, can disadvantage some individuals, often those with little power (McCormick and James, 1983). The element of control of information must be approached.

ETHICS OF EVALUATION

If evaluation is politically non-neutral (Lawton, 1983) and the evaluators' roles vary, then the control of information collected must be established at the outset, for this clearly affects the types of information elicited. The ownership of information can affect the degree of frankness, bias, honesty or the amount of information provided by a subject. Procedures must therefore be established which will clarify the collection, ownership and release of information (Harlen and Elliott, 1982). At the heart of the control issue is a dichotomy between the public's and the evaluator's 'right to know' and the person's 'right to privacy' (McCormick and James, 1983). It is a problem too of the ethics of confidentiality; Pring (1984) sees this as a twofold problem.

Initially if an evaluator has to present a report, for example, to a project director or head of department, then this may be exclusive, debarring those evaluated from seeing the final report, denying them accessibility (MacDonald, 1977). This cedes considerable power both to the evaluator and the recipients; the evaluator may be putting an interpretation in the report which unfairly reflects information from those evaluated or induces features not originally present. Second, the evaluator may be including material which was given in confidence, or given in the knowledge that clearance would be obtained it is were to be used or publicly broadcast—this is particularly true if the comments or opinions are unfavourable, personal or revealing immoral acts, e.g. stealing (McCormick and James, 1983).

In a report whose audience is exclusive the subjects may never know if their confidences have been respected; alternatively, in a report whose audience is wide the subjects may not wish certain comments to appear, particularly if the authorship could be traced without difficulty, be it teachers or children; anonymity may not be enough (Elliott and Adelman, 1976). Pring (1984) sets out five criteria which reconcile the dichotomy and which evaluators would negotiate before commencing evaluation:

1. The evaluator sets out the kinds of knowledge required.
2. The evaluator is open to cross-examination on the evaluation.
3. Information or opinion is treated confidentially, subject to clearance.
4. Interpretation of data is open to critical scrutiny by those evaluated.
5. The evaluator would provide reports which could be examined by those evaluated.

A final consideration in the ethics of evaluation is the profile of the evaluator—does the evaluator adopt an overt or covert style (McCormick and James, 1983), declaring intentions or keeping them unspoken? The latter may elicit information which otherwise may not be forthcoming; the former may elicit information in only a portion of the areas for investigation. Again, here the ethics of confidentiality are addressed and procedures which respect this have to be observed (e.g. Simons, 1982; Pring, 1984).

NATURE AND ROLES OF THE EVALUATOR

Initially this divides itself principally into two concerns: who the evaluators will be and what their roles are. In regard to the former, this concerns external and internal evaluators to a curriculum, school or project; which type is chosen depends on appropriacy to purpose. External evaluators, including teachers from other schools, HMI, heads, deputies, union representatives, staff from higher education institutions, professional consultants, representatives of professional associations, advisers and academics, can claim several strengths; they have the benefit of objectivity, possibly expertise in evaluation, and a view to broad perspectives and constraints in which a curriculum is located. However, they may be insensitive to the complexity or specificity of a curriculum in a particular school; they can also pose a threat a teachers. External evaluation can take the form of testing [e.g. the Assessment of Performance Unit (APU)], consultation, ethnographies, inspections of aspects of a school by national or local bodies, and formal evaluation with a variety of instruments.

Testing, while having the advantage of providing norm-referenced, quantifiable results, poses problems of representing education mechanically, of being arguably invalid measures of education, of casting teachers in powerless positions—having no control over the tests and no rights of redress (McCormick and James 1983), and of being of limited use in suggesting lines along which curriculum development can proceed. Inspections, though they may be superficial, impressionistic and susceptible to personal intervention by headteachers good at public relations, offer a more humane front than testing. It is a more flexible tool than testing, allowing for interpersonal relationships, and premissed on suggesting lines of development and improvement, i.e. having greater explanatory potential than testing.

The notion of internal evaluators—planners, headteachers, curriculum leaders, teachers—has many strengths (Davis, 1983). Such evaluators may have greater commitment to the evaluation and its outcomes; they will be aware of the subtleties and complexities of a particular school; they might have a considerable store of knowledge available to them by having been in the situation for some time. Further, their knowledge of personalities might enable them to elicit considerably more information and participation from staff than an outsider, perhaps because less of a threat is being posed. Against this however are several problems. Insiders may be too familiar with a situation (Eisner, 1985); they may miss significant but day-to-day activities; they may be unable to view matters objectively, whether they want to or not. Being caught up in a situation may prevent honest criticism from being formulated for fear of souring relations or articulating discordant values among staff. The interesting question raised here also is the ability of staff to evaluate each other: will an inexperienced colleague be capable of evaluating an experienced or inexperienced colleague, or will an experienced teacher be able to evaluate colleagues? The issue is raised by Eisner (1985) in his notion of 'connoisseurship'—an appreciation of the qualities of curriculum as practised:

> to be a connoisseur of wine, bicycles or graphic arts is to be informed about their qualities; to be able to discriminate the subtleties among types of wine, bicycles and graphic arts by drawing upon a gustatory, visual and kinaesthetic memory against which the particulars of the present may be placed for purposes of comparison and contrast.
>
> (Eisner, 1985; p. 92)

If a good teacher needs an awareness of the quality of a situation, activity, curriculum or pedagogy to be a connoisseur—evaluator, then the question is raised of the nature or length of teaching experience required for such a task: 'a teacher with years of experience in the classroom...might develop only enough educational connoisseurship to enable [her] to cope at minimal levels with the classroom and school in which they work' (ibid., p. 109). It also raises the question of who is to judge when a teacher is sufficiently experienced as a connoisseur to be able to act as an evaluator. Further, the critical factor of the credibility of the exercise is raised: internal staff may not have the expertise, time, status or legitimacy to perform the task with any measure of credibility. Walker (1981) suggests that of three levels of credibility of evaluators, teachers are ranked the lowest, the other two levels are external agents:

- Level one—high status—professors, university staff, researchers.
- Level two—medium status—college lecturers, LEA personnel.
- Level three—low status—teachers.

This low status or credibility afforded teachers need not mean, of course, that the evaluation is any less rigorous (McCormick and James, 1983), only that in terms of outsider interest it raises questions of validity.

It appears then that a mixed approach is perhaps appropriate, with insiders necessarily complementing outsider evaluation, and outsiders offering objectivity (triangulation) to insider evaluation; they are mutually supportive. In this too comes consideration of externally generated but internally administered evaluation schemes, where guidelines, purposes of foci are laid down perhaps at LEA or national level but interpreted, investigated and reported by schools, and internally generated but externally monitored evaluation schemes.

Given the complexity of the evaluation process it is necessary to determine the roles of the evaluator before the evaluation begins; clarity of conception at the beginning of an evaluation can anticipate and resolve problems of role definition. For example, the question will have to be decided, in advance of implementation, of whether or to what extent the evaluator can shape a curriculum plan or implementation, to make recommendations during the development of the curriculum, or whether the evaluator simply monitors and makes recommendations at the end (i.e. the extent of the evaluator's intervention). The timing of stages and foci here is crucial. Walker (1981) sees the evaluator as embodying several roles, suggesting perhaps that the notion of a single evaluator is better replaced with a notion of multiple evaluators. Roles can be described as: informer; judge; decision-maker; coordinator; report producer; consultant; collector of information; collator of information; monitor; or any combination of these. McCormick and James (1983) add to this the notion of 'critical friends' (be they external or internal evaluators), who have no authority position in relation to schools but have skills, expertise and well-founded relationships with teachers which can promote self-reflection and evaluation in a nonthreatening manner.

TIME SCHEDULE AND TIMING OF THE EVALUATION

The evaluation will have to consider time limits as these will determine feasibly what can and ought to be done in the time available. It will identify priorities and short-and long-term aspects of the evaluation. It will also draw attention to significant omissions occasioned by time constraints—some methods of evaluation take much longer than others. Second, the question of when the evaluation will be done must be addressed. Scriven (1967) suggests two types of evaluation timing: formative and summative evaluation. Formative evaluation takes place during the curriculum development and implementation, it is an ongoing process of monitoring, offering continuous feedback which may or may not shape the direction or course of the curriculum. Summative evaluation is terminal evaluation of the curriculum to ascertain the extent to which it fulfilled its objectives. Clearly, a full evaluation should embody both types; evaluation should be constant (Clemson, 1983). Harlen (1971) expands this notion of ongoing evaluation by suggesting four stages at which evaluation should be done:

1. Stage one—evaluating the suitability of objectives.
2. Stage two—formative evaluation.
3. Stage three—evaluation of individual readiness and progress.
4. Stage four—summative evaluation.

This has resonances with Stake's (1976a) notion that antecedents, transactions and outcomes have to be evaluated; Stake puts this into a two dimensional model which focuses on evaluating intended and observed curricula. Hence the evaluator gathers data on intended antecedents—what the planners intended there to be in the school before the new curriculum came into being. This is matched to the observed antecedents, what actually preceded the new piece of the curriculum, e.g. organization of learning, nature of pupil and teacher interactions, pupils' interests, environmental factors and teaching styles.

Alternatively, the intended antecedents might anticipate certain resources—equipment, time, staffing money; this has to be matched to the level of resources observed before the new curriculum is implemented to ascertain where extra resources need to be provided. At the level of transactions the intentions can be compared to observed implementations, for example, to see if planned activities or learning situations or environments actually happened in the ways intended. Similarly, at the outcome stage the evaluator has to gather data on what outcomes were intended, e.g. knowledge, behaviour, skills, concepts and attitudes, and match them to the observed outcomes, what was actually learned or practised or acquired. This harks back to the earlier definition that 'the effective curriculum is what each child takes away' (Schools Council, 1981, p. 42). At all three levels Stake (1976a) suggests that a measure of congruence between intention and actuality is being sought.

FOCUS OF THE EVALUATION

The issues raised so far point to the need for curriculum evaluators to be clear on the focus of the evaluation, be it persons, e.g. teachers and children, or practices, e.g. curricula, pedagogy, assessment procedures. The focus may well determine the methods of evaluation employed. Stake's foci have already been delineated; additionally, Eisner (1979) suggest three subject-matters of evaluation—the curriculum, the teaching and the outcomes (Norris, 1975; Borich, 1977; DES, 1985c). These are dealt with throughout the book, covering:

- background constraints on the curriculum;
- ideologies, epistemologies, sociologies, cultures;
- aims;
- objectives;
- content;
- skills;
- evaluation and assessment procedures;
- management structures and styles;
- record keeping;
- resources and their utilization;
- the planning and preparation of the learning;
- the sequencing of the work;
- class management, organization and order;
- teaching styles and their variety;

- learning styles, individual differences and preferences;
- motivating children;
- rewards and punishments;
- skills in exposition, questioning, discussion and summary;
- pupil and teacher relationships.

Evaluation of outcomes will look for the match between what has been taught and what has been learnt—specific perhaps to children, teachers and the subject (Eisner, 1985). It is here that there is a strong potential threat to teachers, for attempting to evaluate teacher performance by pupil outcomes is fraught with problems as it slides over the sundry and significant features of pupils and their learning, which may be out of the teacher's control and for which teachers cannot be fully held morally accountable (Kelly, 1982). Gronlund (1974) gives these factors as:

- intelligence;
- past achievement;
- self-concept and self-knowledge;
- acceptance of school knowledge;
- school conditions, resources, ratios of teachers to children;
- out-of-school factors (socioeconomic), community environment;
- interaction of out-of-school and in-school factors

Further, such a model assumes that teachers are only concerned with products and neglect processes, which is a very narrow perspective on the curriculum and on education.

An alternative approach to evaluation, geared more towards self-evaluation, is offered by the Open University (1980) which suggests six main questions which curriculum evaluators may ask of themselves. The evaluation is geared totally to analysis, reflection and, significantly, to action—the characteristics perhaps of the reflective teacher as a model of good practice. For each question there are several contributory considerations.

Given the variety of responses anticipated from these questions, and given the previous debate on effective teaching, the thrust of the implications is to throw into doubt the notion that consensus can ever be achieved other than at a superficial or general level on the constitution of effectiveness in any narrowly prescriptive sense. Effectiveness covers many variables; how total or partial must a teacher's possession of the many possible variables be in order to be judged effective? The term must be used relative to a situation, an individual child, teacher, curriculum or task. In establishing the focus of evaluation, then, the evaluator must be clear on the factors contributing to the particular situation being evaluated.

METHODS OF GATHERING EVALUATION DATA

Techniques of gathering data are not arbitrary; methods are selected on the criterion of appropriacy for eliciting the type of information required—certain methods yield certain types of data. The criterion of appropriacy will have to take account of the purpose, focus. audience, role of the evaluator, model to be used (discussed later), timing and scale of the evaluation. Methods of gathering data lie along a continuum from quantitative to qualitative types; they can be represented in pairs thus (see also Stake, 1976b):

quantitative.................................. qualitative
formal .... informal
intermittent................................. long-term, continuous
objective....................................... subjective
structured.................................... unstructured
measuring .... valuing
assessing .... judging

describing .... interpreting
looking at .... looking for
preordinate .... responsive
scientific .... illuminative
statistical...................................... ethnographic
deductive .... inductive
nomothetic .... idiographic
positivistic.................................... interpretive

Table 6.1
Open University questions for self-evaluation

1. What did the pupils actually do?
   (a) What did they do and what did they not do?
   (b) What I liked/disliked them doing?
   (c) How do I know what they were really doing?
   (d) What kind of evidence do I need to answer (c)?
2. What were they learning?
   (a) How do I know what they were really learning?
   (b) In what terms will I be looking, e.g. personal, academic?
   (c) How does what they were learning match up with my aims?
   (d) What might they have been learning?
   (e) How adequate were the opportunities for the learning? What were the contexts of their learning?
   (f) To what extent was learning actually taking place? Why do I need to know?
   (g) How can I assess it? (Type of evidence; comparing what the pupils do with whatever you think is appropriate.)
   (h) What have I learned from assessing the learning?
3. How worthwhile was it?
   (a) In what terms will I answer this? Overall or context-specific? Short-term/medium-term/long-term?
   (b) How explicit will you make your values?
   (c) In what terms will you judge the worthwhileness (pupils, teachers, etc)?
   (d) What assumptions are you making in your judgements?
   (e) How will you collect and analyse data to answer (c) and (d)?

Table 6.1 (Contd.)

4. And what did I do?
   (a) How fitting was it to the task?
   (b) How will I discuss it—in terms of planning, organizing, resourcing my role during the lesson, evaluation?
   (c) How will I find out what I did?
   (d) What evidence/whose evidence will I use to answer (c)?
   (e) At what level will I answer—general or specific?
   (f) What is the difference between my aims and my practices?
5. What did I learn?
   (a) Did I learn anything? Why not?
   (b) What did I learn about? Myself, the children, the activity, the subject, teaching and learning styles?
   (c) What did I learn about what the children did? What they were learning, how worthwhile it was, what I did? My behaviour with children? My role? My involvement?
   (d) What evidence do I need to answer?
6. What do I intend to do now?
   (a) How will the questions and answers to questions 1 to 5 affect my plans?
   (b) How will I answer questions 1 to 5 for my curriculum development?

Clearly, these parts are not discrete; nor need an evaluation draw on one type of data exclusively. An aclectic approach will use both quantitative analysis (figures, statistics and structured interviews or questionnaires) and qualitative data (opinions, perspectives and depth of response evoked), establishing concurrent validity of the evaluation by using a multi-method approach. Further, no method or type of method is objectively or intrinsically better than another, they are simply different, having their own strengths and weaknesses. For example, while quantitative analysis has the respectability of scientific procedures and can ostensibly measure factors, relationships and their subtleties with a high degree of systematic precision, Ruddock (1981) criticizes statistical methodology for combining 'great refinement of process with crudity of concept' (p. 49)—that the need to operationalize a concept demeans it or fails to encompass all its facets.

Similarly, Eisner (1985) criticizes quantitative methodologies for failing to distinguish between educational and statistical significance. However, qualitative methods, while possessing and reflecting immediacy, flexibility, authenticity and comprehensiveness, have been criticized for being impressionistic, biased, ungeneralizable, idiosyncratic, subjective and short-sighted. In short validity attaches itself differently according to the methods employed (Ruddock, 1981). Given these considerations, evaluators have at their disposal a battery of techniques available for gaining particular types of information: observation; testing; interviews and conversations; questionnaires; rating scales; records (field notes, documents, diaries); group discussions; children's work; reports; appraisal and self-appraisal schedules; personal constructs; Delphi techniques; nominal group techniques; sound and video recordings; photographs; profiles.

It is beyond the scope of this book to discuss each method and its handling in any depth; rather the discussion here briefly illustrates the nature and uses of five key methods—observation, interview, questionnaire, testing and records—revealing their potential for evaluation and their strengths and weaknesses.

Observation (both auditory and visual) is a key method for gathering information and feedback about curricula and children; it is probably the method most used by teachers on a day-to-day basis. It ranges from formal to informal, highly structured to unstructured. Structured observation works on an observation schedule of categories to be completed during the observation period. It might involve time sampling where a record is entered on the schedule of what is observed at fixed regular intervals, e.g. every five, ten or thirty seconds. Alternatively, it might involve event sampling (or sign systems) where a mark is entered in the appropriate category every time a particular event is observed in a given period, for example the child writing, or standing up, or walking around. One-zero sampling requires a mark to be entered in the appropriate category not every time it is observed but just once if it is observed. While event and one-zero sampling can yield frequencies of behaviours, they cannot provide the temporal order in which the behaviour occurred—they aggregate but do not sequence. On the other hand, time sampling has this potential for temporal sequencing, an important factor in tracking a child's behaviour or attempting to trace the causes or developments of a behaviour.

While structured observation clearly operates in a systematic and rigorously analytical manner and presents a wealth of numerical data which can be used to compare children, teachers and curricula, it presents several telling problems, both practical and theoretical. At a practical level the construction of an unambiguous schedule which exhaustively or adequately embraces all the aspects of the construct under investigation is extremely time-consuming, often requiring trial usage to refine the schedule and to ensure that if a team of evaluators is to use it, that there is parity in the way in which behaviours observed are entered in the categories. Further, the possibility of using it to study more than a handful of children at a time is restricted.

At a theoretical level the whole notion of structured observation has been questioned for its inability to take account of each participant's unique perception of a situation; it can only measure observable behaviour rather than intentions and thoughts (Stubbs and Delamont, 1976). Moreover, structured observation focuses on parcels or potentially disjointed fragments of behaviour, neglecting a more holistic view of what is occurring in the classroom. The use of prespecified categories is questionable (ibid.) as this prejudges what the observer will observe, which may only be a poor or partial record of what is actually taking place, i.e. they assume the truth of what they claim to be explaining. Category systems take continual still pictures of interaction and behaviour; they freeze behaviour, however momentarily.

The validity of such a static approach to measuring a fluid, ever-changing active world of behaviour has to be questioned.

Unstructured and semi-structured observation, on the other hand, moves away from categories and schedules towards assessing and understanding the quality of a situation as a whole, hence the observer here (the participant—observer or observer-as-participant perhaps) does not enter the situation with predetermined notions of what to observe, but responds to the situation, allowing key issues and behaviours to present themselves, picking up the flavour of the situation. This requires a lengthy stay in the situation (often measured in months rather than hours). The observer records as much as possible in field notes—comprehensive personal records of behaviour, opinions, perceptions, reactions and understanding—then sifts through the data to decide on the key features, checks with the participants or a neutral party that they are in fact significant, and, sensitized to central issues, investigates these further by observation, the procedure of 'progressive focusing'.

By staying in a situation for a considerable time the observer-effect is reduced, participants become used to the observer; the potential for observing more 'natural' behaviour rather than the 'staged' behaviour observed perhaps in brief periods of structured observation is greatly enhanced. Unstructured and semi-structured observation can be used as a complement to interviews, discussions and other means of data gathering; the data of all these other forms comprising the 'field notes' mentioned above. It underscores the model of 'illuminative evaluation' discussed later. It claims greater potential than structured observation for understanding classroom processes and explaining why situations operate in the way that they do.

Interviews, be they with individuals or groups, can, like observation methods, be highly structured, semi-structured or unstructured. A highly structured interview will have very specific questions requiring specific answers, perhaps of the multiple-choice or yes/no types; the same questions are given to all respondents. The advantage of a highly structured situation is that it provides many responses to the same question—a suitable basis for fair comparative analysis statistically. A completely unstructured interview has no predetermined areas of interest, it is more like a conversation, with the interviewer following the train of thought of the interviewee in an unforced, natural manner; hence in retrospect the interview may prove useful or useless in providing data. Data gathered is generally recorded after the event.

Between these two poles lies the semi-structured interview, where the interviewer has a checklist of items to be addressed, but phrases questions to suit the respondent, tailors the interview sequence to follow the natural flow of the respondent's conversation or thought rather than being bound to an immutable order, and asks open-ended questions which allow a free and full response. In these the value placed on the response lies in the 'candour, depth and richness of the information given. The more involved the respondent becomes in his account, and the deeper the level from which his answer springs, the more genuine and valid his responses will be' (Oppenheim, 1966, p. 76).

The semi-structured interview, then, is a useful instrument for covering the issues to be investigated in a manner which is sensitive to specific situations and which respects the individuality of each respondent. The problems which attach themselves to semi-structured interviews are two-fold. First, in rephrasing questions, the basis for comparison of respondents' answer is reduced; they are different questions and may be interpreted differently. Further, the answers may be given out of anxiety to please or to say something rather than nothing, or may reflect what happens to be in the respondent's mind at the time rather than a fully considered response. All these features are particularly hazardous if interviewing children. Moreover the intonation or phrasing of the question might be given or taken as a clue to the type of response sought. Simons (1982a) offers a useful set of considerations for evaluators approaching interviewing:

1. Establish the respondent's confidence by demonstrating empathy or offering confidentiality.
2. Respond acceptingly.
3. Allow the respondent to shift from topic to topic.
4. Accept unsolicited responses.
5. Be prepared to listen.
6. Use cues from the respondent to prove for depth.
7. Avoid asking too many questions.
8. Avoid accepting the initial response too readily.
9. Avoid summarizing erroneously.
10. Be socially responsive.
11. Recognize the need to be assertive if the respondent is being too repetitive.
12. Look for nonverbal cues.
13. Plan the order of interviewing candidates.
14. Note the number and kind of interruptions accepted during the interview.

Simons (1982a) also identifies problems associated with interviewing children:

1. How to avoid being seen as an authority sympathizer?
2. How to keep the interview relevant and focused?
3. How to avoid summarizing too early?
4. How to get the teacher out of the room?
5. How to interview inarticulate pupils?
6. How to respond to the person who reveals all and immediately wishes he had said nothing?

7. How to evoke pupil responses which are not just responses to the interview situation?
8. How to get beyond the institutional response in a short-time?
9. How to avoid only the headteacher's view?
10. How to deal with reticent pupils?

The interview, then, is a powerful and flexible tool for eliciting data. It can reveal participants motives, opinions, perspectives, reactions, explanations, thoughts and understandings of situations, all of which benefit the evaluator, be it an external agent or the teacher in the school.

Questionnaires may be regarded in some ways as interviews written down, for they too vary from the structured to the semi-structured, allowing for highly structured dichotomous or multiple-choice questions or those requiring a free response. If employing rating scales or Kilert scales (e.g. 'strongly agree', 'agree', 'disagree', 'strongly disagree'), then the categories must be both exhaustive and exclusive. If multiple-choice questions are used then the choices must be exhaustively realistic, i.e. to represent the response with which the respondent can identify. Hence extremely careful devising and phrasing of questions is necessary, which may require a pilot stage.

While questionnaires have potential for supplementing interview or observation data, their inability to offer explanations, clarifications or probes renders them perhaps a weaker tool than the former two methods. There is no way of checking the depth of an attitude or opinion expressed in a questionnaire. There is a tendency for respondents using rating scales to avoid the extreme categories. There is difficulty in identifying how respondents interpret the anchor statements or categories in rating scales, hence the validity of questionnaires may be questionable. Questionnaires used to gather facts may be useful, those used to gather opinion are problematic—though perhaps not insuperably so.

Testing yields data on outcomes, performances and products, which are useful to an evaluator to gauge the success or appropriacy of objectives, programmes and pupils—be they norm-referenced or criterion-referenced tests. They have the clear strength of being objective, controlled, perhaps standardized, susceptible to statistical analysis, and useful for providing data for comparisons. This must not be allowed to cloud the problem of assessment in certain fields, for example, the affective or creative, where a mark is perhaps a crude measure of performance. Like structured observation or structured interviews, their explanatory potential is limited—they only tell an evaluator *that* certain products were occasioned, not why. Similarly, they do not measure all the variables operating upon children's performances which are out of the teacher's control and which cause or constrain a particular outcome.

Records (documentary, formal, field notes or diaries, or informal records) are a valuable data source. Documents can comprise the range of written records, e.g. minutes of meetings, tests results, record of profile form, briefing papers, syllabi, reports, notes or casual observations. Diaries kept by teachers, children or evaluators can record over time data from observations, interviews, questionnaires, or opinions, thoughts, perceptions, feelings, reactions, or facts about curricula and their implementations. They are flexible and open-ended, and if they are comprehensive and structured they can provide invaluable information either to corroborate, illuminate or explain situations or to suggest factors which may not be forthcoming to an evaluator.

Record-keeping informs evaluation and subsequent curriculum planning and decision-making. There are several issues in the devising, keeping and use of records which have to be addressed. Records offer data on which formative and summative evaluation are based. They will differ according to their intended audiences, purposes, format and coverage of curriculum areas: a personal record may be qualitatively different from a stylized record produced for a child's career through the primary school; and a mathematics record could well differ in form from a language record. Decisions have to be taken by curriculum planners on the monitoring of their curricula; these can be approached by addressing key questions.

What are the Purposes of Record Keeping?

As well as informing planing, records serve a variety of purposes, as follows:

1. To record the achievement of children and teachers.
2. To record the experiences of children and teachers.
3. To record children's development.
4. To compare children.
5. To record progress and rates of progress.
6. To ensure coverage of the curriculum.

Seen in these lights, records cover intentions, implementation or trans-actions, and outcomes—which has resonances with Stake's (1976a) countenance and portrayal models of evaluation, outlined later. The School's Council (Clift, Weiner and Wilson, 1981 pp. 22-3) offers a comprehensive list of seven principal functions of record keeping in primary schools:

1. To supply information, to inform the day-to-day planning of the teacher. These could b, for example, running records of attainment and progress in reading, mathematics or language development.
2. To provide summary information to accompany pupils on their transfer from one teacher to another in school. These may be half-termly, termly, half-yearly or yearly.
3. To provide summary information to accompany pupils on their transfer from one stage to another or from one school to another. These may include:

(a) nursery to infant or first school;

(b) infant or first school to junior or middle school;

(c) junior or middle school to secondary school.

4. To provide summary information to accompany pupils on their transfer from one school to another, other than for transition reasons. These could be for geographical moves or for changes within an area brought about for other reasons.
5. To diagnose pupil needs, progress, strengths and weaknesses.
6. To provide information for, or fro, supporting welfare services, for example, school medical, psychological or social services.
7. To provide information for parents: these may be in the form of termly or yearly reports or records discussed at open evenings.

The format and information provided on records, then, will vary according to the purposes for which they are being kept.

What are the Types of Records?

A teacher wishing to plan appropriate curricula will draw on a variety of records. While there is a wealth of types of records they can perhaps be grouped thus:

1. Records 'of content covered, be they by lists, descriptions, flow charts, web diagrams or other forms.
2. Class records—a teacher's weekly record book under various headings in indicative of this type.
3. Summary records—infrequent reports detailing outline information only.

4. Individual pupil record cards, be they formal or informal, where the teacher notes pupil development in detail (in the form of daily, weekly, monthly, half-yearly or *ad hoc* comments).
5. Pupils's self-completion records, where children themselves mark off stages reached, books read, assignments completed, etc. These are the substance of recording in SRA and Reading Workshop laboratories and some mathematics schemes.
6. Teachers' records of group work completed or attempted.
7. Samples of children's work.

While such a list may or may not be exhaustive, it does signal a major problem in record-keeping—that it can easily go out of hand and become a time-consuming occupation undertaken merely for its own sake. This clearly is of limited value; records must be useful. The types of record link to the further question of the forms or formats of records. A teacher can draw on a variety of means of recording information:

1. Record of marks and results of standardized tests.
2. Personal observations.
3. Ticks against statements.
4. Rating scales against statements.
5. Marks against understanding of concepts and skills.
6. Multiple-choice questions.
7. Open-ended areas for comment.
8. Graphs, charts and histograms.
9. Photographs, film, video, slides, audio cassettes.
10. Flow charts and descriptions.

11. Records of significant behaviours or comments by children.
12. Check lists.

Criteria of appropriacy and usefulness clearly operate in selecting which of these methods to use. The reflective teacher will draw eclectically on these to suit purposes most efficiently.

What Areas are Covered by Records?

While to do justice to the primary ethos outlined elsewhere, the whole personality, capability, experiences and all-round development of the child should be recorded (Sharp *et al.*, 1975), in reality the audiences of the records may well determine the answer to this question, as will the formality of the detail required. This ranges from the standard profile card kept by the school for every child, to the working records which teachers keep. Clift *et al.* (1981) found that teachers in the two hundred schools surveyed kept records of the areas shown in Table 6.2. The list is useful in drawing attention to the curricular, personal and social areas which records usefully cover. Again the striking problem is the scope and range of record keeping; too easily it can become an end in itself, exhausting and relatively valueless.

Given such scope the curriculum planer will have to weigh the merits and demerits which attach themselves to questions of record keeping. That they can be time-consuming is clear, hence ease of completion should be the goal. This brings problems in its wake, for while quickly completed tick sheets may reduce the time spent, a standardized format may not reflect an individual's specific profile nor the particular classroom organization and pedagogic styles which obtain in the classroom—a team teaching, open plan or integrated day situation may require a different recording system from a more traditional organization where one teacher works with one class.

Further, there is a tension between comprehensive and unnecessary detail, between specificity and generality. Tilting too far towards comprehensiveness may lead to a plethora of demanding records, many of which will serve little real or enduring purpose for the curriculum planner. On the other hand, too general a record can lead to platitudinous comments or risk unhelpful personal bias. Further, a general grade of C in English may obscure the fact that a child may be excellent in imaginative writing but appalling at spelling or punctuation—the usefulness of highlighting the extremes may be lost in an average.

Table 6.2
Records kept by teachers in the study by Clift *et al.* (1981)

Record	*Percentage of teachers recording in the area*
Reading development	96
List of maths topics covered	81
Social and personal development	55
Writing development (handwriting, spelling, syntax, expression)	35
Oral language development	34
Physical development (and medical notes on visual, auditory, health or motor problems)	31
Concept attainment in mathematics	29
Scientific skills and experiences (areas of study, topics, equipment used)	17
Aesthetic development and craft	14
Study skills	3

(*Source*: Clift *et al.* (1981) *Record Keeping in Primary Schools*, p. 14).

A final tension exists between the alleged objectivity of the tick sheet and the subjectivity of the personal comment. Erring too far from a balance between the two poles can distort records into statistics or anecdotes. While they both have their place an appropriate balance must be struck between them. For the curriculum planner a record must be parsimonious, comprehensive, easy to keep, appropriate to the audiences and purposes, provide opportunity for balancing objective measures with subjective comments, and above all useful, being a springboard to action rather than a monument to pedantry.

With many methods available to evaluators the guiding principles should perhaps be appropriacy and eclecticism in selecting which evaluation techniques to employ. If quantitative and comparative analysis is deemed necessary then structured and formal approaches may be appropriate; if qualitative analysis is required then less structured approaches may be preferable, still maintaining rigour and methodological stringency (Huberman and Miles, 1984). However, the two have been demonstrated to be neither discrete nor exclusive (ibid.). The teacher and evaluator investigating an issue may find it beneficial to draw on many methods yielding many types of data. This attempts to ensure content and concurrent validity to the evaluation; to explore the full spectrum of concerns in an issue requires a full spectrum of methods.

SEQUENCING THE EVALUATION

In approaching curriculum evaluation and taking account of the issues raised, it is possible to suggest sequence of a curriculum evaluation. Eraut (1984) offers a three-stage model: initiation, collection of evidence, and processing and reporting of information. Under 'initiation' one can include (Brink, 1983; Harlen and Elliott, 1982; Harlen, 1983; Eraut, 1984):

- considering the language and metaphors of evaluation;
- compiling an agenda of issues;
- deciding on the type of evaluation—formative to summative;

- deciding the purposes of the evaluation, what it is hoped it will achieve;
- deciding the criteria for the evaluation;
- deciding the focus of the evaluation;
- deciding the audience of the evaluation;
- deciding on the kind of evidence sought;
- deciding on the sources of the evidence;
- deciding on the methods to be used to gather evidence;
- deciding on the constitution, roles, power and responsibilities of the evaluator(s);
- deciding on the executive powers and roles of the audience of the evaluation;
- agreeing the ownership of the evidence;
- agreeing people's rights to gain or prevent access to evidence;
- deciding on the resources required for the evaluation—time, money, administrative support;
- deciding on methods to achieve reliability and validity of data collection and results;
- deciding on the form of the presentation and communication of the evaluation results;
- deciding on the form of the evaluation report;
- deciding on the use of the evaluation report to achieving the expressed purposes of the evaluation;
- deciding on the time scale and timing of the evaluation;
- deciding on the standards and criteria to be used to evaluate and judge the evaluation.

Under 'collection of evidence' will be methods, methodologies, manageability and participants' perceptions of the evaluation and the evaluators' roles.

In processing and reporting the evidence there is a clear need to link evaluation to action (Eraut, 1984), hence the necessity to have previously clarified the nature of the action or intervention of the evaluator, the report and its recipients.

MODELS OF EVALUATION

Curriculum planners and evaluators have diverse purposes and interests. In an attempt to articulate such diversity covered by the term 'evaluation', it is useful perhaps to consider models of curriculum evaluation. Planners can use models to clarify their thinking and to identify issues which surround different conceptions of the evaluation act. Such models will vary according to different evaluation criteria; Lewy (1977), for example, suggests that differences among evaluation studies may be classified under six issues:

1. The developmental stage of the programme—planning to implementation.
2. The entity to be evaluated—components or the whole.
3. Criteria for the evaluation, e.g. outcomes, processes, knowledge.
4. Data type, e.g. judgement, observation, records, interview data.
5. Mode of data summary—quantitative, qualitative.
6. Role of evaluation—formative, summative, for selection or modification or feedback on a programme.

Given such variables, six main models can be described, selected because they interpret the above issues in different ways which planners may find useful.

1. The objectives-based Model

This has its focus on outcomes, the intention of the evaluation being to ascertain how far children have achieved prespecified objectives. It owes its pedigree to Tyler (1949) and his predecessors, and to Bloom (1956). This model exists to detect discrepancies between intended and observed outcomes. While it has the claimed advantage of objectivity, quantitative assessment and precise specification of the focus of the evaluation, it has the disadvantages of assessing and measuring without explaining why children or activities are proceeding in observed ways; it offers only limited-feedback. Further, it neglects processes in favour of products, and risks an oversimplification of curriculum aims and objectives as they have to be specified and measured behaviourally.

2. Classical Research Model

This is similar to the 'objectives' model and is often called the agricultural—botanical model (Lawton, 1980), indicating its origins. This seeds are pre-tested, (e.g. weighed or measured) then sorted into two groups, one experimental group which will receive new different treatments and a control group which will not receive the new treatments, e.g. receiving different types or amounts of fertilization. Subsequently, the experimental and control groups are weighed or measured to compare the relative efficiency of the experimental group with the control group.

Applying the analogy to education, the curriculum planner would pre-test two groups of children—the control and the experimental groups—teach the new piece of the curriculum, re-test the groups and compare the relative advantage or progress of the two groups. While this model appears to possess the attraction of scientific respectability and specificity of analysis, there are difficulties with it. Initially the applicability of a model from agriculture or botany to human behaviour is questionable on practical and ethical ground, smacking of engineering (Lawton, 1983).

Human behaviour is not able to be isolated and controlled like plant behaviour; even if this were possible in laboratory conditions it would ignore the discrepancy between the artificial world of the laboratory and real life which contaminates subjects—regardless of the ethical problems of such laboratory research.

Moreover, the post-test would have limited validity; the control group not having been exposed to the new curriculum, it would be inappropriate to administer to them a test of that new curriculum—they would be certain to perform less well than the experimental group. Alternatively, if it were that the new curriculum offered only a different approach for the experimental group to learn the same content (however framed) as the control group, then this assumes, first, that curriculum projects undergo little or no change during the period of study— a premise rarely upheld in practice (Parlett and Hamilton, 1976) and, second, that variables other than the ones investigated are inoperable for both groups. It may be, for example, that the very fact of being in an experiment or being investigated will have an effect on motivation or performance (the Hawthorne effect). Such a model leans towards quantitative analysis—measures and figures—which may or may not describe the outcome of a curriculum, but which certainly explains very little about why the outcomes were what they were, i.e. it is of limited use to a planner.

3. Illuminative Model

In contrast to the two previous models the concern of the illuminative evaluator is with 'description and interpretation rather than measurement and prediction' (Parlett and Hamilton, 1976). It seeks to illuminate a curriculum in a particular school context experienced by specific teachers and children; in short, to discover the 'learning mileau' (ibid., p. 90). It strives to discover, understand and document what is happening, why it is happening, and participants' perspectives on the programme.

Hence the evaluator attempts to reach inside the group under study, to illuminate the context from within rather than without, to gain as many different perspectives as possible on the curriculum.

Evaluators begin with a broad data base from observations, conservations, interviews, background sources, opinions, and attempt to clarify the central issues in the curriculum as it is experienced by the participants. They do not, then, approach the evaluation with predetermined items for investigation, rather they are responsive to the unique situation or context. By 'progressive focusing'—clarifying, redefining and further investigating what emerge as key issues—evaluators go through a three-stage process of observing, inquiring further and then seeking to explain the curriculum (Parlett and Hamilton, 1976). Such 'progressive focusing' reduces the problem of data overload experienced at the outset of the evaluation. It also has built-in checks for internal validity, for the evaluator presents back the findings to the participants to ensure that a fair interpretation is being given.

Validity is sought through 'triangulation', by seeking as many views as possible on a situation, e.g. teachers', evaluators', and by employing a variety of methods to yield data on central issues, i.e. to provide concurrent validity. By being involved in the situation over a long period of time, and seeing participants in a variety of situations, the evaluator can construct perhaps a more valid picture of the curriculum as practised in a school than can a spasmodic series of short tests, questionnaires or interviews. The strength of this approach lies in the authenticity of the account which it can produce, and the acknowledgement of the significance of the context, interpersonal relationships and unique characteristics of a situation. These can be regarded as weaknesses, for the level of subjectivity is high, the generalizability is low, the sample tends to be small, and until recently only limited legitimacy has been accorded to qualitative measures.

Further, the nature of some of the evidence for the evaluation maybe questioned (Simons, 1984); what will constitute adequate evidence, an uninformed or unsubstantiated value judgement, for example? Perhaps then the illuminative evaluator sacrifices a measure of objectivity and precision of measurement to comprehensiveness, understanding and depth of response.

Countenance or Portrayal Model

This model seeks to utilize features of both ends of the quantitative to qualitative continuum exposed in the preceding three models. It derives from Stake (1976b) who argues that evaluation, in seeking to report different perspectives on a curriculum, must refer to three distinctions: formal and informal analysis, description and judgement data, and analysis and portrayal. His model then is eclectic; it synthesizes elements from other models into a new framework.

Formal analysis is recognized by reliance on schedules and quantitative analysis, observation and interview, structured analysis, measurement and testing, while informal analysis dwells on qualitative analysis, opinions, perspectives, semi- or unstructured observation and description. Stake recommends both approaches as appropriate in his countenance model.

With regard to description and judgement data, both of which have a place in the model, Stake argues for describing and judging data on antecedents, transactions and outcomes (already discussed) in terms of the match between intention and observation. To make a full judgement it is necessary to gather the accounts from five groups of people—spokespersons for society at large, subject matter experts, teachers, parents, children. This, it is argued, will offer a true reflection of the pluralism of values present in a situation. For a full countenance of the evaluation, Stake suggests that evaluators should address five questions:

1. Is this evaluation to be primarily descriptive, primarily judgemental or both descriptive and judgemental?
2. Is this evaluation to emphasize the antecedent conditions, the transactions, or the outcomes alone, or a combination of these, or their functional contingencies (i.e. their interrelationship and associated factors)?
3. Is this evaluation to indicate the congruence between what is intended and what occurs?
4. Is this evaluation to be undertaken within a single programme or as a comparison between two or more curricular programmes?
5. Is this evaluation intended more to further the development of curricula or to help choose among available curricula?

(Stake, 1976b, p. 39)

In analysis and portrayal the question is one of focus. Does the evaluator focus on the curriculum as a whole or on parts of the curriculum—should one attend to the fine grain or to the grand sweep (Stake, 1976b, p. 40)? Stake argues that either components are analysed—objectives, environment, interaction, perceptions, accomplishments—or an overall view is taken, describing and interpreting rather than measuring and predicting, the whole being greater than the sum of the parts. It is impossible, he claims, to do both, as attention to analysis 'distorts the picture as to what the programme is' (Stake, 1977a, p. 161). Analysis and portrayal are, he argues, alternatives of equal status.

Goal-free Model of Evaluation

In this model, formulated by Scriven (1967) the evaluator 'deliberately avoids learning the objectives of the program, which frees him to assess its actual effects....If intended effects are being achieved they should catch his attention' (Taylor, 1976; p. 356). The evaluator then studies the transacted curriculum unhampered by knowledge of the planner's intentions; this enables her or him to itemize significant or peculiar features of a school's curriculum, which then can highlight descrepancies between the perspectives of the planners and the users. To ensure that complete randomness is avoided the evaluator has a checklist of thirteen items which provide the basis of the enquiry—significant features allegedly necessary in any coherent curriculum—e.g. need, market, cost-effectiveness. The checklist thus represents a form of quality control. Hence absences or neglected areas can be identified.

The strengths of this approach lie in their potential comprehensiveness and their ability to release the evaluator from hide-bound adherence to curriculum planners' objectives. The principal weakness lies in the assumption that curricula can be fully evaluated by checklists, and that varieties of curricula can be evaluated by the same single checklist. With such strong criticisms this model is perhaps best used as an adjunct to other models.

Decision-making Model

Teachers and curriculum planners are caught up in the web of decision-making for which information has to be provided [c.f. Cronbach's definition of evaluation (1963)]. Decisions are informed by different types or foci of evaluation, the context of the decisions, and the type of decisions appropriate to that context. An attempt to synthesize this has been made by Stufflebeam (1976) who suggests four foci of evaluation: context, input, process and product evaluation.

Context evaluations, like situational' analyses, identify perceived needs and problems underlying those needs, objectives and the operating context of the curriculum so that decisions can be reached on the setting of the curriculum (Wiles and Bondi, 1984). Input evaluations assess system capabilities—the strategies feasible for achieving the goals. These evaluations inform decisions on procedural designs, sources of support and strategies appropriate to the context. Process evaluations are intended to monitor the implementation of the strategies to detect defects and to inform decisions on refining, controlling and redesigning the curriculum. Product evaluation seeks information on outcomes to determine the match to intentions, goals, objectives, strategies and implementation, so that decisions can be taken to continue, terminate or refocus the curriculum.

Implicit in Stufflebeam's conception is a means—end model of curriculum planning which has similarities to Stake's model of evaluating antecedents, transactions and outcomes. The six models can be presented in tubular form to address issues outlined earlier in the chapter which curriculum planners planning evaluations should address. If models are utilized as focusing tools for elements of curriculum planning and evaluation and as ways of drawing together key elements embraced by the term 'evaluation', then they serve their purpose. If they clarify issues in planners' minds then they are useful. The danger in using models lies in adopting an unreflective stance to them, using them prescriptively and inappropriately. The reflective teacher must sort and select, sift and balance, weigh and decide on which models or elements of models are relevant, appropriate and, above all, useful in planning curricula in the light of critical awareness of problems, possibilities, constraints and freedoms. If evaluation is to be fully integrated into curriculum planning then a measure of rigour and professional insight brought about by developing evaluation has to be cultivated by curriculum planners.

Table 6.3
Models of curriculum evaluation

Model	*Purpose*	*Focus*	*Timing*	*Methodology*
Objectives	Assessing achievement of objectives	Objectives and behavioural outcomes	Summative	Quantitative
Classical research	Measuring gains under controlled conditions	Initial state and outcomes	Pre-test and post-test	Quantitative
Illuminative	Description and understanding of a context-specific curriculum	Participants' and evaluators' perspectives on the curriculum and emerging key issues. The whole curriculum	Formative and summative	Qualitative
Countenance and portrayal	Reporting different perspectives on the curriculum	Participants' perspectives on the curriculum	Formative and summative	Quantitative and qualitative
Goal-free	Objective assessment of effectiveness of the curriculum	The observed curriculum	Formative and summative	Quantitative and qualitative
Decision-making	Curriculum decision-making	Contexts, inputs, processes	Initial appraisal, Formative and summative	Quantitative and qualitative

7

Recent Trends in the Elementary Curriculum Planning

To give an account of particular curriculum developments in elementary schools during the few decades is a comparatively difficult task—by comparison, that is, to that of giving a similar account of developments during the same period in the Secondary sector. There are several reasons for this and these are worth noting before we embark on this task.

This is, of course, partly a confirmation of the fact that changes that occur in Primary education do so in the setting of a separate tradition and one that we have endeavoured to show has been associated over a much longer period—in theory, if not always in practice—with a 'progressive' ideology and a consequent innovatory style. This is particularly true of the curriculum planned for the under-seven-year-olds in the Primary schools, for, as we showed earlier, in Nursery and Infant schools there has occurred, at least since the 1930s, a significant shift from the elementary school tradition with its preoccupation with the utilitarian functions of schooling to an informal, 'progressive' tradition which has sought to develop the capacities of every individual child in a more comprehensive way.

This tradition was well established at the start of the period that we are concerned with here and some of the schools for young children were, by 1960, regarded as providing an education that cam closest to the democratic ideal sought for throughout the public sector of schooling. Indeed, one observer at the time argued that 'in primary education a notable expansion of the curriculum is perhaps the century's major achievement' (Williams 1961, p. 165). Up to the publication of the Plowden Report in 1967 and largely as a result of the changing of the 11+ selection procedures in many local authorities, this tradition was also having an increasing impact on the organization, if not the curriculum, of the Junior departments of Primary schools.

It is not as easy to argue, therefore, that the major advances that have occurred have done so during the last twenty years. Nor is it true to say that these changes have been characterized solely by a response to the three main phases during this period which have shaped the preoccupations of those concerned with curriculum development generally—'the progressive movement' in the early 1960s, 'the curriculum development movement' in the mid-1960s and early 1970s and latterly 'the accountability movement' (Stenhouse 1980). This is not to say that these broad movements have been without their influence, and we hope to show in our later discussion how important they have been in influencing the curriculum of the Primary schools. It is to say, however, that to cite only these elements would be seriously to oversimplify developments in schools that have slowly evolved over a long period of time a distinctive approach to curriculum planning.

The three main movements identified by Stenhouse do not take account, for example, of a fourth influence, 'the child development movement', and we have argued throughout this book that this movement, certainly throughout the twentieth century, has been powerful in influencing any progress made in Primary education. It is important to note here that the 'curriculum development movement', whose relationship had hitherto been secondary to the 'child development movement', gradually became an integral part of that movement during the period that we are concerned to examine. Many of the advances in curriculum planning, therefore, have been either profoundly influenced by, or the direct result of, the work of developmental psychologists, as we hope to show when we examine particular examples.

This leads us to return again to a point made in our Introduction and that is that curriculum innovation was already a well-established concept in some Primary schools (usually in the Nursery-Infant departments) when national bodies such as the Schools Council were being established to create interest in curriculum development and to generate national projects. Indeed, some of the national curriculum movements of the past two decades have tended to constrain rather than advance the development of work with young children, again a point that we will explore more closely later.

Another factor worthy of note is that most of the teachers working in Primary schools during this period had undertaken a more extensive initial professional education than many of their colleagues in other sectors and, although it is true that many have had their 'progressive' ideas 'knocked out of them by experienced colleagues who practised the formal teaching inherited from the elementary schools' (Stenhouse 1980, p. 246), there has persisted throughout the past twenty years a strong nucleus of Primary teachers, headteachers and advisers, again particularly among those concerned with the education of younger children, who have continued to work within and to develop the 'progressive' tradition. In this sense, the initial professional education has had a more profound impact on teachers in Primary education than it has done elsewhere and the study of educational theory and practice has influenced and been influenced by many, if by no means all, teachers even after entry into the profession. In other words, a larger proportion of teachers in this area have shown an interest in the development of their professional expertise.

This receptivity to innovation is also partly due to the size of the institutions within which Primary teachers work. As the schools are physically smaller that Secondary schools, they offer a setting in which it is at least more possible to develop a coherent policy or approach to curriculum planning. It is certainly possible for a teacher to understand and come to know in detail the views, ideas and levels of competence of all his colleagues and in some instances—for example, in schools whose design is open—to be aware of the day-to-day work of colleagues, even if the teachers within a school choose not actually to teach as a team. In this way, professional accountability becomes easier if not inevitable.

Being smaller in scale, it is also possible for the school community to develop a more intimate and informal relationship with the local community and with parents who are themselves at their most responsive to the school when their children are young. It is, in other words, easier to blur the boundaries between the school and its outside community and it is also possible for non-professionals to observe or even participate in the school's work, so that accountability to those served becomes a more personal matter.

We are not suggesting that innovatory activities and open styles of accountability have consequently been widespread, for the natural conservatism of many teachers together with the profound influence of the other traditions—especially the elementary school tradition—have meant that curriculum change does not inevitably occur. Indeed, the small size of the institution can be as effective a factor in halting development as it can be in advancing it and this is particularly true when staffing becomes unduly static, as in the present situation.

It is, however, more possible for teachers in the Primary schools, in comparison to those working in other educational institutions, to be open and responsive to change and development, even in a climate of economic stringency. In reality, although the majority may limit their response to organizational rather than curricular changes (Richards 1980), the fact that non-streaming and vertical grouping has been introduced over a widespread area and into such a substantial proportion of Infant and Junior school classrooms—one of the findings of the HMI's survey (DES 1978)—is some indication that the teachers can have considerable force as agents of change, for there was no obvious external pressure on them in these instances to make these changes.

One further reason for the difficulty in pinpointing curriculum developments during the past two decades is worthy of note. Primary teachers have not been expected until very recently to respond to the same dramatic administrative and political demands that have been made of their Secondary colleagues. The comparatively rapid change to Comprehensive schools and the raising of the school-leaving age naturally placed issues related to the Secondary school curriculum in the limelight of national debate until the late 1970s. These two factors also attracted a large proportion of funding for both the Secondary schools themselves and for large-scale research projects aimed at the development of their curricula.

In retrospect, and in the light of the very political attention given to Primary education, it may be seen as fortunate for the Primary schools that they were, for a large part of this period, left to develop in their usual evolutionary manner. The dramatic changes made in the Secondary sector, however, did provide a stimulus for the discussions of the teachers working there and the theorists, advisers and others concerned to help them. As a result, much of the curriculum theory that was generated came from the practical problems of the Secondary schools. Primary teachers were not until recently required to face such urgent curriculum problems nor were they afforded help in articulating their view of curriculum. This, at least in part, may explain why their conception of the curriculum has remained implicit in their work for so long, has still not fully emerged and is therefore so difficult to delineate. It may also explain why they have been unduly influenced by solutions devised for Secondary schools (Blenkin 1980).

When we look at the Primary curriculum during the past twenty years, therefore, it is apparent that account must be taken of the complex and often subtle factors that are peculiar to this sector of schooling. These factors, we have attempted to show, must be considered in addition to the usual network of constraints and influences that form the more conventionally accepted context for curriculum planning.

It is the intention of this chapter, then, to describe some of the changes that have been proposed or implemented and to evaluate them both against this context and with reference to the framework offered in the preceding chapters. We have structured our discussion into three broad sections: firstly, the response to the move towards increased teacher-accountability, secondly, the influence of a perceived need for subject specialisms, and, thirdly, developments designed to promote attention to process in planning. It is obvious from our remarks above that there is considerable overlap between these three areas and we will note this where possible within the discussion. We will also attempt to show, when we examine particular examples of practice within these sections, that in some instances there are developments that run counter to the process model of planning that we have argued underlies the mainstream Primary approach, whilst in others there is evidence that this approach is being supported and, in some cases, considerably advanced.

The Response to Demands for Accountability

There is much to be said for the assertion that, when one is not formally answerable to others for one's actions, it becomes more likely that one will neglect making any evaluations of one's work (Harlen 1979). Whether this is true of teachers or not, this was certainly the claim that came to the fore in the national debates of 1976 in what must be the bleakest year for 'progressive' education in recent history. Primary teachers were criticized, in some cases hysterically and mostly unjustly, for neglecting to plan for and achieve a reasonable standard of performance in 'basic skills' for young children and it was also claimed that, in some cases, children suffered because their teachers were unclear about their aims. There was widespread pressure that teachers should be called to account.

As a result, it is often assumed that curriculum developments that have been designed to make teachers more accountable for their work have occurred in very recent years and have been produced hurriedly and in response to the demands made by central government on the local education authorities and on schools. To view the responses from the one perspective of national pressures, however, would be to oversimplify events and would not explain the variety of interpretations and materials that have been produced.

Admittedly, most of the work undertaken has been a result of pressures that are external to the profession. These have come from both the national and local government levels. As we noted already, however, there has also evolved a discernible move within the profession, at least since the Plowden Report was published, both to clarify the structure of work undertaken in informal education and to define a more positive role for the teacher in this setting. The main thrust of this work was to take the insecurity out of discovery methods, to ensure, in other words, the value of the work that is undertaken by children and to enable teachers to give an account of this.

The effects of demands for accountability, then, need to be examined in a variety of ways—the national response which is characterized largely by the recent work of Her Majesty's Inspectors and the policy documents from the DES, the local response which is expressed through curriculum policies adopted by the local education authorities and lastly the professional response—the research projects directed at helping teachers to structure, plan and evaluate their work with more clarity and understanding. We must note the influence that each of these has had. The most direct statements, however, have emerged from the Department of Education and Science and we will begin by briefly examining these documents and the view of the curriculum expressed within them.

Recent Publications from Central Government

The pressure from government for the involvement of others apart from teachers in the curriculum has been increasing throughout the past twenty years. There is a risk of oversimplifying occurrences but several incidents are worth noting in order to clarify why teacher-accountability came suddenly to the fore and urgent action in this sphere began to occur.

Firstly, government began to heed and even sympathize with lay opinion which has always been suspicious of informal, so-called 'permissive' movements in education. When the excesses of these were open to public scrutiny (as occurred as a result of the happenings at the William Tyndale Junior School, for example) the whole issue was open to public debate and, as was stated above, it became clear that there was a strong felling that teachers should be made to be more accountable. Secondly, the cost of education was rising, and a mood of dissatisfaction that is still with us developed, as it was generally felt that such an expensive system should yield better—or at least more tangible—results. Very little of direct benefit, for example, had been observed in the schools as a result of the expensive projects undertaken by the teacher-controlled Schools Council. The climate was right, therefore, for a more active intervention on the part of central government.

During this period also, two influencial publications—the Bullock Report on language and literacy (DES 1975) and Neville Bennett's Lancaster research study (Bennett 1976)—were given a great deal of attention by the press. The main recommendations of the Bullock Report were largely neglected by the media, but the publicity that it did receive highlighted the fact that the report advocated the monitoring of standards in literacy at Primary and Secondary levels. The members of the committee were in no doubt that 'standards should be monitored, and that this should be done on a scale which will allow confidence in the accuracy and value of the findings' (DES 1975, para. 3.26, p. 44). This was the first major statement to herald the government's intention to monitor standards.

At the same time, in his research into teaching styles and pupil progress, Neville Bennett was climing that formal teaching fulfils its aims in the academic area without detriment to the social and emotional development of pupils, whereas informal teaching only partially fulfils its aims in the latter area as well as engendering comparatively poorer outcomes in academic development (Bennett 1976), a claim which seemed to offer proof to and to strengthen the case of those who maintained that 'progressive' education was ineffective and had undermined the performance of pupils in schools.

These influences and moods were not without effect on policies being made at local and national level by politicians and administrators and a series of publications began to spell out the government's intention to increase the control over the curriculum.

As a cumulative expression of these policies, the government's Green Paper, *Education in Schools,* marked the beginning of a concern to assess more carefully the work of the schools. Whilst rejecting rigid and uniform national tests of children's performance, it advocated that diagnostic testing should be more widely used in schools and by local authorities, to produce greater consistency of practice and greater accountability. Its main recommendations for Primary schools included that

> (i) in all schools teachers need to be quite clear about the ways in which children make and show progress in the various aspects of their learning...
>
> (ii) teachers should be able to identify with some precision the levels of achievement represented by a pupil's work (DES 1977, p. 8).

It was also argued that the child-centred approach had become widespread in schools (a statement that was to be refuted by the ensuing national survey). It had 'proved to be a trap for less able or less experienced teachers and in some cases the use of the child-centred approach has deteriorated into lack of order and application' (DES 1977, p. 8).

In addition, therefore, it was felt that 'a core of learning' or 'a protected area of the curriculum' should be established throughout England and Wales and that literacy and numeracy should form the most important part of this core for these were skills 'for which the primary schools have a central, and indeed over-riding, responsibility' (DES 1977, p. 9).

To ensure that standards were maintained in this 'protected area', the Assessment of Performance Unit (APU) had been established in 1975 by the Department of Education and Science and three national research projects had been funded—one to investigate record-keeping in the Primary school, another to explore assessment techniques in the Nursery school and the third to help to provide local education authorities and schools with tests in mathematics and language so that they could test their pupils' performance against APU norms should they choose to do so (NFER 1978). In addition it was announced that the DES intended to review the curricular arrangements made by l.e.a.s as a preliminary to defining a new national framework for the curriculum. The details of this review were set out in Circular 14/77 and the aspects that were most relevant to the Primary schools were two requests—to report on aims and to examine and report on record-keeping systems.

The mood of the government's publication, the concern that it expressed for measurable standards of pupil attainment and the ensuing actions that were taken by the DES all indicated a belief 'not so much that teachers cannot be left to choose the right sorts of activity for their pupils as that they cannot be trusted to ensure that sufficiently high standards are attained unless there is some kind of outside supervision' (Kelly 1977, p. 167). This, then, was the first major document to place the curriculum of the schools at the centre of the national concern.

The second was to express a somewhat different mood. *Primary Education in England: a survey by H.M. Inspectors of Schools* (DES 1978) appeared with much less dramatic publicity. This was the report of the work which had been undertaken nationally and in accordance with the inspectors' 'long tradition of observing children at work and forming views on the quality and appropriateness of what they do in school' (Thomas 1980, p. 75).

The survey was concerned with the work of 7-, 9- and 11-year-olds in 542 schools chosen at random to be representative of Primary schools in England. Part of this work was observed at first hand, part was the result of discussion with teachers and headteachers about their planning and record-keeping and part was based on the results of tests in reading and mathematics which had been administered to a subsample of 9- and 11-year-olds in the case of reading, and a subsample of 11-year-olds in the case of mathematics.

The survey offered no evidence to support the view that standards of attainment of pupils in schools were falling. Indeed the results of the reading tests, which it was possible to compare with three earlier NFER surveys (NFER 1955, 1960, 1970), indicated a steady improvement in this sphere. Nor did it offer evidence either that child-centred education was widespread or that the Primary curriculum was usually approached in a 'progressive' or unified way. The practice revealed in the survey was somewhat unimaginative and indicated that the majority of schools planned 'scarcely more than a revamped elementary school curriculum with the same major utilitarian emphases' (Richards 1980, p. 78).

The findings of the HMI's survey largely contradicted the claims that had been made in the Green Paper about the curriculum of the schools and, the inspectors expressed concern not about the neglect of basic skills-teaching but about the fact that the teachers in the top Infant and Junior classes that were observed were, in practice, still too preoccupied with the narrow conception of curriculum inherited from the elementary tradition and were therefore predominantly emphasizing the utilitarian rather than educational functions of schooling. The idea that progressivism was widespread was a widely believed myth not borne out—at least in the Junior departments of Primary schools—by the evidence of this survey (Richards 1980).

The inspectors reported that the teaching of the 'basic skills' dominated the work of many of the schools and they argued that this was often at the expense of provision for a sufficiently wide experience for some children. The consequence was claimed to be, for example, an absence of science teaching in 80% of the classes and they commented on the facts that insufficient attention was afforded to the development of historical and geographical understanding and that craft was making a smaller contribution to the work than was desirable.

On the basis of their findings, they could not support the view that a narrow concentration on 'basic skills' would produce higher levels of performance. They reported that 'the basic skills are more successfully learnt when applied to other subjects and children in the classes which covered full range of the widely taught items did better on the NFER tests at 9 and 11 years of age; also, for all three age groups the work of children in these classes was better matched to their abilities than was the work of children in other classes...there is no evidence in the survey to suggest that a narrower curriculum enabled children to do better in the basic skills or led to work being more aptly chosen to suit the capacities of the children' (DES 1978, p. 124).

Although they expressed support for interest-based work, they criticized topic work that was self-contained and did not include sufficient opportunities for the children to make use of and develop skills and concepts. They also identified the above-average child as the one least likely to be catered for adequately in the Primary schools and suggested that Primary teachers should develop specialist abilities (notably in science) so that the able child could be challenged.

As we have noted before, the survey is an odd mixture of views and recommendations on how the Primary curriculum should develop. On the one hand it is supportive of a flexible, unified approach to planning, where children are encouraged to learn to develop skills and concepts in a variety of situations and by pursuing inquiries; and its findings also support this view. On the other hand, concern is expressed that subjects such as science, history and geography are not adequately covered. They advise that teachers should develop more expertise in knowledge areas and schools should employ subject specialists to take the lead here. It is unclear, when they talk both of subject specialists and of conceptual understanding that goes beyond the content of work, whether the inspectors are promoting a process or product view of the curriculum in their report.

Its findings, as far as the realities of curriculum development are concerned, are also mixed, for, although they refute the wild claims that standards have dropped, they also show that most teachers are still content to plan for and emphasize the utilitarian aspects of schooling. Whether the findings would have been different if the survey had covered predominantly Nursery and Infant classes, the supposed strongholds of progressivism, where the teachers might be expected to have a deeper understanding of the implementation of a unified curriculum, can only be surmised. Their recommendations, which are contradictory and muddled in parts, are however more in line with the 'progressive' than the elementary school tradition, not least because their findings suggested that this may lead to a more raid rise in standards of attainment.

The direction that they envisage should be taken in planning the Primary curriculum is more clearly and succinctly expressed by HM Inspectors in the next document that we must consider.

Having received and reported on the reviews of local authority arrangements for the curriculum, the DES still sought to give a lead in the process of reaching a national consensus on a desirable framework for the curriculum. As a first step towards the achievement of this, therefore, the views of the inspectors were invited and these were set out in *A View of the Curriculum* (DES 1980a), which is perhaps the most sensible and thoughtful of all these recent government publications.

In their discussion of the Primary curriculum the inspectors indicate that, in their view, there are common purposes that can be expressed at a general level and can be seen to be appropriate for every school. They are in favour, however, of schools and classes within schools interpreting these in a highly individual way and they see good reasons why this should be so. They note in particular that the children will bring to the school different experiences, teachers will vary in their interests and competencies and schools may have access to very different resources.

In general they favour the maintenance of 'a wide curriculum', that is, one that is not predominantly concerned with the 3 Rs, for they argue that children achieve a better level of performance in the basic skills if they have many opportunities to use them in a broader context.

The only two areas where weaknesses are noted are 'the provision of observational and experimental science that is seriously lacking in many primary schools' (DES 1980a, p. 11) and the teaching of French which is usually attempted inappropriately. In general, however, they feel that effort should now be directed towards helping teachers to develop to a greater extent the important skills and processes that the children are already engaged in learning. They argue that 'more extensive discussion is required on the levels to which work could and should be taken, at least for some children, in the various parts of the curriculum; for example, the identification of the skills and ideas associated with history and geography that are suitable for primary school children....Working parties of teachers, LEA advisers, inspectors and others have already shown what useful guidelines can be produced' (ibid.).

This seems to indicate that they are concerned with processes—in their terms 'necessary skills or underlying ideas'—rather than describing the 'protected areas' in terms of content. They argue, for example, that 'as children make progress their interests diversity and what is a stimulus to one may be a barrier to another. If the necessary skill or the underlying idea can be presented as well in one way as another then it may create unnecessary difficulties to use the same way with all children' (op. cit., p. 8).

In summary, two kinds of thinking seems to be emerging from central government and to be finding expression in government documents. First there is the viewpoint of the HMIs which urges that ways should be found to develop the existing curriculum by helping teachers both to frame essential processes more carefully and depend their understanding of the skills and concepts that children should be developing in schools. Although confused in parts, the substance of their views focuses on the processes of education and their view of how learning should take place is that it should be essentially unified. One means of achieving this development, they argue, is through discussions of school policy at the local or even school level: discussions which aim to deepen every teacher's understanding. Another mans is to develop a clearer picture of what these processes are and how they can best be learned in a meaningful way by children in schools.

Secondly, there is the view of the curriculum that is being promoted directly from the politicians at the DES. Although there has been a change of government since the Green Paper of 1977, the same desires as far as curriculum is concerned are being expressed, coloured largely by the wish for teacher-accountability and general agreement on a common core of subjects and skills to be taught in all schools.

The most recent expression of their views is found in the consultative document *A Framework for the School Curriculum* (DES 1980b) and here the Secretaries of State detail the form, as they see it, that the curriculum should take. This form is largely defined in terms of content and we are returned to the familiar themes of the political debates of 1976. They see planning as dependent on a clear statement of aims which will translate into achievable objectives. They attach importance to assessment procedures combined with I.e.a record-keeping systems designed to check the achievement of these objectives. They urge the inclusion of 'common elements'—notably English, mathematics and science—which should form a substantial part of every school's work. The emphasis is on the products of education and on clearer means of measuring achievement, particularly in certain skills and knowledge areas.

Unlike the HMIs, the Secretaries of State place emphasis on the work of the local education authorities rather than that of the schools and the teachers. They argue that l.e.a.s are responsible for developing curriculum policies and in addition they are responsible for ensuring that their schools are achieving the aims that the teachers claim to be pursuing. They argue, therefore, that 'authorities should collect information annually from their schools about the curriculum offered, together with school assessments of the extent to which the curriculum matches school aims and objectives' (*op. cit.*, p. 4). They are, in other words, promoting an objective rather than a process model of curriculum.

However confused and confusing these recent publications from central government may be, it is certainly true that, until the DES became actively involved, moves to help teachers to evaluate their work were making slow progress and were having little impact on the schools. It is to a consideration of the impact of demands for accountability on this sphere of work that we must now turn. We will do this by considering first the attempts to monitor nationally the achievements of the schools.

The Monitoring of Standards

The main thrust of central governments's concern has been towards finding means of ensuring that standards of pupil performance are maintained in the schools and, if possible, improved. As we noted earlier, the first widely publicized discussion of how this could be achieved on a national scale appears in the Bullock Report (DES 1975), which addresses itself to standards of literacy.

The members of the committee discuss the fact that a good deal of public attention is given to this area of the school's work and that disquiet has been expressed at the supposed fall of standards. They also show that on the existing evidence, national sample surveys carried out by the NFER (NFER 1955, 1960, 1970), reading standards have improved, although gains tended to level out over the decade 1960-1970. They argue that, although the results from surveys are not disturbing, they leave no room for complacency. In addition, they argue that both the tests and methods employed for measuring the movement in reading standards are inadequate. They strongly recommend, therefore, that a new system of monitoring these standards should be devised and introduced.

In their discussion of the form that monitoring should take, one important point emerges and this is that the scope of assessment should be extended to encompass a more demanding definition of literacy than simple reading performance. They argue, for example, that 'the existing criterion is determined by the reading standards of seven and nine year old children of many years ago on tests whose limitations are acknowledged. It should be replaced by a criterion capable of showing whether the reading and writing abilities of children are adequate to the demands made upon them in school and likely to face them in adult life. What we are proposing, then, is an entirely new approach. We are suggesting that monitoring should be extended beyond the limit of a single dimension to give more information than has ever been available before' (DES 1975, p. 36). They go on to suggest that 'adequate research and development work should precede the introduction of such a system of monitoring' (DES 1975, p. 43).

These ideas of monitoring, discussed here in relation to literacy, are fundamental to the work of the Assessment of Performance Unit (APU) which was established in 1975 within the DES to provide information about general levels of performance of children at school. Although standards in literacy are one component of the work of the unit, its scope extends to cover most aspects of the school curriculum. Each team is investigating means of testing that will give a broader indication of achievement than is possible when only one type of test is used.

It should be noted, however, that the teams concerned to investigate mathematical and scientific understanding are far in advance of other teams in producing and implementing assessment procedures. Indeed, some areas seem to be presenting particularly difficult problems. In a recent paper prepared for the exploratory group on aesthetic development, for example, it is noted that 'many people experienced in this field are convinced that no comprehensive or adequate conceptual model for aesthetic experience yet exists. Nor has any real insight been gained into aesthetic development during childhood and adolescence. Nothing, for instance, exists in the field to compare with Piaget's work on conceptual development.' The paper goes on to argue, however, that 'the whole assessment exercise might, in drawing attention to the need for serious research in this area, prompt new initiatives.'

This problem of devising tests for the more elusive (and some would argue more important) aspects of development also occurs in other areas. The team concerned with science, for example, faces similar difficulties. As one observer argues, 'the science skills which are definable and the outcomes which are precisely measurable will, I expect, be tested well in national monitoring. Only a limited attempt is being made to test the less easily definable skills like creative thinking and imaginative reasoning and their less reliably measurable outcomes' (Brown 1980, p. 79). The science team have, however, gone ahead with the sample testing despite this inevitable bias in their tests.

During the first five years of its existence only one team has both completed a survey and published the report, although others will soon follow. This first report—*Mathematical development. Primary survey report No. 1* (DES 1980c)—covers the survey in 1978 of the performance in mathematic of a representative sample of about 13,000 11-year-olds attending schools in England and Wales. The majority of children took printed tests which required written answers but one subsample of about 1,000 pupils took a practical test, whilst a second subsample of about 1,500 completed questionnaires on their attitudes to mathematics.

In the summary report of this survey it is made clear that the intention of the APU is not to make judgements about or directly influence the curriculum within individual schools or local education authorities. The survey is intended as a 'first step in constructing a picture of children's performance in all aspects of the mathematics curriculum across its range of content, activity and difficulty....Future surveys at both 11-plus and 15-plus will add to the knowledge already gained, and the main value of the APU's assessment programme will, it is hoped, be in the picture of performance which will be built up from a regular series of surveys and reports over the years' (DES 1980d, p. 7). Thus it is clear that the intention is to remain neutral and simply to present facts and therefore the findings of the survey are relevant only when future surveys have been conducted whose findings will serve as a comparison.

The problems with this attempt at neutrality are, however, obvious. Judgements, after all, have been made in order to select the kinds of test to be administered and the very decision that the outcomes of schooling are to be assessed only through pupils' performances implies that certain non-neutral decisions about the validity of this have been taken.

There are further problems with presenting these facts in such a way that they will be professionally useful. The unit was established, after all, to provide government departments with information on performance which would both form a basis for future decisions and provide a measure of accountability for the public. Although in addition, it is argued, the findings will offer useful information for l.e.a.s and teachers, this was not the main intention. Indeed, the very word 'monitoring'—chosen to imply mere information-gathering rather than evaluation—can itself denote that the information is to serve as a warning or at least as a means of strengthening the position of the government (Harlen 1979).

As Brown points out, therefore, one central curriculum issue raised by the existence of APU monitoring is 'the intended or unintended influences on the curriculum of schools' (Brown 1980, p. 80). He shows that already one textbook has been published which claims to help pupils study the science processes which are to be tested by the APU and the claims to have gathered anecdotal evidence that suggests that some l.e.a. advisers are pointing out to their teachers that certain concepts must be taught as these are the ones that will be tested. It is this 'backwash effect', as he calls it, that may increase to such an extent (especially if commercial tests are spawned in the wake of national monitoring) that the impact may have serious effects on the school curriculum.

The influences of the work of the APU, then, remain something of an enigma, for, on the one hand, it seems to be inevitable that a bureaucratic form of accountability is being promoted with this emphasis on national monitoring of standards. On the other hand, the teams working within the unit are taking pains to find ways of measuring processes rather than adopting a narrow view of facts and skills.

It is possible, however, to be more certain of the effects of demands for accountability on the curriculum by examining developments in teachers' record-keeping systems and it is to this that we now turn.

Record-keeping and Assessment

Although formal examinations are largely absent from the Primary schools since the majority are no longer involved in the 11+ examination procedures, there are of course still internal assessments which children undergo before transferring to the Secondary schools. These are mainly tests to assess levels of performance in language and reasoning and are intended to provide the objective evidence which will partly support the appropriate choice of school, although they are not intended to be the sole instrument for making that choice. Similarly, it is common practice to give children standardized tests at the age of seven years in order to assess their reading ages before they transfer from the Infant to the Junior departments of the Primary schools. In addition, a small minority of disturbed or slow-learning children may undergo diagnostic tests under the supervision of the educational psychologist, in order to aid decisions on appropriate action in relation to special education.

Apart from these examples, however, it is unusual to find either standardized tests or external examinations playing a significant part in the work of the schools. This is one important reason why the keeping of records—including the formal procedures required by the l.e.a.s.—holds a particularly vital place in the work of the Primary teacher, since these are the only records of a child's attainments.

The formal records are designed largely to indicate the performance (mainly in reading and mathematics) of the child and also to give, however crudely, a profile of his personality and aptitude for work. These records are required, in other words, to be used at terminal points in the child's school career—at the end of a year or on transfer to a new teacher or school, for example.

There are other forms of records that are also used commonly and may be required of the teacher formally (by the headteacher or even the l.e.a). These are the records of the teacher's planning and his evaluations of the work that has been undertaken with the children.

It is these two kinds of formal record-keeping system that have come to the fore as a result of the pressures for teacher-accountability. It is a clear that the teacher's records—whether they indicate the individual child's achievements or present an evaluation of the teacher's work—are the most direct means of checking on the success or otherwise of the teacher's work. Much of the recent work in this sphere, therefore, has been the result of l.e.a. revisions of these formal records, revisions that reflect their response to the requests for information from the DES.

Local authorities have begun to strengthen and extend their requirements of teachers with regard to the keeping of records and the local advisers have begun to adopt a more active supervisory role in order to ensure that the schools carry out these requirements. With such a flurry of activity from their employers, which has clearly been designed to measure their effectiveness, it is hardly surprising that teachers should be apparently eager to adopt approaches that promise clear indication of progress on the part of pupils. In a situation that demands proof of achievements, teachers can perhaps be forgiven for choosing to ignore whether or not the tangible results are educational in nature.

What is apparent, however, is that the local authority inspectors, who had the opportunity of ensuring that the schools received the best advice available in relation to the keeping of records (a supportive process considered crucial by Plowden), seemed themselves in many instances to be promoting planning styles which were instrumental and out of step with the more advanced educational work that had been developed in some schools. This was reflected in the record sheets produced by the l.e.a.s which tended to be simplistic and gave teachers little scope to indicate the broader aspects of the work that children undertook. The elements that were considered worth recording were narrow and easily assessed and the teacher's attention was directed at the child's achievements rather than emerging processes.

The main line of argument and action of the I.e.a.s hinged on the belief that, if aims could be expressed with clarity and where possible in operational terms, then it would be a simple matter to achieve them. This was certainly an argument expressed in the documents discussed above. It was also an idea that was central to the only large-scale national project that had been concerned with offering teachers a framework for recording in detail the work of the school.

This was the Schools Council's project Aims of Primary Education, whose work we have repeatedly noted. It is now worth examining this work in more detail for two main reason. Firstly, it provides us with an example of work undertaken which typifies the response to the criticism made of Plowden. For the intention is to place the teacher's planning on a more systematic footing. Secondly, it was one of the few pieces of work available from Primary education in the sphere of curriculum planning when the events of the late 1970s heralded a national interest in accountability. Although, like other national projects, it had little direct impact on the teachers in the schools, it did offer the local authorities a model for resolving their urgent problem and its influence can be traced, therefore, through the activities of the advisers in l.e.a.s.

The project team undertook this work in three main phases—they attempted firstly to clarify the constraints on teacher's planning, secondly, to survey the opinions of school teachers in order to help them to clarify what their aims were and, thirdly, to provide the teachers with a model in order to aid them in translating their aims into practice.

It should be noted that, contrary to the claims in Plowden that good teachers were unable to make explicit their aims, the survey found no such difficulty, and listed 2000 aims, collected from teachers in the full Primary range. Admittedly these were uneven in their levels of abstraction, and many would be better described as objectives. It was discovered, for example, that, in the teachers' minds, 'the child should be developing community responsibility is ranged alongside the child should be able to write legibly....In terms of curriculum theory, there is an inadmissible mixture of aims and objectives. But in the teachers' terms there is an equivalence of importance, of concern to them in their work with children' (Ashton, Kneen and Davies 1975, p. 4).

It should also be noted that 'surveys of teachers' opinions on aims may have their uses, but they cannot settle what those aims ought to be (Dearden 1976, p. 29). The Schools Council survey did not set out to do this, but did suggest that it would be useful for much work to be done in this sphere. What the research team did attempt to do (and this element of their work has been one source of influence in subsequent work on assessment, evaluation and accountability) was to help teachers both to formulate their aims and, more significantly, to translate them into practice.

The project team has produced, as part of its material, a guide to assist teachers in this task. The practice of formulating aims is justified by claiming that aims clarify thinking about education, they give a sense of direction, they clarify the implications of apparent incompatibilities in the work undertaken, they clarify in the teacher's mind his own commitment, they enable the best use to be made of limited resources, they aid the selection of the best methods and resources and, finally, they aid evaluation. What strikes one immediately when reading the justification of stating aims in this project is that there is a marked similarity between these justifications and those of Hilda Taba (Taba 1962). Although, as was noted above, the work of the project was not intended to be prescriptive, there is a strong flavour of a behavioural approach in the translation of aims into achievable objectives. In the examples of this approach to planning which were produced by teachers as a result of discussions with members of the team, it is clear that a more formal method is adopted in planning for the older children. For even the Infant age-groups, however, the immediate objective is also behavioural and the intention is to look for the end-product, although the method and grouping to be adopted are both expressed in more informal terms.

In all the examples given, planning is linked to one of the schedules or spheres that we noted already, and is then detailed sequentially under seven headings:

1. Assessment
2. Aims (broken into three levels of specificity)
3. Content
4. Teaching method
5. Time allocation
6. Organization (of materials and classroom)
7. Organization of the children (by age, ability and number)

(Ashton, Kneen and Davies 1975).

Most of the examples of planned work that are given are designed for the development of mathematical learning, but the strategy that is advocated by the project team for the translation of aims into practice (which is as unwieldy as many of the similar strategies attempted in America) is intended to be applied to all aspects of curriculum planning though it is admitted that 'when it came to qualities, the kinds of feelings and attitudes and dispositions that the child should have, the task was infinitely more problematic' (Ashton, Kneen and Davies 1975, p. 5).

The project team does, however, come out in strong support of the behavioural objectives approach. They argue, as we saw, that 'if the teacher's aims are to help to guide his practice, then they should be expressed in behavioural terms. That is to say that they should state what the child will actually be able to do when the aim is achieved....on, also helps the teacher by preventing the intrusion of method into the statement of aims' (Ashton, Kneen and Davies, 1975, p. 15).

In the light of the objections to the behavioural objectives approach, it is worrying to discover that a recent major project, which set out to investigate how aims should be translated into practice in the Primary school, strongly advocates an instrumental approach to curriculum planning. Even more worrying is the fact that the approach was adopted, apparently uncritically, by those responsible for developing effective record-keeping systems for use in the schools. The attraction of the objectives approach is that it ensures that tangible results are achieved and can be measured. Indeed, it is largely for this reason that many of the record sheets produced by advisers and inspectors at the local level imply the use of an objectives approach. A number of contributions to record-keeping at a national level also have adopted, perhaps unintentionally or even inadvertently, the same approach, and it is to a consideration of these that we now turn.

In the NFER research project Record-Keeping in the Primary School, for example, the discussion documents provided for teachers recommend 'a need for aims and objectives' if work is to be assessed effectively. Teachers are advised to consider elements such as,

a Analysis of aims into more specific objectives which can be used as a basis for record-keeping.

b What aspects of behaviour, (cognitive, affective and psychomotor) need to be recorded, i.e., What significant events? (NFER 1977).

This team's approach to the problem is also clearly based on a behavioural objectives model. In fact their analysis is more directly derivative of Bloom's taxonomy than is that of the Aims of Primary Education project described above.

It is interesting to contrast this example with the extreme caution expressed in the Introduction to the parallel work on assessment in Nursery education, for here the stated intention is to serve the needs of teachers not to impose external standards on them. Teachers are warned, therefore, that the assessment procedures produced by this team 'have been designed as a resource to be used not a target at which to aim. It is a recognized danger that assessment instead of producing useful information about children's development and performance may come to determine what is taught' (Bate and Smith 1978, p. 8). It is clear that, although both teams were working to produce materials for assessment, the materials produced for the youngest children were presented with more caution and attempted to support the developmental tradition which, it can be argued, is stronger in the Nursery schools.

It is as well to be reminded again, however, that the work has been undertaken in a climate of economic stringency, when considerable public pressure has been placed on teachers to make themselves accountable for their work with children, and to try to ensure value for money. It is, therefore, understandable that they should seek security in an apparently systematic approach which stresses measurable end-products. When they are presented with a large collection of tasks for children to use and a record sheet designed to record the performances on the tasks, as is the case in the Assessment in Nursery Education project mentioned above, it is difficult to envisage how teachers can avoid the urge to teach for performance.

One further point needs to be added and this is the fact that the most difficult elements of the child's development to assess—his feelings, attitudes and aesthetic awareness—are aside in each of the examples that we have examined so far. We noted the comments made by the team involved in the Schools Council's Aims in Primary Education project. The NFER team argue that 'the possibility of assessing aesthetics was considered but deemed to be almost unassessable at nursery age. It was thought undesirable that teachers should make value judgements of children's aesthetic sense' (Bate and Smith 1978, p. 170). The implication is that the judgements made in other areas (social skills, for example) can be objective and thus are desirable.

A further cautionary note needs to be sounded here, then, for past experience suggests that, if teachers are given means of assessing pupil performance in certain cases only, they tend to focus on these areas or even elevate them above the activities that they are not given assessment procedures for.

It can be argued, then, that, as teachers are pressured into accountability by local and central government, there is 'a return to simple objectives, a reduced "say" for both teachers and pupils in determining the content of their work, a move away from "democratic' towards "autocratic" and "bureaucratic" styles of evaluation and a resultant slowing down or even arresting of the pace of curriculum development' (Kelly 1977, p. 180).

Some of these effects have certainly been noted in the projects discussed above and in the formal records produced by the l.e.a.s., for what they are doing is to advocate that teachers' aims should be translated into behavioural objectives if they are to be of use in practice. It is in the process of doing this that teachers are being misled into a distortion of their aims through the unwitting acceptance of an unsuitable curriculum model.

It certainly seems to be the case that teachers are being encouraged to consider a particular approach which runs counter to the ideology that has in many cases shaped their practice. In adopting the instrumental approach, apparently without considering its serious limitations, they are setting aside, first of all, the strengths of the child-centred ideology—

in Dearden's terms 'the relational aims'—rather than using these aims to advantage and, in addition, developing from them the unified approach. In doing so, they are losing the strengths of the informal approach to education, and adopting instead an approach which restricts the freedom of both the child and the teacher. At the very least, there is an unresolved tension and a fundamental contradiction between this newly adopted behavioural objectives approach and the mainstream ideology of the Primary school.

Before leaving this discussion of teachers' however, we must note that not all of the recent developments have been within an objectives model of planning. There is evidence that the teachers themselves have gone some way towards resolving the complex problem of recording both their own planning and the children's development within the informal, unified approach that we described in earlier chapters, as the examples given here illustrate.

We have included two examples from one teacher's records to indicate how she has devised means of recording both her own planning and the individual child's progress. It can be seen that this teacher's solution avoids the detrimental effects of the objectives approach by adopting a more tentative approach to forward planning.

It is also worth noting several other features that emerge from these examples. Firstly, they are both examples of work developed from an interest initiated by an individual child. Secondly, it is clear how one of these interests was developed in such a way as to involve the whole class. Thirdly, there is much to be learnt from both examples about the extent to which, as well as the means by which, such interests can be developed. And lastly, it is clear that, in order to promote these developments, the teacher needs to be accustomed to observing and studying children and to be skilled at choosing appropriate points of intervention, so that the resultant work is a judicious amalgam of the pupil's own initiatives and the guidance of the teacher. In short, these are good illustrations

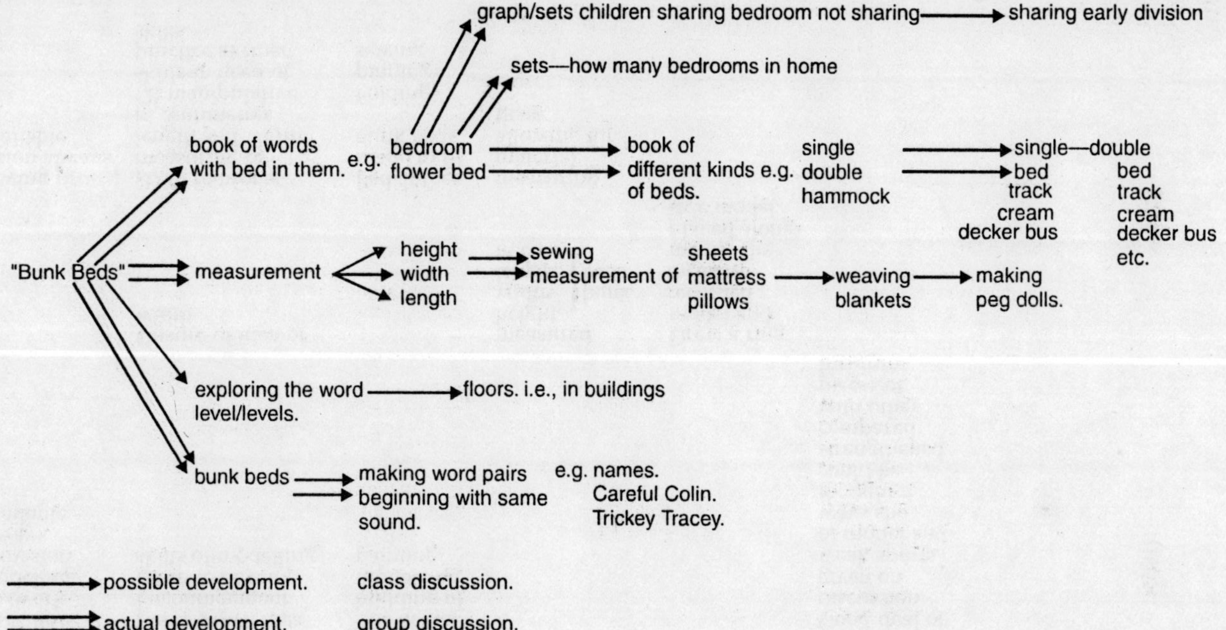

Fig. 7.1: Flow-plan of the development of an interest initiated by two six-year-old girls whilst at boxwork modelling resource area. (M. Bierley)

Kerry. 6 yrs.			Numeracy		Literacy		
Topic and Provision	Reason for Child's Involvement	Practical Activities	Practical and Language	Recorded	Language and discussion	Reading	Written
Bunk Beds Boxwork modelling provision always available.	Kerry's own idea Encouragement given to develop skills of modelling	The actual building of model and painting.			Good deal of discussion given on weak sports of model and ways she thought it could be strengthened compared with other pieces of furniture.		
	Unsure of idea of width		measured height, width, length } bunk beds in cms.	Drew a ring model and recorded measure-ments. Dis-played along-side model.			
Sewing pro-vision always available.	(1) to reinforce measuring of length and width in centimetres. (2) manipulative skills-in need of practice at finer skills.	Bedclothes made to fit bunk beds. Folding-pinning-sewing.	measuring material allowing for them.				

Book made for dictionary of 'bed' words.	To extend language and understanding of building up of words. e.g., bed time—bedtime	Illustrating each word.			Class discussion found 15 words with bed in them.	Used as a resource book for further written work.	Wrote a definition for each word.
Bunk beds.	Kerry is confident with initial sounds, but needs further experience of initial consonant blends.	Each child drew a picture of him/herself and Kerry and other children give labels. e.g. Careful Colin, Trickey Tracey.					Recorded in book in alphabetical order.
Provided cream cartons clothing model railway track model buses.	Understood meaning of single and double bed wanted to extend understanding of single/double in other everyday situations.	Large display board-2 sets children sorted the sets.			Discussion of how meaning of double changes, e.g., cream.		Book made of words meaning two
Class discussion of number of bedrooms in each home.	More experiences of comparative number in set work.		Most least fewer more etc.	Drew sets and wrote information from comparison.			
Class discussion on sharing a room.	Introducing the notion of sharing in mathematical terms.		Sharing objects between 2, 3, 4, 5 people.				

Fig. 7.2: Teacher's record of the work done by one child in the pursuit of this interest. (M. Bierley).

of the approach to education we have endeavoured to outline in our earlier chapters. Finally, to return to the particular issue of record-keeping, it is clear that the teacher keeps a careful note of the pupils' reasons for involvement in a particular area of interest as well as the progress that they make as a result of that involvement in those processes she considers to be important.

Some attempt has been mad by l.e.a.s to extend this school-based approach to record-keeping. This is usually done by offering discussion documents or guidelines so that the staff of a school can developed records of observations to include examples of the child's achievements in addition to his 'experience' in certain areas. It is stated, for example, by one group of mathematics inspectors that 'an item by item assessment is of immediate value to the class teacher in maintaining success for each child. A record of specific achievements, rather than experiences, is also of long term value' (ILEA 1978, p. 1). They go on to argue that records of this kind are more useful as they can be passed on to other teachers, can be used as diagnostic checks when little is known of a child's abilities and can provide a basis for comparing a child's ability with others for grouping purposes.

Schemes of this kind which give focus to school-based discussions are generally to be applauded as they avoid prescription from outside and place stress on support for the teacher, who, in the end, is the one to make the decisions. One major difficulty with such schemes, however, is that, although teachers are not provided with externally devised test items of the kind produced by the NFER team that were concerned with assessment, the guidelines that are offered are based on a confusing mixture of approaches which, at least partly, includes the objectives model.

The inspectors mentioned above, for example, begin by stressing that achievements should be looked for within the normal classroom activities and only exceptionally in specially devised test situations. They also argue that

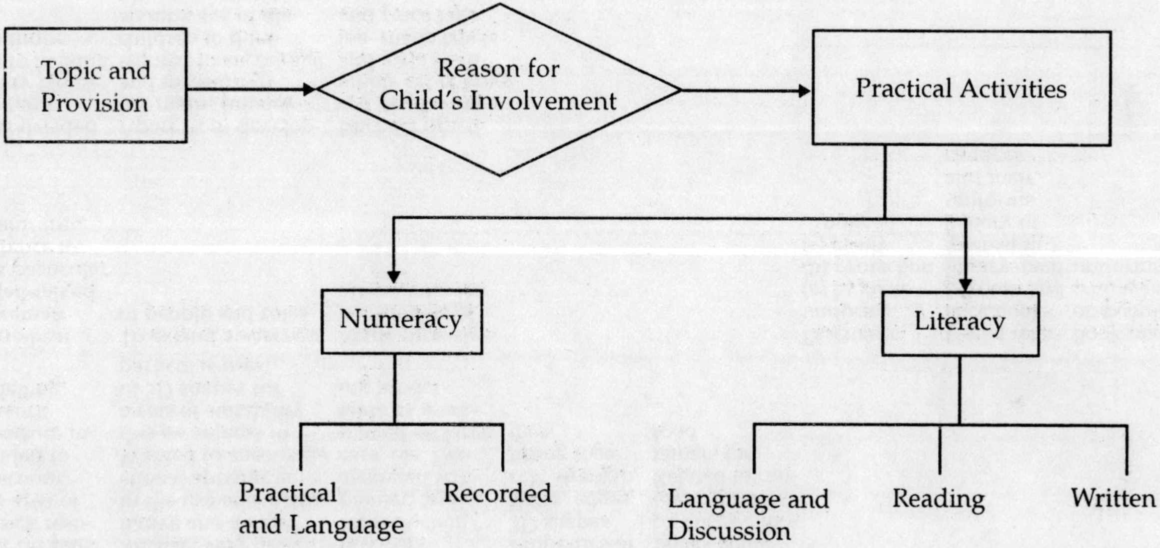

Topic and Provision

Reason for Child's Involvement

Practical Activities

Numeracy

Literacy

Practical and Language

Recorded

Language and Discussion

Reading

Written

Fig. 7.3: Flow-plan of an interest developed for the whole class.

Michael. 6 yrs.			Numeracy		Literacy		
Topic and Provision	*Reason for Child's Involvement*	*Practical Activities*	*Practical and Language*	*Recorded*	*Language and Discussion*	*Reading*	*Written*
Built car park in brick resource area of classroom. Decided to reproduce in boxwork modelling.	Michael very imaginative and aware in the use of constructional apparatus. Wanted to encourage this awareness in terms of suitability of 3D shapes for particular uses.	Boxwork reproduction/ painted and arranged with cars, etc. Displayed on large table as working model.	Properties of 3D shapes. Faces, edges, roll, strength, fitting together.	Books made on cubes cuboides cylinders. Related to containers for food.			
Home-beat policeman visited-talked with particular reference to his uniform.	To extend awareness of people and roles.	Made pipe-cleaner models of attendents, etc.			Discussion uniforms (a) hygiene (b) protection (c) easily noticed	Use of reference books in room and library–own interest in history of uniforms and their changes.	Book made on people who wear uniforms.
Class decided to extend Wendy House area to include a boutique.	Apart from developing maths (money and measuring) wanted to encourage children to think about ways of displaying materials and importance of colour.	Michael practised displaying a whole set of boys and girls clothing–made labels and price tags.					

Boutique set up.	To give him practice in measuring in standards units.		Measurement of head chest waist hips legs feet. Discussion on difference of unit of measure for different items.	Written down in book in shop. Each childs measurements were recorded.	*In dramatic play* encouraging models of language of salesman/girl. Models of:- description persuasion assurance.	Written account of 'If I had £100 to spend'
	To give experiences in adding bills and giving change.	Shop assistant serving.	Counting on to £1 in giving change. Additional help given working in bonds of 10 20 50 100	Each purchase itemised and bill added up. Change to a £1 (all items under a £1)		

Tabulation of one child's involvement in what was eventually a class interest.

Fig. 7.4: Teacher's record of the work done by one child in the pursuit of this interest. (M. Bierley)

conceptual development is a gradual process based on many experiences. They draw attention to the fact that too much stress is placed by teachers on facts and skills and that when these are learned in isolation from understanding they tend not to be applied by the child to new problems. They then go on, however, to arrange their checkpoints into objectives to be achieved. The achievements to be looked for are grouped within one of four areas—the development of underlying concepts, knowledge of facts, performance of skills and application to problems.

A similar mixture of approaches occurs in the work of the Schools Council's Science 5-13 project. We also argued that the objectives model is an approach that persists especially in the work undertaken by those concerned to promote scientific and mathematical understanding.

For this reason it is interesting to take as our final example of developments in the area of record-keeping and assessment a major project which is also concerned with science. This is the School's Progress in Learning Science project.

It is interesting to note that the project's director, Wynne Harlen, had close connections with the team responsible for the Science 5-13 project, who initially adopted an objectives approach and, modified this approach as a result of first-hand experiences of its limitations.

In the Progress in Learning Science project, the emphasis is placed on teacher development and this theme recurs throughout the materials. It is argued that 'the project's aim has been to help teachers gather information about their pupils' abilities, concepts and attitudes and to use this information both for making decisions about classroom experiences and for keeping a record of progress' (Harlen 1977, p. 12). The substance of the work, therefore, is intended to help to develop the teacher's 'diagnostic' abilities, and thus enable him to 'match' the child's level of understanding with appropriate experiences that will challenge and develop his thinking. The emphasis is remove from the end-product of learning and placed on the teacher's developing ability to encourage the process of learning—both his own learning and the children's.

The materials are presented in the form of an in-service course for teachers and therefore consist of discussion documents and audio-visual aids for use with groups of teachers. Materials for use in the classroom have not been produced but the study materials are intended to provide.

— links to everyday work in the classroom so that the practical viability of ideas is immediately explored,

— examples of what various statements mean in terms of real children in real classrooms, which are given on video-tape, audio-tape or tape-filmstrip sequences (Harlen, Darwin and Murphy 1977, p. v.).

The course work is supported by *A Guide to Diagnosis and Development* which offers suggestions for the kinds of experience that would be appropriate for children at different stages of development and guidance on the keeping of records to check these stages of development.

In addition to teacher development, the second recurring theme of this project is the notion of 'matching', for it is argued that an essential part of an effective teaching strategy is an attempt to match experiences to children's development in the various skills, attitudes and concepts involved (Harlen, Darwin and Murphy 1977, p. 7). The team justifies placing the notion of 'matching' at the centre of its work by three main arguments. Firstly, it is central to the views of developmental psychology, secondly, when children repeatedly experience 'mismatch' they are likely to become either bored or bewildered by school, and, thirdly, experienced teachers emphasize the importance of matching from their practical experience.

It is apparent that this project team has rejected the simplistic, mechanistic view of record-keeping that we discussed earlier. Planning and recording processes are intimately linked, in its view, with the professional competence of the teacher as well as with the achievements of the child. The purpose of assessing and recording progress as it sees it, therefore, must be linked with this process of development.

As a result of this, the types of record that it encourages teachers to keep are not only designed to indicate the child's achievements in science but also attempt to provide the teacher with evidence on which to base his future planning. In this sense, the team has produced records to encourage process rather than merely note end-products. In addition, although this work is concerned with the child's progress in learning science, the learning is treated in a unified way. Records focus not just on content but also on the skills, attitudes and concepts that are being engendered as the process of scientific understanding is developed.

From these last two examples it can be seen that record-keeping can not only help the teacher to give an account of his work but also can enable her to develop his professional skills—to 'match' rather than 'mismatch' his planning to the child's level of development. The need to give an account of work thus becomes merely one of many professional reasons for keeping records and assessing pupil performance.

This is by no means true of all the examples of teachers' records that have been devised as we saw earlier. Many of them seem to have been designed to respond only to the demands for accountability and, in doing so, they serve to undermine the unified view of the curriculum that we have argued should be developed in the Primary school.

To a great extent, the development of assessment procedures has been a form of structure for the teacher's work that has either been imposed from outside the school or been encouraged to develop within it in the ways we have described above. This is one important area which has felt the impact of central government's active interest in the curriculum. The desire for a clearer structure, however, goes beyond record-keeping. A more general interest in structuring the curriculum has been a further way in which demands for accountability have influenced developments in schools and it is to these more general aspects that we must now turn.

Structure and the Curriculum

There has been an increasing interest in finding ways of introducing structure into the work of the informal school since the publication of the Plowden Report in 1967. The source of this interest is two-fold.

Firstly, it stems from a desire to place 'progressive' education on a more rational footing. This desire expresses itself sometimes in a general argument for rational curriculum planning as we saw when we examined the work of the Schools Council's Aims of Primary Education project. More commonly, however, it is argued that if the teacher's work is more structured, or at least if the underlying structure of his existing work is identified and described with more clarity, then many of the criticisms of informal teaching could be answered and misunderstandings of this approach rectified. Structure in this case, then, is seen as a means of combatting the arguments of those who oppose the informal work of many Primary schools and is therefore a direct response to demands for accountability.

Secondly, there has developed an interest in structure which stems from the work undertaken in America in the early 1960s. This argument focuses attention on the structure that underlies areas of knowledge and the structure that sequences the child's learning of this knowledge. This American approach depends on 'academic experts within disciplines (notably the sciences) to structure the knowledge and expert planners and psychologists to relate this knowledge structure to the child's level of learning' (Blenkin 1980, p. 57). In this second sense, then, structure is related closely to the structure of knowledge. We will look at examples of this kind of structure when we consider the impact of subject specialisms on the Primary curriculum.

We should note here, however, that in the less Utopian interpretation in Britain the responsibility for structuring the learning is left to the schools. As a consequence, although an interest in structure can be traced to these two sources, the term is now used to refer to many different aspects of the teacher's work. It has been claimed, for example, that it is essential to structure not only knowledge but also experiences and skills. Teachers have been urged also to structure the child's learning, to structure their own teaching styles and to structure the organization of the classroom. It is still unclear, therefore, in many of the discussions of structuring what exactly is meant, largely because it has recently become a fashionable and over-used notion in educational circles.

One practical way in which some teachers have been faced by this general question of structure, however, is through the policy statements which they have been required to make to their local education authorities. As we saw in our earlier discussion of government documents, not only have the I.e.a.s been urged to tighten their school record systems but also they have been advised to collect annually information from their schools about the curriculum that is offered. The need to understand the structure of the work they plan, then, has become a reality to the staff of the schools because of requests to express this structure in a coherent school policy.

The first observation that needs to be made, then, is that the structure can take many forms. We have discussed in earlier chapters that it can be described in a linear and hierarchical form or it can be seen to be modular. We showed that the practical outcomes of adopting a particular structure have a direct impact on the work that is undertaken with children.

The differences in approaches are underlined, for example, in this extract from a discussion of the formulation of a school or classroom language policy which was produced by one local education authority's teachers' centre.

> Teachers will always disagree about what a 'language policy statement' should consist of. The statements that we see at C.L.P.E. vary enormously in their range of attitudes towards language and the types of language activities that they examine....Their purpose is to help teachers to clarify and perhaps also justify the sort of language activities that go on in their schools. If they don't help teachers to think through more clearly the policy of their schools...then they might just as well not be written...I personally prefer to begin with a description of what actually happens and follow this with a statement of why; others prefer to start with a list of aims and objectives and go on to say how they fulfil them (Warlow 1978).

Although it is implicit in theis statement, what is not made clear to the teachers is that the approach that they choose to adopt will influence directly all aspects of their work. If they do choose to begin with a list of aims and objectives and go on to indicate how these will be achieved the very model that they are adopting will, without doubt, determine what will be undertaken.

It is clear, then, that teachers need first of all to be alerted to the dangers of adopting an instrumental model when they are planning their policies. They also need to be helped to clarify what a policy is—which aspects of structure, in other words, they are to be concerned with.

It is an attempt to provide some clarification in this sphere that underlies the work of the Schools Council's Learning Through Science project. The members of the project team attempt to spell out the aspects of planning that need to be considered when formulating a school policy and they offer guidance on the compilation of the policy document.

Although, as we noted elsewhere, they take on the rhetoric of an objectives model, it is clear that they are wishing to help teachers to give coherence to a process model. Attention is given to the place of science in the overall work of the school, stress is on school-based development, where teachers are encouraged and guided to increase their own expertise, and importance is attached to constant revision of the policy. All of these elements are included in the summary of this aspect of the team's work, and we can do no better than to quote this in full.

The following table is a suggested strategy for forming a school policy for science:

The Policy

An intention on the part of a school staff to agree areas of knowledge and experience, enumerate appropriate attitudes, skills and concepts, decide upon methods of evaluation and place these within an organisational framework which will give sufficient guidance to ensure effective and consistent teaching of science throughout the school.

The Strategy

1. Discuss and decide upon what is meant by science.
2. Discuss and decide on the reasons for carrying out science with children in the age range appropriate to your school.

   Make a brief written statement of these reasons.
3. Discuss and decide what experiences are most suitable for the children in your school.

   Give full consideration to:

   Use of source books.

   Thinking about starting points from everyday situations that arise, or can be engineered, in school.

   Use of the school, school grounds and local environment.

   Science from interdisciplinary studies.

   Make a comprehensive, written documentation of such experience.

4. Discuss and decide on ways to organise the work. Give full consideration to:

 The amount of time needed.

 Different methods of organisation.

 Resources.

 General discussion of:

 How to arrange the classroom.

 Finding starting points.

 How to plan investigations or projects.

 The best ways to develop children's enquiries.

5. Discuss ways of evaluating children's progress.

 Try and use the findings from this discussion to agree on a form of record-keeping for science.

The Outcome

A written document that gives all members of staff a clear idea of why they should be presenting scientific experiences to children, and how they should go about presenting such experiences.

Such a document should be subject to periodic review and frequently updated. Then the policy becomes a resource that maintains the school as a dynamic place of learning.

(Schools Council 1980, p. 29)

We can see that intention of this approach is to encourage curriculum development within the school as well as to assist teachers in giving an account of their policies. It is also clear that it is endeavouring to do these things within the context of the informal, enquiry-based approach of the Primary school.

As was true of national monitoring of standards, formal requests for policies which require teachers to structure their work have been a relatively recent phenomenon and so a full evaluation of the impact of work of this kind is a task for the future. Before moving from a discussion of structuring the curriculum, however, we must examine the work of another Schools Council project which has tackled the question of a need for structure from a completely different perspective.

The intention of the Schools Council's project on the Structuring of Play in the Infant and First School was to focus teachers' attention on the play opportunities that they provide in their classrooms and to suggest ways in which play could be developed. The team members view play as of central significance to the school for, they argue, it is 'a vehicle for all aspects of young children's learning, development and motivation'. They go on to claim, however, that 'without structure play cannot be used as a teaching and learning medium' (Manning and Sharp 1977, p. 17).

They recommend, therefore, that, if play in the First school is to promote children's learning it must be 'structured'. Structure is defined as having two components. It refers, firstly, to the organization, provision and use of materials in the classroom and, secondly, to the active role that the teacher takes in joining the children's play and hence in extending the learning opportunities. The members of the team identify three kinds of teacher involvement which they call participation, initiation and intervention. The whole concept of structure as used in this project refers to the way in which the teacher shapes (or, some would say, manipulates) the spontaneous play of the children.

It could well be that this team has been too anxious to respond to those who wish for control over every aspect of the child's work. It can be argued, for example, that to intervene in and use children's play in the way suggested here is one way of ensuring that play does not occur in the classroom. Play, by definition, is spontaneous and, 'more an enjoyment of means than an effort to some particular end' (Garvey 1977, p. 10).

There is no doubt that the members of this project team have produced an excellent resource of materials which they recommend for play but which also could be used as starting-points for the enquiries of young children. They also offer sensible advice in relation to all aspects of general classroom organization. They reveal important contradictions, however, when discussing the teacher's role in promoting play in education.

They seem not to have made the important distinction between the role of play in the child's learning and his pursuit of enquiries which have been promoted through activities that are of intrinsic interest to him. They are thus led to strange view of play. They make constant references, for example, to the teacher's use of the child's play, they claim that children who are left alone to play do not develop imaginatively and they imply that play that is not developed by the teacher is worthless. In doing so, they give an impression of the kind of teacher control that we also drew attention to already and that quite rightly attracts the criticisms that we noted there. When they argue that play for many teachers is the basis of the curriculum and is to be used as 'the central agent and motivating force for all the child's learning' (Manning and Sharp 1977, p. 26), they are expressing a curious argument which confuses play with enquiry-based learning.

The worrying aspect of this for the purposes of our present discussion is that play (a component that has always been seen as important in informal education) has been devalued, not only because of the need to express the structures inherent in interest-based approaches to learning but also because of the felt need to make all things respectable by endowing them with teacher-imposed structures. The importance of play opportunities for young children has, as a result, been neither acknowledged nor explained. What the project team has achieved, however, if unwittingly, is an interesting discussion of how interests can be initiated and enquiries developed through first-hand experiences in the classroom.

We have shown, through the above examples, that there has been an increasing interest in defining the structures of both the teacher's planning of the curriculum and the child's learning, and that a main feature of this interest has been the need to give an account of the work undertaken in school and, in some cases, to defend it against the severe criticisms of those outside the school. We have also revealed, however, that this interest has not always been pursued with complete clarity concerning what precisely it entails. It is crucial that efforts be directed at achieving such clarity in what is a very important aspect of this approach to education.

In summary, we have indicated that demands for accountability have influenced many of the recent developments in Primary education. We have examined these developments in some detail and have argued that, although it is right that teachers should be called to account and this process can be of positive value in clarifying and developing their understanding of their work, in most cases the means by which accountability is being sought is undermining the more advanced work of the schools. In other words, in reality, the demand for accountability in some cases is promoting instrumentalism and detracting from the processes of education.

Throughout our discussion of the effects on the Primary curriculum of increased demands for accountability, we have made constant reference to a related influence, the pressure of subject specialisms. This also has the effect of undermining the unified approach to curriculum that has been developed in the Primary school. It is to a closer examination of this influence that we now turn.

The Influence of Subject Specialists

The usual approach in the Primary school, unlike that of the Secondary school, is to adopt a one-teacher system—that is, an arrangement that assigns to one teacher the responsibility for most of the work of one class. Exceptions may be made in the case of music, physical education, modern languages or religious education, but, even with these exceptions, the majority of the child's programme is planned by one teacher. Indeed, as we argued already, this complete responsibility has been an important reason for the advancement of a unified curriculum.

Recently, however, as we saw at the start of this chapter, this one-teacher system has become a source of concern, particularly in government circles, for it has been argued that, as the scope of the curriculum widens, many teachers are finding difficulty in coping and are reducing the quality of their work as they increase the quantity. This is the first source, therefore, of an interest in the introduction of subject specialisms into the Primary school.

This argument takes broadly two forms. The first claims that the range of work that remains to be covered, even if the above exceptions are made, places heavy demands on the teacher's knowledge and skills and many teachers are not able to meet these demands. As we saw earlier, this was a reason given by the HMIs in their survey (DES 1978) for the general neglect or poor teaching in certain important areas of human experience. Subjects such as science, history, geography and craft were all cited by them as generally suffering from this neglect.

Within their recommendations, therefore, the inspectors argue that subject specialists should be employed in Primary schools. They also argue that the existing teachers should be encouraged to develop their particular strengths for the purpose of extending the experiences of all the children in the schools by teaching certain aspects of content to classes other than their own.

They take note of the strengths of the 'one class to one teacher' system (op. cit., p. 117) and acknowledge the dangers of undermining these advantages by introducing measures that will fragment the child's experience at school. They argue, however, that 'when a teacher is unable to deal satisfactorily with an important aspect of the curriculum, other ways of making this provision have to be found. If a teacher is only a little unsure, advice and guidance from a specialist, probably another member of staff, may be enough. In other cases, more often with older than with younger children, and much more often in Junior than in Infant schools, it may be necessary for the specialist to teach either the whole class or a group of children for particular topics...perhaps more subjects, in particular science, should be added to the curriculum list, at least for the older children' (op. cit., p. 118).

Some attempt to combat such weaknesses in a school's facilities has been made, of course, by establishing posts of special responsibility. The inspectors express disappointment at the fact that, in the great majority of cases, teachers holding such posts have made very little impact on either the school's work in general or on the work of individual teachers.

The HMIs, then, are tentatively advancing the cause of subject teaching as one way of combatting the weaknesses of the school curriculum. In the context of their overall recommendations, and in the light of their warnings about fragmenting the curriculum, however, it is obvious that they do so somewhat reluctantly.

We also saw earlier that the politicians at the DES in general have shown no such reluctance in trying to advance subject teaching. Their reasons for doing so, however, are somewhat different and provide the second administrative argument for introducing subjects.

It was made obvious in their latest document (DES 1980) that they are seeking national agreement on a common core of subjects and skills that will form the substance of the school's work. In the Primary school, in their view, the core should include the 'basic skills', science and religious education, and a large proportion of the child's time at school should be devoted to learning these common elements. Their main arguments for establishing agreement on the common core are those to do with accountability and national consistency which we have already discussed. In addition, however, a concentration on the core areas (the basic minimum of schooling) is seen as a means of ensuring that children who have weaker teachers will be at less of a disadvantage, as the scope of work of these teachers could be reduced to cover only the core areas.

Although this latter argument is not in itself concerned with the educational reasons for establishing a common core, since it stems from a concern to preserve and promote at the centre of the school's work the knowledge and skills whose importance derives from their social and economic utility, it does restrict educational discussions. It is clear that the DES is determined to establish agreement on the 'framework of the curriculum' or the 'common core' so that discussion can only focus on the content which is to be included. Unlike the approach that we argued was distinctive of the Primary curriculum, which stresses those processes that develop from the unity of the child's experience, this desire for national consensus is placing the stress on separate bodies of knowledge and skills which must be promoted in all schools and acquired by all children.

The view of both the HMIs and the DES assume that the widening scope of the curriculum is the result of an increase in content. However, curriculum development does not inevitably mean an increase of or change in content. It is the process that underlies the content that is important.

The second way in which an interest in subject specialisms is influencing the curriculum is also partly administrative and based on the same assumptions. This time, however, it is linked to administrative and organizational factors that are internal to the teaching profession. Most of the recent large-scale attempts at curriculum enrichment, as we noted in our Introduction, have taken as their points of reference the curriculum theory that has been generated by those whose interests lie in Secondary education.

In the Schools Council, for example, which is still the largest sponsor of curriculum projects, most of the committees have hitherto been linked to a subject or discipline. Admittedly there has always been one committee responsible for developments in Primary education and some of the projects therefore have been enabled to explore more general curriculum issues. (The Aims of Primary Education project that we have already discussed is one example of work dealing with wider issues than those of content.) In general, however, the projects of the Schools Council have been limited to curriculum development within subjects and, in the recent past at least, have relied heavily on subject specialists (usually from university departments) for advice and guidance. This, in turn, has led Primary teachers to see curriculum development in terms of content only and has encouraged them to 'look to subject programmes, again usually constructed in behavioural terms, in order to develop work in content areas' (Blenkin 1980, p. 63).

These subject areas have not only been given prominence by national bodies like the Schools Council. They have also proved to be a lucrative source for publishers who have had considerable success in promoting commercially produced programmes in particular subject areas.

The two subjects which have had most attention in this respect, as we have constantly pointed out, are, of course, science and mathematics. We have already noted that these two areas are likely to be the weak points in the work of most Primary schools and this view has been reinforced—in science, at least—by the findings of the HMIs survey. Indeed, most Primary teachers would admit to finding the teaching of mathematics and science difficult. We will begin, therefore, by examining two programmes that have been produced for the teaching of mathematics.

The first is a commercially produced programme called Mathematics for Schools which has had such an impact on the work of the schools that the author's name has become synonymous with mathematics for many teachers. It is not uncommon, for example, to hear the children in many schools being asked by their teachers to work at their 'Fletcher books' rather than at mathematics or number.

The authors claim to be concerned with 'more than the results of mathematics. ... Rather, we have stressed the thorough understanding of concepts and then the application of those concepts to new situations.' They go on to claim that their series is concerned with 'the course of all mathematical experiences, and the logical and psychological processes involved, from the reception class upward in all types of schools' (Fletcher 1970, p. 2).

The workbooks for children which they offer are designed to build on and extend the existing practice in informal schools. They depend, therefore, on the teacher's first arranging activities for the children with real materials and then discussing these activities with the children. The books are intended to be used to practise the concepts which the teacher judges have been newly acquired by the children as a result of the activities.

In reality, however, this is rarely the case, as teachers tend to rely entirely on the children's workbooks supported by as a small amount of practical materials, such as counters. The same problem of misuse applies to this material as that we noted earlier when we discussed the practical tests produced by the NFER. As we argued then, placing sequenced material of this kind is schools in unlikely to improve the teacher's practice. The evidence of those who have tried to do so suggests that good teachers become inhibited by the sequence and weak teachers become over-dependent on the materials. It would be a comfort if the activities asked of children by these books were at least a substitute for poor teaching, but many children (and adults!) quite rightly become confused by the instructions which are given, because they depend largely on two-dimensional sketches, a very difficult medium for expressing with clarity what is expected.

It is claimed by the authors, however, that the books fulfil five purposes. They 'aim to provide learning situations, use stimulating methods of presentation of the pages, show the structural development of mathematics, provide practice and consolidation and make evaluation possible' (Fletcher 1970, p. 4). And so teachers who do not read beyond this will gain the impression that the series of books constitutes a full course of mathematics. However, the teacher's guide goes on to give detailed suggestions for practical work to supplement and reinforce that required by the workbooks. Thus teachers often fall between the two stools of, on the one hand, using the scheme to support their own, informal teaching of mathematics and, on the other, relying on the children's books to provide a complete and sequentially structured programme of learning. In this, they are reflecting an ambivalence that can be observed in the scheme itself.

For, although it is said in the teachers' manual that the children's books are intended to assist in the learning of concepts when such learning has been sparked off by other activities or experiences the children have been having, they are arranged so that the mathematical concepts to be learned are sequential. Each book is sectioned so that various concepts at a certain level can be practised and the sections within one book are all linked to a discussion of the objectives of the work which appears in the teacher's guide. 'The objectives for each section,' the authors explain, 'are stated for the most part in terms of child behaviour. We have used this form of statement so that you can determine by discussion and observation when the children are familiar with the concepts detailed in each section and are ready to move on or conversely, when they are not ready and are in need of further activities and discussion' (Fletcher 1970, p. 4).

'Fletcher' mathematics, then, is an attempt to introduce a sequenced programme of mathematics into an informal setting. The materials are devised in such a way that the logical structure of the subject forms the sequence of learning for the child. It becomes, in other words, the blueprint for practice. Before each level is attempted, objectives are prespecified in behavioural terms and these form the basis of assessing the child's success. There is, however, some attempt to encourage teachers to use this programme in conjunction with a more integrated approach based on the child's exploration of the environment.

No such concession is made, however, in our second example, the Kent Mathematics Project. For it aims to present an independent programme in the form of the kind of 'teacher-proof' material that is a typical product of the objectives model as used by specialists to plan a system based on the demands of subject, despite the claim that it is teacher-produced in all aspects of material, system and classroom organization. It is, therefore, a mathematics programme in its purest form and is packaged in such a way as to enable it to be used quite separately from other aspects of the school's work.

The project is designed for children between nine and sixteen years of age, so that its main impact is on work at the later Primary stage. The build-up to acquire the necessary 'entry concepts and skills', however, has some inevitable influence on the work undertaken by younger children in the schools that are using the project.

The tasks are presented (mainly in workcard form) in 'a material bank' and this includes work at nine mathematical levels which form 'a hierarchy of concept development'. The authors argue that concepts are developed through linear sequences of tasks, although these sequences interweave in a highly complex way. They claim that their 'material bank' takes full account of all these inter-relationships and they try to illustrate this by using as an example the position in 'the grand framework' of 'the Pythagoras task'.

'This [the Pythagoras task] assumes understanding of area and requires the pupil to calculate squares and square roots. Also, the pupils have been introduced to Pythagoras through a concrete stage involving construction, cutting out and fitting triangles' (Kent County Council 1978, p. 10). They then go on to indicate the number of concept lines in Level 2 in flow-plan form:

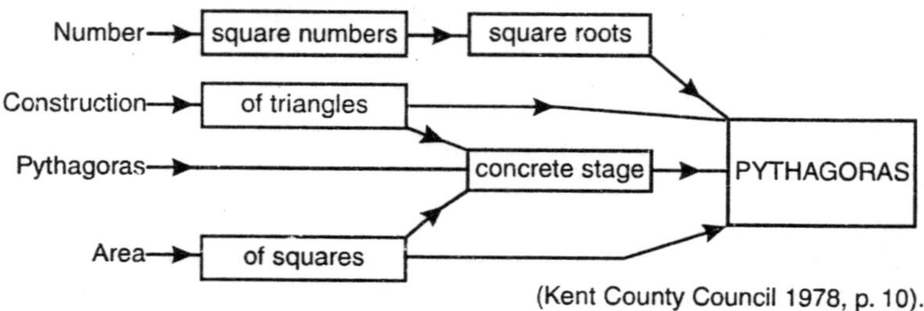

(Kent County Council 1978, p. 10).

The tasks themselves are derived from the 'concept hierarchy'. Each task is preceded by the task objective and it is explained that these usually describe briefly what the pupil should be able to do after working through the task. They go on to argue that it is not always possible to describe precise changes in pupil behaviour, and so some objectives describe the intention of the task in terms which do not describe the end-state 'but what should happen to the pupil during the task' (op. cit., p. 11). 'Objectives have been designed in a form intended to be the most helpful to the teacher' (ibid.), that is, by expressing them in terms of the mathematics rather than in terms of the children's learning.

The project team has, of course, devised a system which provides a record of the pupil's work—'the network'—which is based on the concept framework and incorporates codes to indicate the successful completion of tasks. The team explains that 'the position of a task in the framework is therefore an identification of the level of mathematics learning in an objectively designed structure of concept development and can be used for monitoring a pupil's progress and, if needed, for assessment purposes' (op. cit., p. 13).

We can see, from the above evidence, that this project's approach is even more strictly behavioural than that of the Mathematics for Schools programme. Taken together, however, they constitute examples of materials in use at both ends of the Primary school. The first is widely used in work with young children and the second with older children. They also typify both in approach and content a wealth of other material that has been produced recently by mathematicians. This is despite the supposed success of the child-centred 'new mathematics' which many thought would transform the teaching in this sphere of the work of the Primary school.

One reason for the popularity of these programmes is, of course, that teachers feel more inadequate in this area than in others. This certainly was one finding of a recent Schools Council survey, where it was found that

> some teachers would favour a stronger centralized direction to mathematics teaching. For example, one suggested:
>
> ...a manual, nationally accepted, showing the step-by-step procedure in the teaching of each phase of mathematics.
>
> Although few teachers would want to go as far as this...such views are evidence of a widespread feeling of uncertainty in the present situation.
>
> (Ward 1979, p. 57)

This survey also showed, however, that a large number of teachers are not looking to experts to pre-package material for them, but are anxious to develop their own expertise and improve their own teaching. It was found that 'understanding' was a key word which constantly recurred in the replies to the questionnaires and it was sought for both teachers and pupils.

It should be noted, however, that projects like the ones discussed above are unlikely to offer teachers an opportunity for developing their understanding for the reasons. It is also unlikely that they will enable children to become mathematically educated in the widest sense, for concept attainment is stressed at the expense of the process of concept development and the pupil is passively guided through the logical structure of the subject.

Finally, we must draw attention to the fact that the designing of materials that are to be learned strictly in accordance with the logical structure of the subject is likely to undermine or neglect other important elements. Mathematics, of course, being the most logical of the areas of human understanding, lends itself well to treatment of this kind. If teachers are encouraged to emphasize only the cognitive component, however, they are unlikely to generate a commitment to mathematical understanding in their pupils, for a mathematical education is not only to do with the achievement of understanding of abstract concepts, it should also 'awaken in children the significance of mathematics to their lives—an appreciation of its aesthetic qualities; its role in the maintenance, protection and development of society; its use in their ordinary lives' (Choat 1978, p. 125). No doubt the subject specialists who structure materials for teachers have this kind of commitment themselves, but children need to have day-to-day contact with teachers who have such understanding and commitment if they are to be helped to it themselves. It is also important that, as with all learning in the Primary school, we keep in mind the contribution that the learning of mathematics can make to the child's overall development.

Although the teaching of mathematics has been a major concern of teachers during the 1970s, the opposite is claimed to be true of science. We noted earlier that it was constantly referred to by the inspectors in their recent report (DES 1978) as an area of human experience that is neglected in Primary education. As a result of the findings of this report, there has been considerable interest in the teaching of science recently, although, as yet, there has not been the proliferation of programmes that has occurred in mathematics.

We have already referred in detail in earlier sections of this chapter, however, to aspects of the work in this sphere undertaken by the Schools Council and it is our intention now briefly to review the three projects together as they form an interesting picture of the development of ideas about curriculum within one area.

The team working on the first project, Science, 5-13, began with the belief that science 'could contribute to educational ends which transcend subject boundaries, e.g. "self-realisation", "broadening experience", "educating the whole child" '(Elliott 1980, p. 98). They recognized, however, that these loosely expressed aims offered little guidance in planning day-to-day experiences. Their solution, as we noted already, was to adopt an objectives model of planning and to combine this with a Piagetian framework for matching appropriate objectives to the child's stage of development.

From the start, however, their objectives approach was somewhat different to the strict behavioural model. This is explained by one member of the team as due to disagreements among team members about the value of objectives. She tells us, for example, that 'one objection was that "they destroy everything we are trying to do in the classroom", that "one was making precise what was not precise", that "where you were making statements about objectives you were fitting on a veneer of structure which was inappropriate in the classroom situation"' (Elliott 1980, p. 105).

It was also found, especially in the courses that were conducted by the team for practising teachers, that the response to the use of the objectives of science as a starting-point for planning was disappointing, whereas their use as a guide for open-ended work with children brought enthusiastic responses from the teachers. Indeed, the project director acknowledges that this put objectives in perspective, for they were unlikely to be used in a mechanistic form by teachers who were seeking guidance rather than an externally imposed structure. By way of contrast, however, the team was under considerable pressure from teachers to produce pupil material, a contradiction that again draws attention to the confused thinking on the part of some teachers in the area of curriculum planning.

The project team resisted this pressure, however, and produced, in addition to its guide, 26 source books for teachers. There were intended to support teachers' planning of work, to give them ideas for extending topics which children were already enthusiastic about and to provide them with information. They were intended, in other words, as resources to enrich the scientific aspects of the work of teachers who were developing interests in the way.

The evaluation of the project revealed, however, that 'the project's books do not on their own give as much help as many teachers need in starting children learning science activity for the first time', and that they 'did not significantly change teachers' willingness to adopt methods for enabling children to learn more active inquiry' (Harlen 1975, p. 89). It was, in fact, generally agreed that the dissemination of the project's ideas had been minimal.

The attempt at resolving this lack of impact, however, has not so far led to the employment of science specialists to package science programmes for teachers. Rather, the Schools Council has placed emphasis on two quite different ways of solving the problem—first on finding ways of developing the class teacher's expertise and second on offering advice for school-based development. In an attempt to pursue these lines of development, therefore, the Schools Council sponsored the two further projects, Progress in Learning Science and Learning through Science, which we discussed earlier in this chapter.

In our discussion of these two ensuing projects, we noted that in both cases the teams support a unified approach to the curriculum. The evaluation of the Science 5-13 project had led to the belief that there is a close relation between mathematical and scientific activities for young children and that, in the view of the project evaluator at least, it makes little sense to continue to develop curriculum materials for these areas separately. And so neither of these subsequent projects seeks to promote science as a discrete area of knowledge or subject specialism. Both are concerned, however, to promote first the processes upon which scientific development depends and, second, the contribution that experiences of a scientific kind can make to the child's overall development. They are moving, in fact, from a concern with the objectives of science to a study of how the scientific process is advanced and how educational processes in general can be forwarded.

By using examples from the two areas of mathematics and science, we have tried to show the impact that can be made on the curriculum by an over-emphasis on the particular needs of one subject. We have also indicated what is likely to occur when the demands of the subject are dealt with in isolation from both the child's needs and the teacher's understanding. Finally we have shown that in one subject area, that of science, there are clear indications that the considerable experience of attempting to develop the curriculum is causing some specialists in this field to shift attention from the demands of the subject to the processes essential to educational development.

This, we would argue, is to be applauded, as it is our contention that, when special expertise in an area of human understanding (regardless of which area this is) is used to support and guide the understanding of teachers and to reveal the means by which children develop, then the unified approach to curriculum planning can be considerably advanced and the practical implications of the process of education are clarified. If this special expertise is used, however, to plan and structure the work for the teacher and prespecify the experiences to be undertaken by the children, then both the unified curriculum and the process of education are undermined.

This leads us finally, then, to a discussion of some developments by which a process model of curriculum development is being promoted.

Planning for Process

We argued in our previous section that, when teachers feel that their own understanding is particularly weak (as is the case with mathematics), then this aspect of work is likely to be vulnerable to the kind of external influence and isolated treatment that we described earlier. It is not unreasonable to assume, therefore, that the converse is likely to occur in areas where the teachers feel that they themselves have a degree of expertise and as a result feel more confident.

This certainly appears to be true, in theory and, quite often, in practice, of the work that has been undertaken in the area of language and literacy. Consequently, it is in this aspect of work that the understanding of processes is advancing most rapidly. In addition, the practice of schools changes more often in this sphere than in any other.

It was clear, for example, that, when the Bullock Report was published in 1975, a healthy and informed debate was being conducted within the profession concerning the best approaches to adopt in this important area of education. This was reflected in the report which, far from being concerned narrowly with 'basic skills' or subjects such as English Literature, used, as its terms of reference, all the aspects of language and argued that the development of oracy and literacy was the responsibility of all teachers. Although the discussions within the report indicated that there was by no means agreement on how improvements could be achieved (particularly in the area of the teaching of reading), it was clear that many changes had been achieved already and this was apparent not just in the theoretical back-ground but also in the work of teachers, publishers of children's books and so on.

It is also clear that Primary teachers, unlike many of their Secondary colleagues, recognize the importance of a wider view of language and are concerned to encourage children to talk as well as read and write. It is unusual, in fact, to find a silent Primary school class, as the teachers now see the various forms of communication as important, however incompetently they themselves may set about communicating with children.

We will begin, then, by examining one example of the influential work undertaken recently in this sphere—the Schools Council's project, Communication Skills in Early Childhood.

The main thrust of the work of this project is towards helping teachers to cope more adequately with children who are disadvantaged in school. Although the project's director goes to great pains to separate her work from the obviously instrumental language programmes developed by the early interventionists (for example, the Peabody Kit, Talk Reform etc.), she advises that teachers should deliberately encourage children to develop educationally desirable language skills. She argues that these skills are important to all children, but are particularly so for disadvantaged children. She claims, for example that 'what is seen to be desirable content for learning may change, but the means of achieving it will be the same. It is the strategies that children of educated parents have learned that provide them with the important means of learning: it is not necessarily the goals of such parents that should be recommended' (Tough 1973, p. 126). She goes on to claim that it is the tools and strategies of language that are the basis of every child's means of learning, and she explains that these are 'the skills in using language as a means of examining the detail, the relationships and the structure of the world . . . the skills of logical argument, of examining a range of possible solutions to problems, of anticipating and planning, and of framing questions which will bring the kind of information required' (ibid).

Joan Tough's approach is based on a model of language use that, it is claimed, promotes the kind of thinking that will be encouraged and valued in schools. Various kinds of language use, therefore, support different thought processes that in turn support the overall process of education. Later in the child's school career these different processes will underlie the subjects, areas of experience and so on that he will be engaged in. She argues that, if he is underfunctioning in any of these areas, he is likely to under-achieve at school, because he will be unlikely to develop the thought processes required to make sense of the areas of human experience that the school attaches importance to.

Joan Tough's model incorporates seven functions of language:

1. Self-maintaining—maintaining the rights and property of the self.
2. Directing the child's own activity and that of others.
3. Reporting on present and past experience.
4. Logical reasoning.
5. Predicting and anticipating possibilities.
6. Projecting into the experience of others.
7. Building up an imaginative scene for play through talk.

(Schools Council 1976).

She argues that all teachers should foster language usage in these seven areas, especially with children who are not encouraged to make use of all these functions in language usage in their homes.

A major criticism of such an approach is that it advances a deficit theory of language, i.e. that certain children are not fully equipped or competent in the kind of language usage that is crucial to school learning (Spencer 1976). Joan Tough proposes, however, (in much the same way as Smith does in connection with the teaching of reading, as we noted elsewhere that it is in the interests of all the children they teach that teachers should deepen their own understanding of the process of language development and its link to thought.

The essence of her approach is to encourage teachers to use her model to appraise the children's language. Appraisal is envisaged as a diagnostic process on the part of the teacher. In this way, her work is similar to that of the Progress in Learning Science project, for it again attempts to extend the tradition of child study and observation which has been a long-established practice of teachers of young children.

She goes on to argue that, if sensitive dialogue between child and teacher is part of the day-to-day life of the classroom, it becomes possible for the teacher to use her appraisal of the child's strategies to encourage an extension of his language skills. This she terms the fostering plan and she expresses the view that 'fostering begins with the recognition of an opportunity for meeting what the teacher judges to be the child's needs. . . . .Appraisal is a continuous process of recognising the child's skills: fostering is a continuous process of recognising opportunities for extending the child's skills' (Schools Council 1977, p. 24).

The materials produced, then, are directed at the in-service education of teachers (again in the same way as the science projects). The intention is that the teacher should plan to develop an 'enabling curriculum', using the model of language and the teaching strategies that derive from it to support her understanding of and response to the children. Cognitive development in the view of this project team is intimately connected with linguistic development which in turn is dependent on both the strategies that the child can employ in the new situations that he meets and the dialogue that he can sustain as he learns from these new situations.

Joan Tough fiercely defends this approach against those who claim that it encourages teachers to perpetuate a middle-class verbal tradition. She argues, for example, that 'to those who cry that this is a middle-class model we would retort that if the skills of thinking are to remain a middle-class monopoly, education will remain accessible only to the middle classes' (Tough 1977a, p. 78). She also defends her use of structure by distinguishing it from the objectives model and pointing out that

> structure may not be most usefully conceived as a linear sequence in the acquisition of concepts and skills. In looking for a structure for the curriculum it may be more useful to recognise three dimensions upon which it should be based:
>
> 1. Knowledge of the potential that the child has for learning...
> 2. Recognition of the potential of the environment...
> 3. Knowledge of communication strategies...
>
> It is not the structure of the content which should be the main focus, but the total structure of the enabling environment, at the centre of which is the tutoring adult (Tough 1977a, p. 80)

This work aims, therefore, to cover the development of all thought processes by emphasizing the importance of the process of communication. It is admitted that all concepts are not dependent on language but that 'higher order concepts. . .are likely to be far more dependent on language for their development. . . .Such concepts must await a necessary level of maturation, but the child's experiences contribute to the process of maturation, and amongst those experiences the language used by others plays its part in directing attention and placing experiences within a structure' (Tough 1977b, p. 141).

This particular project's work is directed at teachers in Nursery and Infant schools, but the underlying ideas have also found their place in work undertaken with older children. The 'model of communication and learning' proposed by Douglas Barnes, for example, has much in common with this general approach, although his concern is with the later stages of education. The themes of 'meaning' and 'strategies for learning' also recur in his discussion and he similarly argues that 'language must enter into the curriculum in two ways: (1) as the communication system of the classroom and school; (2) as a means of learning' (Barnes 1976, p. 31).

We can see, then, that studying the use and functions of language is one way of clarifying the underlying processes of education. When this is done, it can be argued that these processes are supportive of and can be supported by various modes of human understanding. If we look in detail at one of the functions of the Tough model, for example, this point becomes clearer:

4. Towards logical reasoning

 Strategies

1. Explaining a process.
2. Recognizing causal and dependent relationships.
3. Recognizing problems and their solutions.
4. Justifying judgments and actions.
5. Reflecting on events and drawing conclusions.
6. Recognizing principles.

(Schools Council 1977, p. 23).

It is obvious that this has importance in the areas of mathematics and science but it is difficult to think of areas of human experience where such qualities do not have application.

The model that Joan Tough offers us, therefore, has application in most areas of human experience, but there is one area to which a study of language development provides no explanation—that of visual imagery and artistic development.

This is an area of human experience which, up to now, has been afforded no obvious utilitarian value, although the increasing importance given to Craft, Design and Technology may alter the circumstances in this respect. It is also an area that has held a prominent place in the work of the Primary school. Recently, however, it has become threatened for, as a result of demands for accountability, it is tending to be regarded as unimportant and teachers are being encouraged to feel that an interest in graphic work is not completely academically respectable but is a 'frill' rather than a critical skill (Goodnow 1977).

In addition, it is an area that is threatened by the attitudes of many teachers to art as a subject. It is not unusual for children who are not talented artists to become quickly self-conscious and modest about drawing and painting so that, as a result, many become reluctant to engage in work of this kind even in the early years of schooling. In other words, many teachers do not recognize the importance of artistic experience to the development of every child.

For these reasons, therefore, it is interesting to look in more detail at the views of Elliott Eisner (1979) for the explains the role of visual communication in human development in a similar way to those whose main interest and concern is with language. He does so by considering why art is important before concerning himself with how it should be taught. Eisner begins, therefore, by asking what it is that children learn when they make visual images, and proceeds to discuss nine aspects of learning that can occur. These can be summarized as:

1. Children learn that they can create images and that this provides intrinsic satisfaction.
2. Children learn that the images that they create can function as symbol, both as public images and as personal symbols.

3. Children learn that symbolic images can be used as a vehicle for symbolic play so that symbols become one means of imagining and empathizing.
4. Children learn that the process of image-making requires them to make personal judgements in an area where external and rigid standards do not exist.
5. Children learn that images can be related to other images to form a whole and so are encouraged to consider spatial relationships.
6. Children learn that they can develop skills which will enable them to create illusion and form images that are visually persuasive which will in turn provide a vehicle for transforming ideas, images and feelings into a public form.
7. Children learn from making images that ideas and emotions that are not physically present can be symbolized.
8. Children learn from making images that there are ideas, images and feelings that can only be expressed through visual form.
9. Children learn that the world itself can be regarded as a source of aesthetic experience and as a pool of expressive form.

(Eisner 1979)

Eisner argues, therefore, that, far from being a 'fringe' activity or trivial hobby, visual representation can not only make its own unique contribution to the process of education but can also have significance in the child's more general cognitive development.

We have shown in this last section that there is evidence that progress is being made in clarifying the processes that underlie education. It has been argued in this recent work that the educational process is complex and subtle, and its aims cannot be achieved by a straightforward application of learning principles to direct and deliberate shaping of behaviour. If attempts are made to do this, as happens when the objectives approach is adopted, the educational process is reduced to training, the curriculum is fragmented, and important, long-term aims are set aside in order to achieve measurable results. In these examples, therefore, this approach has been deliberately rejected.

Finally, this work has been based on the view that progress in the Primary school is more likely to be made if attention is given to the processes to be pursued in teaching. The mainstream Primary school tradition has already developed some practical expertise in this respect, but in the past teachers have failed to make explicit their approach to education, and have relied too much on intuitive understanding. The work that we have described in this last section attempts to help teachers to achieve more clarity in their planning for process development.

At a time when demands for accountability are being made on them, it is encouraging to find that teachers are being warned against the excesses of instrumentalism, and helped to find other approaches which are more demanding but more likely to promote education. This work has, therefore, placed much stress on the teacher's developing expertise as it has shown that it is upon the skill and understanding of the teacher that education depends.

Summing Up

In this chapter we have attempted to make an evaluation of some recent developments in the Primary curriculum in the light of the theoretical discussions of our earlier chapters. We began by drawing attention to the fact that curriculum development in the Primary sector of education is not a recent phenomenon. Nevertheless recent years have witnessed a number of attempts to accelerate that process for a variety of reasons and it is these attempts that we have been concerned here to examine.

It seemed to us that these developments could be best viewed under three headings; firstly, those that appear to have been prompted by demands from various quarters for teacher accountability, secondly, those that appear to be prompted by a desire to emphasize a subject specialist approach to the Primary curriculum and, thirdly, those that appear to have acknowledged the kind of concern with the processes of education which we have attempted to argue in earlier chapters is an essential ingredient of the Primary curriculum.

Under the first of these headings we looked in particular at the recent publications that have emerged both from Her Majesty's Inspectorate and from the Department of Education and Science since these seemed to us to be prompted by demands for increased public control of education. However, we also felt it appropriate under this same heading to examine some of the projects that have been concerned to encourage teachers to adopt a more structured approach both to planning and the keeping of records, since these seemed to be motivated by the same desire to increase external control of the curriculum and to make possible greater external monitoring of standards, and they seemed likely too, if not handled properly, to result in the same kind of limitation on the freedom of the teacher and the school to attend to what seem from the inside to be the educational needs of their pupils.

We found ourselves looking again at official publications when we came to examine recent developments under our second heading, pressures for the introduction of subject specialisms. Here in particular we noted the ambivalence of these publications which while recommending an increased emphasis on teaching in certain traditional subject areas also from time to time were to be noted extolling the merits of a unified approach to learning. We also here devoted attention to some recent projects in specific areas such as science and mathematics. Again we noted some internal inconsistencies not only between the ideas of, on the one hand, teaching these subjects as subjects and, on the other, attempting to see them as part of a unified curriculum but also between an approach to the teaching of them which emphasizes subject-content and one that views them from the standpoint of what they can contribute to the overall development of the individual child. Those that seemed to have most to offer and to fit most naturally with the established ethos of the Primary school were those, like the Learning Through Science project, which have come to acknowledge the primacy of the second of these two possible roles.

This, we argued, was the main source of the strength of those projects we saw as falling appropriately into our third and final category which embraced those developments that have recognized the centrality to Primary education of a process model of curriculum. We found it interesting to note that developments under this heading have been more commonly found in those areas of the curriculum where, unlike in mathematics and science, Primary teachers have for a long time felt more confident of their abilities, in the humanities, for example, and especially in the area of language development. Developments such as those that followed the publication of the Bullock Report and the work of Joan Tough have, in our view, been free of the major inconsistencies of some of the other developments that we have considered, in so far as they have started from a recognition that education is concerned with development and that planning a curriculum for such education must begin from a consideration of processes rather than intended behavioural outcomes. They thus have the merit of internal consistency and, in our view, the added merit of being in harmony with the basic principles of Primary education.

Any such attempt at categorization of these recent developments, however, is bound to bring its own difficulties, not least in that there will inevitably be a good deal to overlap whatever categories one chooses. This overlap we have tried to draw attention to as and when it has occurred.

It is also inevitable that, when attention has been devoted to the curriculum of the Primary school by different groups of people viewing it from different standpoints, there will be conflict between the views offered. This too we have tried to highlight.

What is more serious and less excusable is the conflict we have detected within some of the views expressed. We hope we have been able to show both that this conflict exists and some of the forms that it takes. We have also endeavoured to demonstrate that to a large extent it stems from a failure to appreciate the fundamental principles which our earlier chapters have been designed to pick out, for example, a failure to recognize the implications of adopting an instrumental view of the curriculum and a corresponding failure to distinguish between the ideas of education as the promotion of certain kinds of development and as the acquisition of certain bodies of knowledge, a failure which in turn leads to certain confusions about the role of subject-content in education.

This confusion and conflict within and between recent developments in the Elementary curriculum can only lead to a similar lack of clarity in the minds of teachers themselves as they attempt to respond to the demands made of them. What is required, therefore, is a good deal of rethinking about both the theory and the practice of Primary education not only by the teachers themselves but also, and perhaps even more importantly, by those who have become increasingly concerned in recent years to advise those teachers on what they should be doing. Greater accountability and external control over education can only be effective if those who are demanding the former and attempting to exercise the latter have a clear view of what it is they are demanding.

Index